The New Template for Recovery:

How to Quit Drinking
and
Build a Better Life

Revised Edition

T. Christopher Portman, Ph.D.

This edition published by
Dog Ear Publishing
4010 W. 86th Street, Ste H
Indianapolis, IN 46268

www.dogearpublishing.net

ISBN: 978-160844-583-7
This book is printed on acid-free paper.

Printed in the United States of America

Contents

Preface   vii
Introduction: A Template for Recovery   ix

Part 1: Get Square with What You Need to Do   1

Chapter 1: Are You Safe to Quit Drinking?   3
    Withdrawal Risks   3
    Withdrawal Assessment   4
    Options for a Safe Withdrawal   9
    Nutrition and Detoxification   12
    Medications That May Help You Quit Drinking   12

Chapter 2: Do You or Do You Not Have a Problem?   15
    Brief Screening Tests   16
    Treatment Center-Based Assessment   20
    Assessment with a Private Practitioner   21
    Doing Your Own Assessment   22

Chapter 3: Getting Ready to Change   45
    Are You a Good Candidate to Quit on Your Own?   45
    Finding the Motivation to Change   47
    Stages of Readiness to Change   48
    Phases of Recovery   51
    The Hero in You   58
    Recommended Reading   59

Part 2: What Happened to You?   61

Chapter 4: A Drug Called Alcohol   63
    What Alcohol Is   63
    Where Alcohol Came From and How It Spread   64
    Health, Societal, and Economic Costs of Alcoholism   67

Contents

The Advance of Conflicting Beliefs about Alcohol
    Addiction   68
The Disease Concept   70
Nature versus Nurture in the Development of
    Alcoholism   71
A Progressive Disease?   73
A "Chronic" Disease?   73
The Bio/Psycho/Social Model   74

Chapter 5: Physical Addiction to Alcohol: Process and Effects   77
The Biology of Alcohol Dependence   77
Damaging Physical Effects   82
Experiential Effects   86

Chapter 6: The Psychology of Addiction   91
You Are Not to Blame!   93
Alexithymia   97
The Psychological Addiction Process   98
Social and Cultural Factors   102
Recommended Reading   102

Chapter 7: The Backward-Gazing Model   103
What's Up with Standard Treatment Programs?   103
An Office-Based, Individual Approach   111
What's Up with Alcoholics Anonymous?   112
The Medical Model   122

Part 3: The New Model: Finding Your Pathway with the
    Recovery Template   125

Chapter 8: A Forward-Going Approach   127
Quitting versus Recovery   127
Finding a Model to Live By   128

Chapter 9: The Life Areas Model of Recovery   135
The Template for Recovery   135
How to Use the Template   137
Eight Roadblocks and How to Overcome Them   141

Part 4: The Areas of Recovery   149

Chapter 10: Health and Fitness   151
    Overcoming Your Health and Fitness Discouragement   152
    Your Own Action Plan   157
    Recommended Reading   159

Chapter 11: Emotional Recovery   161
    Where Feelings Really Come From   161
    How to Prosper from Your Moods   180
      Strategy # 1: Learn to identify your feelings, without
        fear or judgment   180
      Strategy # 2: Learn to change how you feel by changing
        how you think   184
      Strategy # 3: The faster-than-a-martini-mood
        adjuster   189
      Strategy # 4: Self-validation   189
      Strategy # 5: Changing maladaptive coping patterns   198
      Strategy # 6: Building a positive inner voice   202
      Strategy # 7: Defeating the three P's   206
    Co-occurring Mental Health Problems—Dual Diagnosis   212
    Recommended Reading   218

Chapter 12: Leisure/Recreational Recovery   219
    What to Do   222
    Further Considerations   224

Chapter 13: Relationships Recovery   227
    About Primary Partner Relationships   228
    Recovery of Your Existing, Though Damaged, Primary
      Partner Relationship   234
    Starting a New Primary Relationship in Recovery   256
    Family Relationships   259
    Friendship Recovery   262
    Co-Worker Relationship Recovery   268
    Recommended Reading   270

Chapter 14: Career/Occupation Recovery   271
    Let the Past Go   272
    Develop a Sense of Entitlement   273

Contents

Do Not Be Too Risk Averse   274
Building Your Courage   274
Strategize Using the Life Areas Template   275
Capitalize on Happenstance   275
Use Job-Getting Strategies   277
Recommended Reading   282

Chapter 15: Living-Place Recovery   283

Chapter 16: Philosophical/Spiritual/Religious Recovery   289
Philosophy, Spirituality, and Religiosity   290
The 12-Step View   290
Why Believe in Anything?   291
Building Your Own Philosophical/Spiritual/Religious
      Recovery   292
Recommended Reading   293

Part 5: The Art of Staying Sober   295

Chapter 17: Understanding Relapse   297
The Paradox of Relapse   298
Relapse Dynamics Demystified   300

Chapter 18: Relapse Prevention Strategies   307

Afterword   319
References   321

Preface

Writing *The New Template for Recovery: How to Quit Drinking and Build a Better Life* has not been as much an inventive process as it has been a straightforward expression of the information and strategies I have learned and used over more than three decades of working with thousands of people experiencing alcohol use problems. Through these years, there has been relatively little that I invented. Rather, I have relied on the brilliance of others. To name only a few: William Miller, Allen Marlatt, and Carlo DiClemente for their hard scientific work in the field of addictions; Terrance Gorski for bringing relapse prevention strategies to millions of recovering people; Jack Trimpey for his brave trek beyond the status quo; Donald Meichenbaum, Albert Ellis, Martin Seligman, David Burns, and Wayne Dyer for their inspired brands of cognitive therapy; John Gottman for showing us how to help troubled relationships; Jeffery Young for his insights on how people can reinvent themselves; and Anne Fletcher for her illuminating investigation into how people quit drinking and detailed exposé on the strengths and weaknesses of organized treatment programs.

I greatly appreciate the editorial assistance supplied by Brooke Warner, Carolyn Acheson, Dixie Cheek, and Nicolle White. And, I dearly thank my wife, Dr. Ellen Walker, for her constant encouragement and educated suggestions. Without her unflagging support, the book would not have been written.

Ultimately, I want to acknowledge gratitude to the thousands of amazing men and women who have honored me by allowing me to have a part in their recovery from alcohol addiction. Your struggles, your courage, and your heroic achievements, have humbled me, educated me, and have enriched my life beyond anything I could ever have imagined.

Introduction

The New Template for Recovery: How to Quit Drinking and Build a Better Life is for people who want to overcome alcohol use problems but either are turned off by standard treatment programs and Alcoholics Anonymous or endorse those systems but want something more. This book also is for those who might attend treatment programs but find them prohibitively expensive. The self-directed approach I have developed is practical, progressive, logical, easy to follow, and, above all else, exciting. People tend to fear that giving up alcohol will only be a sacrifice they must live with. Nothing could be farther from the truth. It is, in fact, a liberation, and this book will show you how to make it happen for yourself.

If you are the sort of person who is not content to simply have things done for you, but rather the sort who wants to know, and who thrives on discovery and on personal accomplishment—in short a person who is a seeker rather than a follower—*The New Template for Recovery* may be just what you are looking for to help your quitting drinking become a personal triumph.

The book is quite comprehensive and detailed for a very good reason—for most people, successfully quitting drinking becomes a far greater challenge than they would ever have imagined. You are likely to need every edge, every bit of knowledge and every strategy you can get. Fortunately, the central concept and how it is laid out in the book is not at all complicated. The first half is about alcohol addiction and effects. The second half consists of individual chapters for each of the life areas in which you may wish to focus your recovery—how to find fulfillment in health and fitness, relationships, careers, leisure pursuits, living place, spirituality, and in psychological wellbeing. Unlike other approaches, this is a going forward approach that reinforces sobriety by getting busy reinventing your life.

Over the past 35 years, I have directed both inpatient and outpatient treatment programs, written program curricula, and taught and supervised hundreds of counselors. I have been deeply involved in the development and delivery of standard treatment programs, as well as in direct client services. In addition, I have been privileged to assist several thousand individuals with alcohol or other drug problems through my private practice as a psychologist.

I also have been a proponent of Alcoholics Anonymous and its 12-step system. At the same time, I have kept my mind open and followed research. To my initial consternation, then wonder, and to my eventual delight, I have seen scores of people who have bucked the system, colored outside the lines, and somehow found lasting sobriety on their own. In research, this is called "natural recovery" or "solo recovery." It is not the equivalent of "spontaneous remission," in which the symptoms of an illness mysteriously disappear. In natural recovery, people actually *do something* that works against the disorder.

In my experience, and as now has been well documented in extensive research, many—possibly most—people who recover from alcohol use problems manage to do so on their own, without treatment or AA. Here is a sampling of what research has been discovering:

- An analysis of two surveys involving thousands of people, published in the American Journal of Public Health, indicated that among people with prior alcohol problems, 77% were successfully abstaining without any treatment program or AA involvement (Sobell, Cunningham, & Sobell, 1996).
- The vast "Wave 1, 2001–2002 National Epidemiologic Survey on Alcohol and Related Conditions," painstakingly interviewed more than 43,000 people. Of the 10% who had met criteria for an alcohol dependence problem at some point in their lives, 75% had made improvements, yet only 25% of those with a *prior* alcohol dependence problem had participated in any level of treatment. That is, 75% apparently had quit, were quitting, or had made significant improvements on their own (Dawson, 2005).
- In a voluntary survey of 222 people who overcame drinking problems, professional health sciences writer Anne Fletcher found that 56% had resolved their problems in "non-conventional" ways. Her book *Sober for Good* (Fletcher, 2001), is a widely read self-help bestseller, and in some ways provides a springboard for this book.

- A careful study of a group of people who had gained sobriety *without treatment or self-help groups* showed that 92% remained stable in their recoveries at a 2-year follow-up (Rumpf et al., 2006).
- A study involving 4 and 10 year follow-ups of 51 to 65 year-old adults with alcohol use problems found a natural recovery rate of 73% (Schutte et al. 2006).
- Studies from Germany and Sweden found 53% and 80% respectively of formerly alcohol dependent adults had not sought professional help in becoming sober (Klingemann et al. 2010).
- Meta-analysis (pooling data from many studies) of the efficacy of different types of substance abuse therapy has not found any approach to be superior or inferior to another (Imel et al., 2008).
- A meta-analysis of studies of people required to attend Alcoholics Anonymous indicated that it is *less effective than no treatment at all* (Kownacki & Shadish, 1999).

Although research clearly documents the phenomenon and prevalence of natural recovery, I can appreciatively say that treatment programs and AA are a great help to many thousands of people each year. In fact, I strongly encourage all of my private clients to try *at least* two AA meetings. Whether out of naïveté, irrational fears, and/or shyness, it is never wise the reject something out of hand that may ultimately serve as a great support. If you have ever attended meetings, at least you know that AA provides an organized set of teachings and potential base of social support for recovery.

I have also spent much of my adult life motivating people to try treatment programs and have trained families for countless interventions. I am convinced that for some people, treatment programs and/or participation in AA is the only way to succeed in recovery. Yet, equally clearly, treatment programs and/or AA do not appeal to everyone and can be toxic for some. Many people can only gain a quality recovery if they do it on their own. A combination approach works best for others.

I have constructed *The New Template for Recovery* for those of you who thrive on taking *the major role* in the direction of your own lives. Even people with strong religious faith agree that God imbued us with a practicable modicum of freewill, and expects us to exercise good judgment *independent* of constant divine steerage.

The Correlates of Recovery

Research shows that the *venue* for recovery, be it an organized treatment program, an AA hall, or one's own living room, is not the most important factor for success. Other factors correlate more strongly with successful recovery. For example, having at least one close person in your life who knows and supports what you are doing appears to be a strong contributor to success. With such a person, or persons, in your life, you may be a good candidate for a self-directed recovery.

Another import factor appears to be having what is referred to in psychology as an *internal locus of control* (Rotter, 1966, 1992). In research, a correlation has been found between this characteristic and successful recovery (Kivlahan et al., 1983; Koski-Jannes, 1994). This is the perception that good and bad things affecting one's life, rewards and punishments, come from one's own doing. People with an internal locus of control automatically expect to do things their way, and forcing them to do otherwise often leads to resistance. These individuals tend to believe in adages such as, "There is greater wisdom in honest doubt than in all of your creeds" and, "Questions unanswered are far less dangerous than answers unquestioned." These individuals benefit from information, strategy, and help where necessary from people *they* select—not the judgment or direction of others, or being held hostage to what someone else orders for everyone cookie-cutter style without regard for individual differences.

On the other side of the spectrum are individuals who have what is referred to as an *external* locus of control—the perception that good and bad things in their lives, rewards and punishments, are caused by forces outside of themselves and beyond their control. These individuals are more likely to expect or hope that other people and events will either cause or solve their problems. People with an external locus of control, therefore, may be better off in standard treatment programs because they may benefit from the externally delivered information and directives to follow. There is no shame in this. If you believe that you have an external locus of control, please feel free to participate in a structured treatment program of your choice. In Chapter 7, I describe different types of treatment programs and how to decide which may be most appropriate for you. This does not mean that you will fail in recovery if you have a more *external* locus of control, but suggests that it may help if you try to embrace the idea that you yourself have the capacity to make good choices and positive behavior changes.

From another perspective, this book is likely best suited for people with reasonably good *self-efficacy*. People with self-efficacy perceive that for any given challenge ahead, they have the right stuff to succeed, it will be a positive experience, it will be worth the effort, and it will pay off (Bandura, 1977, 1997). The antithesis of this is *learned helplessness* (Seligman, 1991)—perceptions of hopelessness and helplessness about being able to produce the behaviors that will be necessary to succeed in any specific challenge ahead. Research on recovery from alcohol use problems shows a significant correlation between positive self-efficacy and successful recovery (Greenfield et al., 2000). This means that simply believing that you can succeed increases significantly the likelihood that you will.

Obviously, if you have had a lot of positive early-life experiences, you are more likely to possess a greater degree of self-efficacy. But having had life experiences leading you to a place of hopelessness and helplessness does not mean you cannot develop self-efficacy. The many shelves of popular self-help psychology books broadcast countless ways to do this. Consider Wayne Dyer, a long-time and well-respected cognitive behaviorist, and his idea of "attractor energies" (Dyer, 2002). This concept points out that attraction, like the force of gravity, is the most powerful force of energy in the universe. If thoughts are a form of energy, it follows that negative thoughts attract more negatives into our lives, whereas positive thoughts bring things that are more positive.

If you think this is all a bunch of mumbo-jumbo, consider this: A little boy sees another kid pedal through his neighborhood on a shiny new bike. If this little boy says to himself, "What a beautiful bike! Too bad I'll never get one of those," what do you think the chances are that he ever will get one? If, instead, he says "Wow! What a fantastic bike. I'm going to get one of those no matter what it takes!" Now what do you suppose the chances are that he will get the bike he desires? Positive wishes tend to motivate us to take action.

Specifically related to recovery, try to catch your disparaging beliefs—the thoughts that you cannot do it. Toss them out and think positively for a moment instead. This would seem to be common sense.

of course, but it is not necessarily easy to do. Realistically, though, there is every reason to think positively—to believe that you can succeed in overcoming an alcohol use problem. Millions of people do. Odds are that you simply have been *discouraged* rather than *encouraged* by others— that is, other people have been telling you that you that you are a failure or will fail if you do not go to AA or to a group treatment program. So, of course, you become doubtful. Take heart! The research is there. Countless individuals recover on their own—and helping them succeed is their own belief that they can.

If you have an internal locus of control, reasonable self-efficacy, and a preference for doing things on your own, you may be asking yourself why you should even read this book. My response is that even the most rugged individualists need to capitalize on the experience and knowledge of others. I once decided to build a lawn shed after a storm blew down my old shed made of tin. I recognized that I am not a carpenter, but I consider myself to be a handy, self-sufficient guy. I got five or six books at the library on how to build lawn sheds. I talked with people at hardware stores and lumberyards. Then I carefully designed my own shed, set up a schedule, and went to work. Several weekends later, I had a beautiful shed, solidly built by my own two left hands, with no prior experience whatsoever. Were there a few mistakes? Sure, but I corrected them with a little more study and advice. If I had tried to build the shed without reading a book on how to do it, it would have turned out looking like a kid's driftwood beach fort.

Indeed, you can do many things, even complicated things in which you have little or no experience. But when it comes to lawn sheds and sobriety, if you are not going to contract out the job, you must study-up on how to do it. Overcoming an alcohol use problem can be much more complicated than most people will ever imagine and a much greater challenge than building a lawn shed. You can definitely succeed without formal treatment programs or AA, but it will be important to seek information and resources to build your recovery plan in a way that is specifically effective for you.

In the treatment field and in AA, it is thought that when people do manage to stay sober on their own, the quality of their recovery is often poor—that they show little or no improvement in their emotional control, relationships, productivity, etc. Indeed, I have met many individuals who have quit drinking on their own but seem to remain their old depressed, irascible, critical, or avoidant selves. On the other hand I have met many individuals who are also "dry but not in recovery" who have long participated in treatment and 12-step programs. And I have met many self-directed abstainers in solid recovery with admirable lifestyles, optimism, productivity, and relationships. The important point is that, regardless of the venue, some people are able to see quitting drinking as an opportunity for personal growth, and they work toward changes in important dimensions of their lives. It is this attitude, along with real behavior changes, that make for a positive and enduring recovery.

A Template for Recovery

I am increasingly excited about the self-directed approach I have developed. It is elegantly simple in concept, yet vastly comprehensive. I liken it to the principle of Occam's razor: The simplest, most obvious, uncluttered answer is usually the right one. *The New Template for Recovery* is based on the concept that quitting drinking and recovery are two different things. Recovery is an on-going, self-liberating, life experience far beyond the mere act of quitting drinking. A recovery built around constantly reviewing the past and just waiting to see if life gets any better is stagnating and depressing. So the self-directed approach is about *you* building *your* life *your* way, starting *now*, in a rewarding and self-sustaining process. It places your alcohol use problem in the past where it belongs, so at some point in the future, if you glance back, you will see the old addiction at a great and safe distance behind you.

The structure of this approach is based on an anthropological, as much as a psychological, understanding that human life is not a singular endeavor but, rather, is played out in different functional domains. Life is about finding fulfillment in physical health, mental health, relationships, productivity, recreation, choice of where you live, and finding a philosophical or spiritual position to live by. These are all areas of life that eventually are affected by alcohol dependence and, therefore, become the areas of recovery on which to focus. What this means is that there is not just one recovery; there are many. And the recovery I am talking about is not merely recovery from the effects of alcohol but also from all the assaults against your self-esteem, your losses and perceived failures, your inhibitions and self-doubts, across your whole life. It is about discovering your needs, who you really are, or want to be, and how you want to live. It is about the humanistic psychology holy grail of *self-actualization*.

A comprehensive recovery plan focuses on building or rebuilding some or all of these life areas. This book offers a template for this process that is adaptable for each person as he or she deems appropriate. After some self-assessment and important information about addiction, separate chapters are devoted to how to gain recovery based your unique goals and plans for each area of life.

This is a forward-going approach, progressive rather than regressive, proactive rather than reactive—and it is under your control. If someone wants or needs to know what your recovery plan is, you will be able to confidently tell them about each component. This can be impressive, and as comprehensive and as detailed as you like. You can peruse the chapters as you wish and build your own strategy. I present the information in sections and in an order that is intuitively logical. If you do not need or wish to follow my suggested arrangement of sections, feel free to jump ahead to any sections that appeal to you. Please forgive my many redundancies. These are intentional because I realize that some people will not read all the chapters.

This book makes liberal use of different terms to describe drinking problems. *Alcohol use problem* is the current preferred expression in scholarly literature because it is broad and non-political. It does not assume a cause and is not attached to any particular theory of addiction. In fact, although controversial, the latest addition of the Diagnostic and Statistical Manual of the American Psychiatric Association—DSM-5 (2013) has shed the terms "abuse" and "dependence" in the new chapter on Substance-Related and Addictive Disorders. With this change a person will no longer be diagnosed with either an Alcohol Abuse Disorder or an Alcohol Dependence Disorder, but rather with an Alcohol Use Disorder. Nevertheless, in this book I take the liberty of using a variety of terms in order to convey understanding in different contexts including: alcohol use, abuse, dependence, addiction, alcoholic, alcoholism, and problem drinking. Each of these terms actually has somewhat different implications which will become clear as you begin to read.

Before going any further, it is also important to me that you know about the limitations of what I am presenting. I strongly support research-based concepts and strategies. Thus, I have tried to incorporate into this work as much research-based material as I reasonably could.

Much of the material I am presenting, however, is based on my many years of experience with thousands of people with alcohol and other drug use problems, and drawn from my study of the fields of addiction research, sociology, cultural anthropology, psychology, and medicine. Although I have not included comprehensive documentation on nearly as many topics as I might have, I believe there is more than enough documentation to be helpful. Clearly, what I am presenting are not the ultimate, always correct, definitive answers about recovery. Rather *The New Template for Recovery* should be seen as an optimistic work-in-progress. And if you are the sort of person who is already attracted to the concept of a self-directed recovery, I trust that you will naturally question many things I have to say in a healthy way.

Part 1

Get Square with What You Need to Do

Chapter 1

Are You Safe to Quit Drinking?

Problem:	*Alcohol withdrawal can be physically and mentally unsafe.*
How to win:	*Evaluate your withdrawal risk and follow through on the appropriate help option.*

Withdrawal Risks

While most people can quit drinking abruptly (cold turkey) without harm, it is not always safe. Depending on how much you have been drinking, for how long, how old you are, and other health factors, you need to be aware of the risk of harm from withdrawal and options for safely quitting. Most people realize that *getting* intoxicated is dangerous. Acute intoxication can lead to delirium, coma, convulsions, respiratory arrest, and death. And of course, long-term, there are myriad deleterious effects throughout the body—organs, muscle tissue, circulatory and nervous systems, brain and cognitive functions are all compromised and eventually damaged.

What most people do not know is that the *withdrawal* process also can be damaging. Once the brain is accustomed to being bathed in alcohol, it does not like having the alcohol removed. Heart attacks and strokes are possible as blood pressure can rise precipitously. Seizures and a phenomenon known as delirium tremens (the DTs) can occur. Cognitive damage also can result—in some cases permanently—and repeated withdrawals are especially challenging to the brain. A "kindling" phenomenon occurs as symptoms of withdrawal and its effects worsen with repeated detoxifications.

Anyone who has a tolerance to alcohol will have some level of withdrawal upon quitting drinking, although only about 50 percent will notice symptoms. Research indicates that the incidence of *noticeable* withdrawal symptoms in the general U.S. population is low, whereas *most* people in treatment programs for alcohol use problems report withdrawal symptoms (Caetano, Clark & Greenfield, 1998; Saitz, 1998).

Actually, each drinking episode is followed by withdrawal. Many people experience this as a hangover. If you are habituated to alcohol from regular use, however, and have increased tolerance, you may not notice significant hangover symptoms. It is important to know that the absence of symptoms does not mean the absence of damage. This may well be the case, but you just do not feel it. Because of this tolerance phenomenon, many alcohol dependent people do not realize the danger both from drinking and from withdrawal each time they quit. As one of my patients put it, "I thought I had developed an *immunity* to alcohol because I could drink so much, and without hangovers." Big mistake!

Withdrawal Assessment

Whether or not you are safe to quit drinking may require a professional medical assessment. If you have any concerns at all, see your primary care physician, or an American Society of Addiction Medicine certified specialist, or go to a hospital emergency room or treatment center. This book can only begin to explain some of the symptoms and individual characteristics that suggest your risk of experiencing withdrawal problems.

Cutting to the chase—here are the alcohol withdrawal symptoms identified in the widely used Clinical Institute Withdrawal Assessment of Alcohol Scale, Revised (CIWA-Ar) (Sullivan et al., 1989), along with my discussion of what some of these symptoms might mean for you. Remember—the items on the scale are designed to be asked and observed by a medical professional. I offer the scale here so you get some idea of what is or could be happening to you. Habituation and withdrawal are discussed further in Chapter 5, on the physical addiction process and effects.

Clinical Institute Withdrawal Assessment of Alcohol Scale, Revised (CIWA-Ar)

[Many of the numbered response options are blank intentionally because they represent a subjective range of responses between extremes.]

NAUSEA AND VOMITING—Do you feel sick to your stomach? Have you vomited?

0 no nausea and no vomiting

1 mild nausea with no vomiting

2

3

4 intermittent nausea with dry heaves

5

6

7 constant nausea, frequent dry heaves and vomiting

TACTILE DISTURBANCES—Have you any itching, pins and needles sensations, any burning, any numbness, or do you feel bugs crawling on or under your skin?

0 none

1 very mild itching, pins and needles, burning or numbness

2 mild itching, pins and needles, burning or numbness

3 moderate itching, pins and needles, burning or numbness

4 moderately severe hallucinations

5 severe hallucinations

6 extremely severe hallucinations

7 continuous hallucinations

TREMOR—Arms extended and fingers spread apart.

0 no tremor

1 not visible, but can be felt fingertip to fingertip

2

3

4 moderate, with patient's arms extended

5

6

7 severe, even with arms not extended

AUDITORY DISTURBANCES—Are you more aware of sounds around you? Are they harsh? Do they frighten you? Are you hearing anything that is disturbing to you? Are you hearing things you know are not there?

0 not present

1 very mild harshness or ability to frighten

2 mild harshness or ability to frighten

3 moderate harshness or ability to frighten

4 moderately severe hallucinations

5 severe hallucinations

6 extremely severe hallucinations

7 continuous hallucinations

PAROXYSMAL SWEATS

0 no sweat visible

1 barely perceptible sweating, palms moist

2

3

4 beads of sweat obvious on forehead

5

6

7 drenching sweats

VISUAL DISTURBANCES—Does the light appear to be too bright? Is its color different? Does it hurt your eyes? Are you seeing anything that is disturbing to you? Are you seeing things you know are not there?

0 not present

1 very mild sensitivity

2 mild sensitivity

3 moderate sensitivity

4 moderately severe hallucinations

5 severe hallucinations

6 extremely severe hallucinations

7 continuous hallucinations

ANXIETY—Do you feel nervous?

0 no anxiety, at ease

1 mild anxious

2

3

4 moderately anxious, or guarded, so anxiety is inferred

5

6

7 equivalent to acute panic states as seen in severe delirium or acute schizophrenic reactions

HEADACHE, FULLNESS IN HEAD—Does your head feel different? Does it feel like there is a band around your head? Do not rate for dizziness or lightheadedness. Otherwise, rate severity.

0 not present

1 very mild

2 mild

3 moderate

4 moderately severe

5 severe

6 very severe

7 extremely severe

AGITATION

0 normal activity

1 somewhat more than normal activity

2

3

4 moderately fidgety and restless

5

6

7 paces back and forth during most of the interview, or constantly thrashes about

ORIENTATION AND CLOUDING OF SENSORIUM—What day is this? Where are you?

0 oriented and can do serial additions

1 cannot do serial additions or is uncertain about date

2 disoriented for date by no more than 2 calendar days

3 disoriented for date by more than 2 calendar days

4 disoriented for place/or person

Total **CIWA-Ar** Score _____
Maximum Possible Score 67

Patients scoring less than 10 do not usually need additional medication for withdrawal. The ratings are necessarily subjective. Nothing beats actual medical assessment by a doctor, and the scale's recommendation that people with a score lower than ten usually do not need medical attention is really a moving target. What about scores only slightly higher than 10? Again, about half of those who are habituated to alcohol—that is, having a tolerance—do not experience any of these symptoms. If you have not noticed any withdrawal symptoms, this does not mean that you are safe. In general, the older you are, the more you have been drinking in quantity and frequency, the more times you have been through withdrawal, and the more health problems you have, the greater your risk for withdrawal-related problems.

Apart from feeling ill, anxious, and/or shaky, as mentioned above, more serious withdrawal problems include convulsions or seizures and/or delirium tremens (the DTs). Seizures are a definite sign that you need immediate medical attention. One or two seizures are unlikely to harm you seriously, but back-to-back seizures can cause death. The DTs can have a rather late onset, occurring up to a week after the person has stopped imbibing. The DTs are dangerous. Symptoms may include disorientation, losing touch with reality (psychosis), intense anxiety, severe agitation, accelerated heart rate (tachycardia), high blood pressure, and fever. Persons can lose touch with who they are, where they are, and who they are with. One patient several days after being admitted to our treatment program, walked into my office believing that it was his bank and that I was a teller rather that a treatment program director. Be aware that the "shakes" that drinkers commonly develop within the first day after quitting, although not insignificant, are not the same as the DTs.

Options for a Safe Withdrawal

Faced with a possible withdrawal problem, what should you do? Here are the options:

Option 1: Continuing to drink as you have

This option would only delay your withdrawal and is a decidedly poor choice in the long run. The longer you wait, the more complicated your withdrawal will become. Costs and eventual losses certainly will worsen across time. That way madness lies.

Option 2: Quitting cold turkey

This also is a bad choice if you have been drinking several times per week, drinking more than three or four drinks on each occasion, have a tolerance, are over age thirty, have any other health problems, or have a history of withdrawal problems. Your withdrawal could be physically and mentally damaging, and unnecessarily uncomfortable.

Option 3: Self-tapering

Slowly, evenly, decreasing the amount you drink each day across two or more weeks is a physically safe way to quit drinking, but it is surprisingly difficult to do. People who try this almost always fail. They tend to get a one- or two-day start but then blow it by overdrinking and having to start their taper again (See the "loss of control" element in Chapter 2). For some individuals, even a small decrease in their nightly intake of alcohol can cause withdrawal problems. In hospital detoxification units, alcoholics often have to be medicated to offset their withdrawal symptoms even before their blood/alcohol concentration has dropped below the legal limit to drive.

Option 4: Community-based social detoxification

This is a good option for anyone, but especially for those who do not have much money or health insurance. Social detoxification programs are usually community-funded residential centers or small clinics where persons, generally without other resources, go for help with withdrawal. Trained personnel monitor withdrawal symptoms and may send individuals to a hospital emergency room if they appear to be in trouble. In some social detox centers a doctor is present. People generally spend from one to five nights at these centers. Otherwise they are free to come and go as they please.

Option 5: Clinic or office based, medically supervised detoxification

Recommended! This option usually involves going to a doctor's office for a physical examination or just a vital-signs check if you are a patient of record. Then, if you're not admitted to a hospital detoxification unit, you can quit drinking at home while taking a protective medication. The type of medications used most often are benzodiazepines, such as Librium, Valium, or Klonopin. These medications have proven to be effective at protecting the brain and easing anxiety during withdrawal. They are tried-and-true anti-anxiety medications. Generally, low dosages are sufficient and do not prohibit most people from doing ordinary things such as driving a car and going to work. But the benzodiazepines are addictive in and of themselves. Therefore, it is generally a good idea not to use these medications for more than a week.

If you are considering this option, it is crucial that you *do not drink while on the medication.* If you are unable to abstain while taking benzodiazepines, you run the risk of becoming overly sedated and potentially dying in the process. If you think you may not be able to stop drinking at home, for any reason, or if you have other physical health issues such as a compromised liver, heart disease, or brittle diabetes, you must not try this option and instead go with Option 6.

Option 6: Hospital-based inpatient detoxification (medically managed)

Also recommended. Hospital-based inpatient detoxification provides the widest margin of safety. Again, it becomes particularly important to have detoxification managed at this level for those with a history of heavy and prolonged drinking, elderly people, and people with other health issues, such as diabetes, heart conditions, or liver problems. Understand that detoxification and treatment are two different things. Being treated for detoxification is a medical procedure and does not obligate you to participate in a treatment program, although treatment options will likely be offered to you as you complete detoxification.

Nutrition and Detoxification

Whatever approach you take to quit drinking, it is important to help your brain and body recover with good nutrition. Alcohol use seriously impairs the body's ability to utilize vitamins and nutrients. This can result in an array of problems including a compromised immune system, brain and peripheral nervous system damage, osteoporosis, muscular atrophication, coronary artery disease, and increased cancer risk. In order to counteract these problems, nutritional supplements are widely recommended. For example, regular drinking depletes thiamine (vitamin B-1), and this is what causes Korsakoff's disease—a serious type of brain damage from heavy drinking. Thus, it is found to be helpful to take a multiple vitamin that includes the B complex, to help the brain recover. Many medical sources—your allopathic or naturopathic doctor, medical websites, etc.—will advise you to increase vitamins to assist detoxification and your continuing recovery. In addition to the B complex (B-1, 2, 3, 5, 6, 12) important withdrawal/detox vitamins and supplements include: Vitamins (A, C, D, E, K), folic acid, choline, magnesium, zinc, calcium, and many others.

Even a quick search of the Internet produces a barrage of medical and commercial information about vitamins and minerals that may be helpful in detoxification and recovery. What can be concluded is that it is a good idea to make sure you are getting adequate amounts of important nutrients through diet and supplements. Unfortunately, the American credo that more is better has led vitamin manufactures to tout "mega" dosages often in excess of what are needed or healthy in order to compete for market share. From vitamin A to zinc, some supplements are known to be toxic in high amounts. So don't overdo it. The dosages in most daily multiple vitamins are probably all you need. My advice is to consult with your own doctor on appropriate supplements for you. Also, see Chapter 10 on recovery of health and fitness.

Medications That May Help You Quit Drinking

There are now several drugs marketed to help quit drinking. These include:

- Naltrexone, marketed in its pill form as Revia and Depade, and as Vivitol in its once a month injectable form
- Acamprosate, marketed as Campral
- Topiramate, marketed as Topamax

These medications are thought to help support total abstinence by decreasing one's urge to drink. Research to date indicates that the drugs are moderately more effective than placebos (Latt et al., 2002; Johnson et al., 2003; Bouza et al., 2004; Mann et al., 2006). They appear to be most effective when combined with recovery counseling and close medical management. Thus you may want to investigate the use of such medications. Side effects are generally very mild. But be aware that these medications are not cheap and can only be a small part of a possible recovery. My view is that if you are going to spend that kind of money, spend it instead on healthy nutrition and fitness activities, or on recovery counseling sessions.

Another medicinal resource is Antabuse (disulfiram). This is the one that will make you sick, even violently ill, if you drink after taking it. That's because it inhibits the liver from producing cortisol and prolactin, which are the hormones needed to break down acetaldehyde (a toxic metabolite of alcohol) before it poisons you. There is a concern about possible liver damage with this drug for some individuals, but in most cases this risk is low compared to the effects of alcohol on the liver. Like a cast on a broken arm, Antabuse can powerfully deter a person from drinking in the early weeks and months of recovery—until one's mind and life patterns have sufficiently healed. It works best if monitored daily by one's doctor, pharmacist, or family member. The problem is, if not monitored by someone else, it is too easy to put aside or forget to take over a weekend—then it's off to the races with drinking again.

Of course, there are myriad natural products available on the Internet touted to make withdrawal and abstinence easier. As with any medication or supplement, may the buyer beware.

In summary, if you think you may have any withdrawal issues related to your drinking, do not hesitate to contact your doctor or go to an emergency room or treatment center for evaluation. Also, you must realize that the level of withdrawal management you may require does not necessarily correlate with the type or level of overarching drinking problem you may have. To understand this, you need a meaningful assessment.

Chapter 2

Do You or Do You Not Have a Problem?

Problem:	*Alcohol abuse/dependence can be difficult for the drinker to recognize.*
How to win:	*Complete the self-assessment or assisted assessment options described.*

There are several ways to assess whether you have an alcohol use problem and to get a handle on the type and extent of the problem if you have one. Here are four options:

1. You can start with standardized brief screening questionnaires that have been developed for research purposes and for use by helping professionals in doctor's offices, hospitals, medical clinics, and schools.
2. You could go to a treatment center and undertake an assessment process that includes a face-to-face interview with a certified or licensed substance-abuse professional.
3. You might do the same thing with a counselor or a psychologist in private practice who specializes in substance abuse.
4. You could *self-assess* by learning how good professional assessments are actually done.

Option 1: Brief Screening Tests

As a more recent standard of care in the medical field, questions about alcohol use have become part of the medical history that people routinely are required to fill out on intake forms. Like other medical screening tests, however, these questions only suggest to doctors and their patients that they may have a problem. Then to determine the actual presence and extent of a problem, more advanced tests are ordered or recommended.

Three of the most commonly used screens for alcohol use problems are included here. Each has a proven record in research. They have credible validity to the extent that they are more often correct than incorrect at identifying who does or who does not have a drinking problem. If your answers on any of these three questionnaires indicate a positive result, or are negative but you still are concerned, you need to consider undertaking a more comprehensive assessment. The problem with brief screening questionnaires is that they produce many *false positives* (they indicate a problem when one does not exist) and *false negatives* (missing a problem that really exists).

The CAGE Questions

Have you ever felt the need to cut down on your drinking?

Have people annoyed you by criticizing your drinking?

Have you ever felt guilty about drinking?

Have you ever felt you needed a drink first thing in the morning (eye-opener) to steady your nerves or to get rid of a hangover?

The *CAGE* has been around for many years and has considerable validity, but only as a screen. A "yes" response to any of the four questions recommends that you seek further assessment.

The AUDIT

1. How often do you have a drink containing alcohol?

(0) Never (Skip to Questions 9-10)

(1) Monthly or less

(2) 2 to 4 times a month

(3) 2 to 3 times a week

(4) 4 or more times a week

2. How many drinks containing alcohol do you have on a typical day when you are drinking?

(0) 1 or 2

(1) 3 or 4

(2) 5 or 6

(3) 7, 8, or 9

(4) 10 or more

3. How often do you have six or more drinks on one occasion?

(0) Never

(1) Less than monthly

(2) Monthly

(3) Weekly

(4) Daily or almost daily

4. How often during the last year have you found that you were not able to stop drinking once you had started?

(0) Never

(1) Less than monthly

(2) Monthly

(3) Weekly

(4) Daily or almost daily

5. How often during the last year have you failed to do what was normally expected from you because of drinking?

(0) Never

(1) Less than monthly

(2) Monthly

(3) Weekly

(4) Daily or almost daily

6. How often during the last year have you been unable to remember what happened the night before because you had been drinking?

(0) Never

(1) Less than monthly

(2) Monthly

(3) Weekly

(4) Daily or almost daily

7. How often during the last year have you needed an alcoholic drink first thing in the morning to get yourself going after a night of heavy drinking?

(0) Never

(1) Less than monthly

(2) Monthly

(3) Weekly

(4) Daily or almost daily

8. How often during the last year have you had a feeling of guilt or remorse after drinking?

(0) Never

(1) Less than monthly

(2) Monthly

(3) Weekly

(4) Daily or almost daily

9.   Have you or someone else been injured as a result of your drinking?

(0) No

(2) Yes, but not in the last year

(4) Yes, during the last year

10. Has a relative, friend, doctor, or another health professional expressed concern about your drinking or suggested you cut down?

(0) No

(2) Yes, but not in the last year

(4) Yes, during the last year

Add up the points associated with your answers above. A total score of 8 or more indicates harmful drinking behavior.

The Short MAST (Michigan Alcoholism Screening Test, Seltzer et al., 1975)

1. Do you feel you are a normal drinker?	yes	**no**
2. Do your spouse or parents worry or complain about your drinking?	**yes**	no
3. Do you ever feel bad about your drinking?	**yes**	no
4. Do friends or relatives think you are a normal drinker?	yes	**no**
5. Are you always able to stop drinking when you want to?	yes	**no**
6. Have you ever attended a meeting of Alcoholics Anonymous?	**yes**	no
7. Has drinking ever created problems between you and your spouse?	**yes**	no

8. Have you ever gotten into trouble at work because of drinking? **yes** no

9. Have you ever neglected your obligations, your family, or your work for 2 or more days in a row because you were drinking? **yes** no

10. Have you ever gone to anyone for help about your drinking? **yes** no

11. Have you ever been in the hospital because of drinking? **yes** no

12. Have you ever been arrested even for a few hours because of drinking? **yes** no

13. Have you ever been arrested for drunk driving or driving after drinking? **yes** no

Scoring: 1 point for each of answers in bold.
  2 points = possible alcohol problem.
  3 points = *probable* alcohol problem.

Once again—these tests are only screens, so if you have concerns about your drinking or your score, get a more comprehensive assessment.

Option 2: Treatment Center-Based Assessment

This option makes it easy for you. All you have to do is look in the Yellow Pages under "Alcoholism," or do an Internet search for alcoholism treatment centers, and you will see all the inpatient and outpatient treatment programs, usually state certified, in your area. Be assertive and call them. They are reasonably confidential. You do not even have to say who you are. In general, they are aware that those who seek them out feel unsafe and they are unlikely to ask for more than a first name. There is no cost in calling several programs to ask about the availability of assessments, how they are conducted, and what they cost. Each state monitors the assessment and treatment protocols of certified programs, and this provides some reliability.

At the same time, you will have to trust that the person you see is not overly biased or under pressure to fill beds or treatment group spaces. I have directed both inpatient and outpatient treatment programs, and have been president of a treatment programs director's consortium. Sad to say, I'm fully aware of the so-called "pocket-book assessment"—if you have the insurance or the cash, the treatment center will just happen to have the right treatment program for you. And when courts order individuals to get assessments at treatment programs and require that they follow any resulting treatment recommendations, this becomes tantamount to the fox guarding the henhouse.

I have, however, observed improvements over the years. For example, some states will not allow treatment program owners themselves to do assessments. But there is still considerable competition and pressure to fill treatment programs. Following an assessment at a treatment program, those being assessed are often asked to sign a form acknowledging that their condition likely will worsen if they do not participate in the prescribed course of treatment. This is a questionable practice because it is not backed by credible research. To the contrary, as I have said, research supports that millions of people recover on their own.

In addition, if you are assessed at a treatment center, you should be aware of a peculiar dynamic: Throughout the field of mental health counseling and therapy, it is understood that people may hold back a little. This *resistance* is a natural part of the initial therapeutic process, thought to result from clients not trusting how therapists will respond to private information, and/or unwittingly protecting themselves from their troubling internal experience. In general, when people fear that they may not be able to control a novel situation and risk losing freedoms, they may begin to sound defensive and/or angry. In psychology, this is referred to as "normal human reactance." Unfortunately, in treatment programs when individuals being assessed show normal human reactance this can be misinterpreted as evidence of denial of a more significant alcohol problem than actually exists. Thus, people can be referred to higher levels of treatment than they really need (Portman, 1987).

Option 3: Assessment with a Private Practitioner

While working in treatment centers I have done countless assessments. I have taught assessment strategy, and have done myriad assessments in my private practice. With a private practitioner, as with a treatment center, you can run the risk of getting a financially driven assessment (e.g., the counselor has to make payments on his Jeep Cherokee). But the benefit of this option is that the private practitioner, who is not financially affiliated with a treatment program, is at greater liberty to suggest that you do not have a substance use problem if you perhaps do not. A private counselor also can refer you to *any* program that may specifically meet your individual needs, or can provide office-based treatment with you on a private schedule.

Often, people feel safer in a private office setting—safe that they are not going to get their arms twisted to participate in something they do not want to participate in. Again, look in the Yellow Pages or on the Internet for counselors and psychologists who specialize in substance abuse. But be careful. In her book *Inside Rehab*, Anne Fletcher points out a tendency for therapists at all levels to list as many specialties as they can on their websites although they may not necessarily be fully qualified in each, (Fletcher, 2013). So make sure you find out what their actual experience is in addictions counseling. As with treatment centers, simply call and ask questions about the practitioner's experience, processes, and fees.

Option 4: Doing Your Own Assessment

If you have an internal locus of control, or are simply mistrusting, or are "in denial" (resisting self-acknowledgement of an alcohol use problem), you are not likely to take anyone else's word about the extent of your possible drinking problem. You will want to learn how any result was arrived at. It then behooves you to learn about how assessments are really done and what substantiates a diagnosis. I believe it is entirely possible to do a reasonably accurate self-assessment regarding an alcohol use problem, but, I implore you to understand at least one big caveat: The trouble with an alcohol dependence problem is that it is not merely physical but also psychological. The drinker seldom understands the extent to which the alcohol has become his or her emotional manager. In Chapter 7, I discuss this phenomenon carefully—how it occurs and why the drinker is the last to know. For the moment, just be aware that addiction involves a hijacking of one's mind, with the victim not realizing that this has happened. Thus, you may have difficulty comprehending and honestly responding to a self-assessment, *even if you think you can.* I can only suggest that you back up your self-assessment with an opinion from a credible professional.

That said and well in mind, here is how you can gain a good understanding of whether you have an alcohol use problem, and if you do, the extent of the problem. This self-assessment system has three components: (1) the self-assessment grid; (2) DSM criteria; and (3) misunderstandings about what is or is not a substance use problem

The Self-Assessment Grid

I have introduced the self-assessment grid to many groups in treatment programs and to many individuals in my private practice. Those who do this tend to find it educational and meaningful. Here is how to use it:

First, we make a distinction between three types of drinkers:

1. Social drinker
2. Problem drinker
3. Dependent/Alcoholic drinker

Then we compare each of these three levels of alcohol use on four dimensions:

1. Quantity and frequency of drinking
2. Reasons for drinking
3. Costs associated with drinking
4. The element of loss of control

Instructions for using the grid are as follows:

1. Do a quick read-through of the grid to get an understanding of the concept.
2. Read the discussion that follows about each dimension.
3. Write down what your own drinking experience has been for each dimension.

Self-Assessment Grid

	Social drinker	*Problem* drinker	*Dependent/Alcoholic* drinker
Quantity and frequency of drinking	From rarely to daily. Very rarely more than 2 drinks per occasion.	From occasionally to daily. Sometimes 1 or 2 drinks, sometimes quite a few more.	From occasionally to daily. Sometimes at inappropriate times (e.g., before work or during childcare). Rarely just 1 or 2 drinks. Often multiple drinks per occasion.
Reasons for drinking	To enhance the good times socially on a take-it-or-leave-it basis. To unwind in an evening. For health (e.g., keep good blood pressure and cholesterol).	Important to feel socially confident. To self-medicate moderate depression or anxiety in general.	Because at times without it, mood, anxiety, and/or social problems would seem unbearable. To avoid withdrawal symptoms.
Costs associated with drinking	None	May include costs to one or more life areas: Health/fitness Relationships Work Leisure activities Financially Legally Emotional management	Includes costs and losses in several life areas: Health/fitness Relationships Work Leisure activities Financially Legally Emotional management
Element of loss of control	Doesn't happen	Happens sometimes	Happens way too much

In this self-assessment guide I use the term "dependent"/alcoholic drinker rather than "addict"/alcoholic drinker. I have done so because although the current *Diagnostic and Statistical Manual of Mental Disorders* (American Psychiatric Association, 2013) prefers the word "addict," for many people that word conveys an exclusively *biological* meaning. In this book, the *psychological* component is emphasized. To me the term "dependent" has a broader meaning than the term "addict," including both psychological and physiological components.

Dimension 1: Quantity and Frequency of Drinking

Surprising to some, the quantity and frequency of alcohol use is probably *not* the most important dimension in the assessment of drinking problems. Nonetheless, it is a serviceable starting point because there is, in general, a direct linear correlation between how much and how often a person drinks and that person's alcohol use problem. Typically the more a person drinks the more problematic it is likely to become. Still, there are always some people who drink frequently but have no problem and others who drink infrequently, yet have significant problems. In the graph below, point A is the unusual case of a person who drinks a lot but evidences no problems or costs in his or her life. The person at point B is the unusual example of someone who drinks very little but has significant costs in major life areas, e.g., to health and fitness, relationships, work.

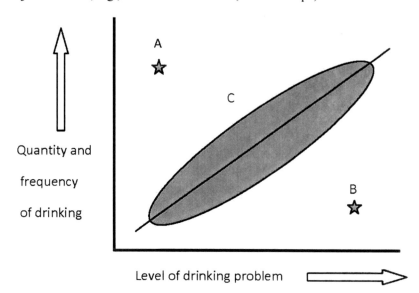

C = Most cases

A and B are unusual "outliers"

For *social drinkers,* the frequency may be as low as once or twice a year or as much as every evening. In the overall population, the frequency of drinking may be increasing somewhat in recent years. Doctors, emboldened by a considerable amount of research, are recommending small or moderate amounts of alcohol intake regularly for health benefits. Research over several decades suggested that light or moderate drinking can be healthy for most people. But there is no agreement among international health organizations on the level at which drinking becomes unhealthy. Recommended upper limits tend to range from two to four drinks per day for men and one to two drinks per day for women. Why the difference between men and women? The general assumption is that men on average are significantly larger than women. Any larger person will have a larger volume of blood and therefore a lower percentage of alcohol drink-for-drink compared with a smaller person.

In any case, researchers are persistent and restrictive about these drink limits. They do not mean "on average." Many people mistakenly assume that since they often, or even usually, stay within those limits, that they are healthy drinkers. Unfortunately this is not so.

Research in America generally supports that two drinks for men and one drink for women per day is healthy and that anything over this is unhealthy. Benefits at the lower limits include healthier heart, brain, metabolism, immunity, cognitive functioning, emotional health, and longevity. Drinking above these limits is associated with the reverse: increasingly compromised heart, brain, metabolism, immunity, cognitive and emotional functioning, and a shorter life-span. It is important to note that not all researchers agree that alcohol use, at any level, is healthy (Fillmore et al. 2004). You will find more discussion of this and related research in Chapter 5.

In their adult lives, *social drinkers* rarely exceed one or two drinks at each occasion. This is excluding the experimental abusive alcohol use typical of Americans in their teens and young adult years. As a side note, an estimated 70 to 90 percent of high school seniors and college freshmen drink abusively episodically. Imbibing more than four drinks per occasion is termed "binge drinking." This has not changed significantly over the past fifty years that researchers have followed such parameters. Perhaps one of the downsides of the "zero tolerance" approach advocated in American school systems is that without adult modeling and introduction to *appropriate* alcohol use, the old adage that *suppression breeds deviance* is borne-out—kids just can't wait to try it with their peers as soon as they can get their hands on it unsupervised. Also contributing to massive amounts of alcohol abuse by secondary school and college aged young people is their struggle to gain a positive social identity. Inebriation makes them feel socially confident, and social confidence is seen as sexy or sexually attractive. In a term that was coined about sixty years ago for what happens to most of these young abusive drinkers, they "mature out." But some do not, and continue as active alcoholics in their adult lives.

In any case, whether someone drank abusively as a teenager or young adult or not, as adults, social drinkers rarely drink more than one or two drinks on each occasion. The exception might be a special occasion such as a family member's wedding, but even then, four for five drinks would be the maximum. In that rare situation, the otherwise social drinker would be noticeably inebriated for lack of significant tolerance and hungover all the next day. This would be decidedly uncharacteristic of his or her usual pattern of non-problematic alcohol use.

If this has been your experience, you likely are a social drinker. But if you are an adult and drink more than four drinks (male) or two drinks (female) more than once every three or four months, you *may* have a problem. Remember—one drink equals 5 ounces of wine, 12 ounces of beer, or 1-1/2 ounces of liquor. People often tell me that they have just a couple of glasses of wine at night but as it turns out, they are drinking by the tumbler! If you have any question about your level of consumption, get out your measuring cup to see how many drinks you really are taking in per glass. A standard wine glass can hold from 9 to 10 or more ounces. So you may be drinking doubles without knowing it. A typical bottle of wine contains 750 milliliters which equals 25.36 ounces. So if you drank the whole bottle you will have had five drinks. Regardless, if you get intoxicated more than once or twice a year, and on occasions that are not truly special, this is not social drinking and you might have a problem.

Thus, for *problem drinkers*, the quantity of alcohol consumed per occasion is sometimes higher than four drinks for men or two drinks for women. But any exact cut-off numbers would be misleading. Practically speaking, problem drinkers have episodes of intoxication whereas social drinkers do not. However, there are also many problem drinkers who drink regularly but seldom, if ever, show signs of intoxication and, due to tolerance, would not say that they feel intoxicated. Such persons are referred to as "functioning," or in some cases even, "high-functioning" problem drinkers or alcoholics. They may be dependent on moderate amounts of alcohol nightly but evidence few problems in their lives. This, of course, does not mean that problems aren't brewing beneath the observable surface or that there won't eventually be deleterious effects.

Further out on the scale are the *dependent or alcoholic drinkers* who tend to drink at higher quantities and frequencies, although, again there is considerable variance. Additional factors determine the existence and extent of a problem. Contrary to popular assumptions, the dependent/alcoholic drinker does not necessary drink too much on all occasions. Most alcoholics who go to treatment are best characterized as *episodic over-drinkers*. Actually, this single erroneous perception—"I don't drink too much every time"—keeps millions of alcoholics from recognizing their addiction problem. They think that because they have only one or two drinks much or most of the time, they must not have a problem. Episodic over-drinking is still a problem. Drinking too much daily is simply an indicator of a problem that has progressed further and is more severe.

If you think you really don't have a drinking problem, or if you otherwise need to be clearer on the *quantity and frequency* of your drinking, try the following exercises:

1. Complete a personal quantity/frequency history below.

Your Personal Quantity/Frequency History:

Write down in all honesty your history of quantity and frequency of alcohol use for each stage of your life—as a child, teen, young adult, currently. Are there any patterns? Has your use changed at different times in your life based on age, geographies, school, jobs, relationships, or other changes?

_____

_____

_____

_____

_____

_____

_____

_____

_____

_____

_____

_____

_____

_____

_____

_____

_____

2. Ask your mate, other family member, or trusted friend for his or her opinion. This can help, but you have to be aware of a couple of things: Other people will not necessarily be honest, especially if they themselves drink too much, but also because they may not want to offend you.

3. Be an "anthropologist"—a *participant observer* in own life—and record or track your drinking for a couple of weeks. Make a copy of the following tracking sheet, which you can fold to keep in your wallet or purse.

Alcohol Use Tracking Sheet

	Type of Drink	Quantity	Start time	Finish Time	Where	Who with	BAC Estimate
Monday							
Tuesday							
Wednesday							
Thursday							
Friday							
Saturday							
Sunday							
Totals							

You'll notice that the last column has a space for your blood alcohol concentration (BAC) estimate. To document your BAC, use the chart below.

B.A.C. Estimations for Men and Women

Number Of Drinks	100 lb	120 lb	140 lb	160 lb	180 lb	200 lb	220 lb	240 lb
1								
Men	.04	.03	.03	.02	.02	.02	.02	.02
Women	.05	.04	.03	.03	.03	.02	.02	.02
2								
Men	.08	.06	.05	.05	.04	.04	.03	.03
Women	.09	.08	.07	.06	.05	.05	.04	.04
3								
Men	.11	.09	.08	.07	.06	.06	.05	.05
Women	.14	.11	.10	.09	.08	.07	.06	.06
4								
Men	.15	.12	.11	.09	.08	.08	.07	.06
Women	.18	.15	.13	.11	.10	.09	.08	.08
5								
Men	.19	.16	.13	.12	.11	.09	.09	.08
Women	.23	.19	.16	.14	.13	.11	.10	.09
6								
Men	.23	.19	.16	.14	.13	.11	.10	.09
Women	.27	.23	.19	.17	.15	.14	.12	.11
7								
Men	.26	.22	.19	.16	.15	.13	.12	.11
Women	.32	.27	.23	.20	.18	.16	.14	.13
8								
Men	.30	.25	.21	.19	.17	.15	.14	.13
Women	.36	.30	.26	.23	.20	.18	.17	.15
9								
Men	.34	.28	.24	.21	.19	.17	.15	.14
Women	.41	.34	.29	.26	.23	.20	.19	.17
10								
Men	.38	.31	.27	.23	.21	.19	.17	.16
Women	.45	.38	.32	.28	.25	.23	.21	.19

If you're honest, this tracking experiment can be enlightening. It is important to record every incidence of drinking and to be accurate in the quantity. Record a 12-ounce beer, or a 5-ounce glass of wine, or 1-1/2-ounces of hard liquor as one drink each. With beer these days, you have to be careful. Many types of beer have significantly higher *alcohol content by volume* (ABV) than others, from a low of about 0.4 percent (O'Doul's) to 10 percent (Expedition Stout). Sam Adams Triple Bock has an unbelievable 17.5 percent ABV. The beers with higher alcohol content tend to be the malt liquors and some of the microbrews.

Otherwise, most beers tend to be around 5 percent ABV. So a 12-ounce Budweiser (5 percent ABV) is counted as one drink, whereas a Double Cream Stout (7.5 percent ABV) must be counted as 1.5 drinks, and a Sam Adams Triple Bock (17.5 ABV) as 3.5 drinks. See the helpful list at: http://www.realbeer.com/edu/health/calories.php.

Wines tend not to vary as much in alcohol content. Most wines have from 11 to 14 percent ABV. The alcohol content of wine actually is self-limiting because as it increases, the yeast necessary for fermentation is destroyed. Be aware, however, that "fortified" wines can be much higher in alcohol content, simply because the manufacturers add alcohol after fermentation.

I do not recommend taking a baseline of your drinking if you already have a hunch or know that you have a drinking problem. If this is the way you feel, even ahead of the self-assessment described here, you are well advised to act on one of my recommended choices about safe withdrawal management and to take the steps to quit drinking straight away without tracking your drinking for any length of time.

Dimension 2: Reasons for Drinking

Social drinkers imbibe on some social occasions, and occasionally alone, to enhance a good time on a take-it-or-leave-it basis. That is, they are comfortable if alcohol is not available and often are involved socially without the use of alcohol or even thinking about it at all. Social drinkers also may drink to *unwind* before or with dinner. Most social drinkers, however, do not drink nightly and have many other ways of unwinding. Some social drinkers imbibe as much as nightly in the belief that it has health benefits, but, again, this is not more than a couple of drinks per evening.

Problem drinkers may drink for the above reasons but for additional reasons as well, including drinking to *alter their state of consciousness*. This has a slightly more nefarious connotation than simply to *unwind*. For instance, they may want to drink to overcome a depressed, angry, or anxious mood. A social drinker would rarely do this or endorse self-medicating a bad mood as a reason for drinking.

In addition, for the problem drinker, alcohol becomes more important in social situations. To feel adequate social self-confidence, they tend to rely on alcohol and are distressed if it is not available. In some cases this can lead to what is called "pre-drinking"—in which the individual is concerned about whether sufficient alcohol will be available at a social function, or with not wanting to appear to be a heavy drinker, so he or she drinks privately before attending the function. These behaviors do not fall into the category of social drinking.

Dependent drinkers drink because they need to. The no-drink option becomes more difficult or not possible at this stage. Usually, the effect of alcohol has become their primary emotional management system, and in many cases their social manager as well. The ability to adroitly identify and cope with various moods, even within normal range, is seriously compromised. Without alcohol in their system, their social self-confidence flags and their social skills fall by the wayside. They cannot imagine that anything will work as well to unwind, relax, or overcome a vague and growing sense of depression. In the extreme, they drink because they have to. Physical and psychological withdrawal symptoms compel them to continue imbibing.

Dimension 3: Costs Associated with Drinking

The dimension of costs is where the proverbial rubber hits the road. Ultimately, this is the most useful dimension by which to access a potential alcohol use problem. It is *the-proof-is-in-the-pudding* dimension because it refers to the negative outcomes or *effects* of one's drinking in different areas of life and functioning. This dimension takes some detective work, requiring us to ask questions about the effects across various areas of functioning: health and fitness, relationships, work, leisure pursuits, mood, financial, and legal costs. At an extreme, one could drink large quantities daily, but if everyone agrees that the person's mood is great, work is going well, relationships are thrilling, and health and fitness are fantastic, there simply is no alcohol use problem.

So what are the costs, or negative effects of drinking for *social drinkers*? The answer is zero, zip, none. Think about it. Any sort of cost, automatically and by definition, makes it problem drinking. All right— that's a bit of an exaggeration. We can make a few exceptions. Clearly, social drinkers spend money on alcohol, and some may spend more than is prudent for their income or budget. Consider the wine hobbyist who may not be a problem drinker or dependent drinker but spends a great deal on money and time on his wine hobby. Also, although problem drinkers and alcoholics are overrepresented in the DUI (driving under the influence) population, most DUI recipients are social drinkers who made a thoughtless mistake. A single DUI, stand-alone, does not a problem drinker or alcoholic make. Nevertheless, generally speaking, the Costs category is blank for social drinkers.

Problem drinkers, in contrast, will evidence costs in one or more areas of life. If someone keeps drinking despite identifiable health costs, this constitutes problem drinking. If someone keeps drinking despite negative effects in relationships, work, leisure activities, or ability to cope emotionally, this is problem drinking. When someone continues to drink despite negative life effects, he or she likely is facing at least a diagnosis of problem drinking.

Costs vary considerably from individual to individual on this dimension, as they do on the other dimensions. Someone may have had three divorces related to drinking but manage to keep a professional career on track. Another person may have a great marriage but has been fired three times. One person may have health costs while another person seems to be perfectly healthy. If there is a single linchpin cost, it is to *emotional regulation.* Most people do not realize that the first associated feature of an alcohol use problem is not relationship problems, lost jobs, or compromised health. It is increasing depression, or more general emotional deregulation that may include difficulty coping with anxieties, frustration, and anger. See Chapter 11: Emotional Recovery, for a more complete understanding of this phenomenon.

The difference between *problem* drinker and *dependent* drinker on the dimension of costs is one of degree. On average, the dependent drinker simply experiences more profound costs than the problem drinker, and ultimately not just *costs* to life areas but also *losses*—lost marriages, lost jobs, or no further participation in leisure or recreational pursuits.

Here again we see the impact on life areas that can be compromised by and are indicative of a substance use problem. You need to honestly appraise what costs may be associated with your drinking. I suggest that you try to write down possible costs per area on a sheet of paper, and ask a trusted friend or family member for feedback on the issue.

Areas of Life and Functioning Potentially Affected by Drinking:

- Health and/or fitness (a fall-off in basic health care activities, overweight, acute or chronic illnesses developing or poorly managed)
- Relationships (problems with family members, friends, co-workers, or romantic relationships)
- Work (productivity, working intoxicated, hung over, calling in sick, getting fired, staying in a job you don't like too long because you self-medicate at night with alcohol)
- Leisure, recreational, or hobby pursuits
- Emotional management (increased depression and/or anxiety)
- Financial
- Legal (alcohol-related driving offenses, disorderly conduct, domestic violence,
- Lawsuits stemming from your misbehavior or lapses in judgment)
- Any other costs

Before we continue, I want to further clarify the term I have been using: dependent/alcoholic drinker. The field of addictions treatment tends to assert that alcoholics are born—that by genetically endowed metabolic processes, alcohol affects alcoholics differently than it does social drinkers and makes them more prone to overdrinking. And to some extent research bears this out--but not completely. I discuss this more fully in chapter 5. The point to be made here is that in the broader bio/psycho/social model of addiction, alcohol use problems can have many causes. Anyone can become alcohol-dependent (or alcohol *addicted* if you prefer), if he or she imbibes at a sufficient quantity and frequency. Anyone can become physically and/or psychologically habituated. Although sometimes confusing, it generally does not take an expert to realize who among dependent drinkers is genetically predisposed and who is not. A look at one's parents, aunts, uncles, and grandparents, plus certain components of one's own drinking, usually tells the story. In effect, of course, the point is moot because the outcome is the same. Whether biologically predisposed or not, once psychologically and/or physically habituated, life falls apart. An argument can be made, however, that an alcohol dependent/addicted drinker who is not genetically set up to be alcoholic, may be able to become a limited or social drinker once the *psychosocial* causes that drove over-drinking have been resolved. Whereas, if the cause is *genetic*, attempting to control drinking is likely to be a script for disaster.

Dimension 4: The Element of Loss of Control

Loss of control does not apply to social drinkers—only to problem drinkers, and to a greater extent, to dependent/alcoholic drinkers. Although the meaning is broader, in the simplest sense it is the experience of intending to have a couple of drinks but winding up having more and getting intoxicated. Alcoholics, by genetic endowment, metabolize alcohol differently than social drinkers do. As a result, they do not seem to experience the unpleasant sensations that social drinkers get after a couple of drinks.

At a molecular level, beverage alcohol is known as ethanol. It is the same molecule in beer, wine, and hard liquor. It functions as a central nervous system depressant because it slows neural transmissions, effectively slowing thought processes, reaction time, and briefly lowering blood pressure, among other effects. But the ethanol molecule also is a pure carbohydrate. Thus, for all drinkers, the first effect of alcohol is not as a depressant but, instead, as a stimulant because it spikes blood glucose—it raises blood sugar. At first, heart rate and blood pressure go up, respiration increases, memory is enhanced, and, if in the company of others, verbal output increases. Many drinkers are thought to have their first drink after work, not so much to unwind as to get a bit of a pick-me-up.

For social drinkers, these positive effects are short-lived. A common myth among alcoholics is that social drinkers control their drinking. They do not. It is self-limiting. After a couple of drinks, the positive effects evaporate and the central nervous system depressant features start kicking in. They begin to feel slower, dull-witted, and tired. Thus, when offered a third drink they'll say, "Oh no, I'm tired." or, "No. I want to get something to eat." or, "No thanks. I think I want to get going now."

For the dependent drinker/alcoholic, however, two drinks feel good, and so do three. Four or more drinks are even better. This is part of the element of loss of control. These drinkers do not experience the negative effects until it is way too late. They can be in a blackout and still not have significant negative effects, even though they won't remember a thing the next morning. By genetic endowment, they are more alcohol-tolerant than social drinkers, so they do not experience the naturally limiting effects that stop social drinkers from over-imbibing. You may notice in a group of people that after a brief increase in a social drinker's conversational output, there comes a rapid decrease in verbal participation after a couple of drinks. In contrast, the verbal output of alcoholics continues to increase the more drinks they imbibe.

This element of loss of control is closely associated with a natural tolerance that alcoholics are thought to be born with, and it becomes diagnostic. It is an important element in assessing teenagers with possible drinking problems. After all, regarding costs as a primary assessment device, they have not had wrecked marriages, lost jobs, and the like, because they have not been married, have not had professions yet, and their health seems indefatigable. Therefore, we look at this issue of tolerance to help identify budding alcoholics. These individuals may get sick, vomit, and have a hangover on a first or second experience, but unlike social drinkers, tend to get over this quickly.

Active alcoholics, as a rule, do not get sick and they do not get significant hangovers. Thus, we worry about the teenager who knocks back ten beers and laughs at the other kid who throws up after drinking five beers. The myth that it is healthy to get a tolerance begins during the teen years. This makes intuitive sense to the uneducated, as it seems similar to gaining strength for a sport by working out more. With alcohol use, however, tolerance is habituation. It enables one to imbibe more ethanol but without noticing increasingly damaging effects on mind and body. It's a lot wiser to avoid tolerance so you can get the positive effects at the lowest, least damaging level. With habituation, you have to drink more to get the same results, and eventually there will have to be withdrawal. My advice to wannabe social drinkers is this: Never let your tolerance build up.

To explore another aspect of the element of loss of control, some therapists engage a client in a simple experiment that goes like this: The drinker is asked to drink a limit of two drinks each night for one week, and a follow-up appointment is made. Social drinkers have a high return rate. When asked how the experiment went, they typically report, "Yes, I had two drinks on the night after our appointment last week, but the next night we were doing something else and I didn't drink at all. On the weekend we went out of town and I had one beer at a restaurant. Then I didn't drink again until I remembered our appointment last night, so I had two beers." That's a social drinker. Alcohol has little importance in the lives of social drinkers.

Alcoholics—if they come back at all—have a different story to tell. The counselor asks, "So how'd it go last week?" The response typically is: "Great! I had two drinks each night last week." This is followed by a pause, and the counselor asks, "Okay, how about the weekend?" Then the response is something like, "Oh! Well, yes, Fred dropped by on Friday night, and we had a couple of six-packs, and, come to think of it, we partied pretty hard Saturday night and, well, I got drunk on Sunday, too, but last night I just had two drinks before our appointment, so you see I can do it."

In other words, folks, they just cannot do it. It's not their fault really, but they cannot *consistently* limit their drinking. Even when a person does manage to go a whole month on a set limit, an interesting phenomenon occurs. I might say to one of my clients, "So, Marty, it looks like you did just fine. You may be on your way to being a good social drinker." Then Marty will say, "Well, Doc, to tell you the truth, I don't think so." Then I say, "Well I don't understand. You did it, didn't you? You went all month without going over the drink limit?" Then Marty says, "Yes, but it wasn't so easy. To be honest, when I have to stop at two drinks *I just feel deprived.*" This is an important distinction. Social drinkers *never* feel deprived when they stop after a drink or two.

Another important consideration in assessment under the category of "loss of control" is that of a possible genetic propensity. Research from many quarters suggests that alcoholics metabolize alcohol differently than social drinkers. Therefore, we must look back. In all good assessments, we ask people about alcohol use histories among their siblings, parents, aunts and uncles, grandparents, and beyond. Here again, you have to be honest. Most of the time, if you had a family member whose drinking was a topic of conversation, this relative had a problem; otherwise, it would not have been talked about. If both parents are alcoholic, there may be as much as a fifty-fifty chance that their offspring will be alcoholic.

Many times, people tell me that none of their family members even uses alcohol. Then I find out that the family is of a religious orientation that forbids drinking. In these cases, potential genetic risks may be obscured. Whenever someone tells me that a family member does not drink at all, my follow-up question is, "Why is that?" The question is a good one because there is often a reason behind someone's tee-totaling. For example, the person may have had an early problem but was able to quit. Or, the parent was an abusive alcoholic so the person has a strong personal commitment to abstinence. Also, an extended family member may be abstinent because of a health issue.

DSM-IV-TR

Continuing with your self-assessment, let's look at how you might see yourself against the most widely accepted criteria in the medical and mental health professions—the DSM-IV-TR, the *Diagnostic and Statistical Manual of Mental Health Disorders* (fourth addition text revised, 2000) published by the American Psychiatric Association. The DSM-IV-TR has established the criteria by which insurance companies, treatment centers, and the entire mental health profession agree on a diagnosis of a mental health problem. For substance use, there are established criteria for two possible disorders: Substance Abuse and Substance Dependence. I include the DSM criteria here because these can be useful in your self-assessment. First, here are the criteria for Substance Dependence.

As mentioned, the DSM-5 has recently been published (American Psychiatric Association, 2013). Again, in the new volume the terms substance "dependence" and substance "abuse" have both been thrown out in favor of diagnoses expressed as substance "use" disorders in the chapter on *Substance-Related and Addictive Disorders*. So we now have, for example, *Alcohol Use Disorder, Cocaine Use Disorder*, etc. The designers of the DSM-5 wanted to reserve the term "dependence" for a person who by necessity becomes habituated to a medication for treatment of conditions such as chronic pain or anxiety disorders, verses the "compulsive, out-of-control drug use" characteristic of *addiction*. This, of course, is highly controversial.

The blanket term "substance use disorder" has the advantage of avoiding assumed causes or endorsement of specific theoretical models, but also loses some important nuances that help understanding. The DSM-5 does not include criteria for an *abuse* category at all, and the criteria for *alcohol use disorder* are pretty much the same as in the DSM-IV criteria for *Alcohol Dependence Disorder* anyway, so I've chosen to focus on the latter, with both *abuse* and *dependence* criteria for our self-assessment purposes.

DSM-IV-R Diagnostic Criteria for Substance Dependence

A maladaptive pattern of substance use, leading to clinically significant impairment or distress, as manifested by three (or more) of the following, occurring at any time in the same 12 month period:

(1)   tolerance, as defined by either of the following:
(a) a need for markedly increased amounts of the substance to achieve intoxication or desired effect
(b) markedly diminished effect with continued use of the same amount of the substance

(2)   withdrawal, as manifested by either of the following:
(a) the characteristic withdrawal syndrome for the substance
(b) the same (or closely related) substances taken to relieve or avoid withdrawal symptoms

(3)   the substance is often taken in larger amounts or over a longer period than was intended

(4)   there is a persistent desire or unsuccessful efforts to cut down or controlled substance use

(5)   a great deal of time is spent in activities necessary to obtain the substance (e.g. visiting multiple doctors are driving long distances), use the substance (e.g. chain-smoking), or recovery from its effects

(6)   important social, occupational, or recreational activities are given up or reduced because of substance use

(7)   the substance use is continued despite knowledge of having a persistent or recurrent physical or psychological problem that is likely to have been caused or exacerbated by the substance (e.g. current cocaine use despite recognition of cocaine induced depression, or continue drinking despite recognition that an ulcer was made worse by alcohol consumption)

specify if: with the physiological dependence: evidence of tolerance or withdrawal (i.e. either item 1 or two is present)
without physiological dependence: no evidence or tolerance or without withdrawal (i.e. neither item 1 nor two is present)

Notice that according to these criteria, one need not have withdrawal symptoms to qualify for having a substance dependence problem. Also notice that only three of the seven features have to be present to establish a diagnosis.

The criteria for a substance *abuse* diagnosis are somewhat different. The classification of an alcohol use problem assumes a class of drinkers who have some alcohol-related problems but who are not dependent or addicted. Consider the college freshman who gets intoxicated several times at parties but is neither physically addicted nor psychologically dependent, but rather is naively exploring the new world of quasi-adult living. Many individuals who may meet criteria for an alcohol abuse problem, however, may well be headed for an eventual alcohol dependence problem. If a person is biogenetically prone, this likely would be the case. Here are the criteria for a substance abuse problem.

DSM-IV-R Diagnostic Criteria for Substance Abuse

A.   A maladaptive pattern of substance use, leading to clinically significant impairment or distress, as manifested by one (or more) of the following, occurring within a 12 month period:

(1) recurrent substance use resulting in a failure to fulfill major role obligations at work, school, or home (e.g. repeated absences or poor work performance related to substance use; substance related absences, suspensions, or expulsions from school; neglect of children or household)

(2) recurrent substance use in situations in which it would be physically hazardous (e.g. driving an automobile or operating a machine, when impaired by substance use)

(3) recurrent substance related legal problems (e.g. arrest for substance related disorderly conduct.)

(4) continued substance use despite having persistent or recurrent social or interpersonal problems caused or exacerbated by the effects of the substance (e.g. arguments with spouse about consequences of intoxication, physical fights)

B.   The symptoms have never met the criteria for Substance Dependence for this class of substance.

An interesting operative term within these criteria is "recurrent." This means that one drinking episode that may result in some sort of social, legal, academic, or other life-area problem is not sufficient, stand-alone, to warrant the diagnosis of a substance abuse problem.

Before you draw conclusions based on the above assessment strategy, several more bits of information are important.

- That one drinks only at set times, such as only after 5:00 p.m., does not rule out a problem.
- That one drinks only beer is irrelevant. It's all the same ethanol molecule, whether in wine, beer, or distilled liquor.
- That alcoholics always lose control when they drink is a myth. The largest subset of alcoholics entering treatment programs does not consist of daily drinkers but, rather, episodic over-drinkers. Some of these would become daily drinkers eventually.

Summarizing Your Self-Assessment

So where do you see yourself at this point? You may see yourself as a social drinker. This means that you could identify no quantity/frequency excesses, no inappropriate reasons for your drinking, no costs in any life areas, and no loss-of-control issues around your drinking behavior. But you still may have reason to abstain—for not liking the taste of alcohol or its effects, or because of a health issue that has come to your attention for which alcohol use is inadvisable, such as liver disease, heart disease, or incompatible medications. Other reasons for which a social drinker may want to abstain could be to show support for a family member in recovery, or because of a legal issue from an alcohol use-related offense, such as a DUI or domestic violence charge, which may require abstinence whether one has an alcohol use problem or not.

For the Dependent Drinker

If you find in your self-assessment that you are a dependent drinker/alcoholic, you need to quit drinking. This is usually much harder than it seems, and if you are disinclined to participate in standard treatment or AA, it is with you in mind that I have created this book. But if you are interested in a mainstream treatment program, you will want to know what level of treatment is appropriate for you. The American Society of Addiction Medicine has worked out a system called the ASAM Patient Placement Criteria (Mee-Lee et al., 2001). This is not an assessment system. The criteria are consulted *after* an alcohol abuse or dependence problem has been diagnosed by any other means. The criteria ask us to rate each individual case on the following dimensions:

1. Withdrawal risk
2. Biomedical complications (the relative stability or fragility of one's health)
3. Behavioral and psychological issues
4. The person's readiness to change
5. Relapse risk
6. Absence or presence of a supportive recovery environment

Based on the individual's status in each dimension, an estimation is made regarding different levels of detoxification and outpatient or inpatient treatment services that may be needed. The idea is to place a person in a level of care that provides a high margin of safety but at the same time is not higher than necessary. If you are interested, I recommend that you consult a professional because considerable knowledge and experience are necessary to apply the criteria in a useful way. Regardless, it's not a bad idea to obtain and peruse a copy of the ASAM Criteria for yourself. You can order a copy at www.asam.org.

For the Problem Drinker

If you find in your self-assessment that you may be a problem drinker, or have an alcohol abuse problem that is short of a dependency problem, you probably are hoping that you are not a genetic alcoholic— meaning that you do not metabolize alcohol as an alcoholic. You probably are hoping that you can control your drinking and become a social drinker rather than have to quit drinking entirely. For you, I must say that you may be playing a risky game. The majority of alcoholics I see at first want very much to see themselves in the problem drinker category. They want to work at controlled drinking but discover after a series of sincere and frustrating attempts, not to mention additional drinking-related life problems, that it will not work for them.

Nevertheless, if you find yourself clearly in the category of problem versus dependent drinker, you do have a couple of options—well, actually three. The third option is to continue your problem drinking. Once again, however, that way madness lies. The other two options are: (1) quit entirely and avoid ever having any alcohol use related problems again, or (2) learn to control your drinking at a safe limit in terms of quantity, frequency, and situations. You must realize, however, that this latter option may be much more difficult than you can imagine.

Regardless of how you decide to classify yourself, I encourage you to read on. If you think you are a social drinker, then perusing the information will constitute a further self-assessment. If you see yourself as a problem or dependent drinker you will need all the knowledge you can attain, and a positive and practical, personal plan for recovery.

Chapter 3

Getting Ready to Change

Problem:	*Many people fail to create a successful recovery because they do not know what the process of changing requires, and they lack sufficient motivation.*
How to win:	*Learn about the stages of readiness to change and the phases of recovery, and build your motivation to succeed.*

Are You a Good Candidate to Quit on Your Own?

A lifetime of health and happiness versus years of compounding misery hang in the balance as you answer for yourself the following question: *Am I a good candidate to quit drinking on my own?* Fortunately, considerable research over the past few decades can shed some light on this question and increase the odds of your answering it correctly. Some factors have been identified among problem drinkers—and even *dependent* drinkers in some rare cases—that predict or preclude who may succeed at controlled drinking. For our purposes here, however, we're going to explore who may or may not be a good candidate for succeeding at *total abstinence* without participating in treatment programs or AA. Here is a list of factors that may *preclude* success at quitting on your own, or at least make it a lot more difficult.

- If you have a history of failed attempts to quit on your own.
- If you have other psychiatric problems that may exist independent of your drinking problem, such as depression, anxiety, attention difficulties, or personality disorder, which

if not resolved, will complicate quitting (see "Co-occurring Mental Health Problems—Dual Diagnosis" in Chapter 11).
- If you do not have a family member, mate, or at least good friend who closely supports your attempt to quit.
- If you clearly have an *external* locus of control and usually need others to direct you through needed changes.
- If you are not personally committed to total abstinence.
- If you lack a sense of self-efficacy for the task of abstaining, or otherwise feel like you will not have what it takes to succeed.

Researchers tend to observe that in general, the more severe one's alcohol dependence—the more protracted and profound—the more likely he or she will not succeed at solo recovery (Klingemann et al., 2010), and for that matter, the less likely they will succeed with treatment programs. Conversely, effective self-change seems to correlate with several factors. These sorts of potential success-predicting factors have been referred to as "recovery capital" (Cloud & Granfield, 2008). It may be helpful to peruse the following list to estimate how much recovery capital you may have.

RECOVERY CAPITAL

- Less severe dependence
- A shorter period of time in active addiction
- Fewer mental health problems
- Good health
- Financial assets
- More educated
- Cognitively intact—no memory, reasoning/problem-solving, or judgment limitations
- Stable living place
- Well employed or good vocational skills/credentials
- Dramatic wake-up calls (e.g., divorce, injuries, DUI, getting fired)
- Formal and informal significant other or medical professional interventions
- Positive social environment and social skills

- Spirituality
- Self-esteem

My additions to the list:

- Self-efficacy (one's belief that they can succeed)
- An internal locus of control (believing that change comes from within)
- A strong personal commitment to quit
- A belief that quitting will pay off—that there will be benefits

The more recovery capital you have the better the odds that you will successfully quit drinking. But unfortunately, there are no precise guidelines here. Many other factors may help or hinder you. I have often seen the unpredictable—less severe cases who eventually could only gain sobriety through inpatient treatment program participation, and severe cases who quit on their own.

My recommendation is that you try to assess what recovery capital you personally have that may enhance your chance of success at solo recovery. You don't have to have them all. Where you may be missing several of these success predictors, perhaps you can build them up. If missing social support, for example, you can work at developing a friend or two who will honestly support your quitting drinking. Of course, if you have any confusion about your personal recovery capital and your odds of successfully quitting drinking, I recommend that you consult a recovery specialist for help.

Finding the Motivation to Change

Now let's return to the concept of self-efficacy—a person's perception that he or she has the right stuff to succeed in any given challenge ahead. Some people have had the good fortune of succeeding at most of the challenges in their lives. Others have not. If you believe you have not been among the fortunate ones, you will have some work to do. Fortunately, self-efficacy is a learned perception, and you can make significant advances if you practice. First you need to practice believing that you can succeed, or at least acting as if you can succeed when faced with challenges in your life. In his book *10 Secrets for Success and Inner Peace*, Dr. Wayne Dyer (2002) points out that our thoughts are, in fact, a powerful form of energy. What he calls "attractor energies" are healthy, positive thoughts that operate at higher frequencies than unhealthy, negative thoughts. Dyer encourages us to turn our thoughts to positive ones such as love and joy, and in this way attract these positive experiences back to us. "These higher and faster frequencies that empower you will automatically nullify and dissipate the lower energies in the same way that the presence of light makes darkness disappear." The way I interpret this, for our purposes, is that the more strongly you desire to recover from your drinking problem, the greater is the likelihood that you will succeed.

Stages of Readiness to Change

If you want something to increase your motivation to change that is a bit more scientific you are in luck. There is beaucoup research on how people make behavior changes. The current understanding is that people typically go through the following *stages of readiness to change*, with each stage involving different strategies (DiClemente, 2003):

1. People who need to make a change such as quitting drinking or smoking, or losing weight but are not really ready, linger in a *Precontemplative* stage. At this point they may realize that what they are doing is not healthy, but they're not really considering doing anything about it. The pros and cons seem to favor continued drinking.
2. Even ahead of any definitive decision to change, people tend to move through a *Contemplative* stage. During this time the pros and cons get a more serious look as individuals are increasingly troubled by the effects of their drinking and wonder if quitting may be possible and beneficial. The person's thinking process may include recognizing that the change is really needed and at least the internal understanding that it ought to be done. A problem at this stage is that the mind can be lulled into complacency, relieved by the illusion that because change is being

considered it will surely happen one day, thus effectively delaying any actual change.

3. Effective change requires moving beyond the Contemplative stage to the *Preparation* stage. This phase is characterized by a tip in the scale to make an actual decision to change, the development of a plan to do so, and a commitment to that plan. Plans are best if they include details such as when one will quit drinking, how detoxification will be managed, who will offer support, and what alternative behaviors will be initiated (e.g., going to a gym, watching moves or reading). Plans should also take into account and make accommodations for any foreseeable obstacles such as social, family, and work commitments. Through the experiences of my own life, and having witnessed the lives of countless others, when it comes to making any behavior change, the single most powerful step is pinning down an actual calendar date. For example, "Monday the 20th, I will quit smoking" or "Beginning Tuesday, I will start going to the gym three nights per week." If it gets on my schedule I am highly likely to do it—if not on my schedule, probably not. There is an inherent resistant to making plans for change because at least subconsciously we fear change. Yet, as you begin to formulate a plan to quit drinking you are likely to experience a reduction in anguish and confusion and a growing sense of empowerment. So if you have not already quit drinking, be brave. Honestly explore the pros and cons of drinking, imagine self-liberation, and start planning.

4. The *Action* phase is entered when you actually initiate the plan and quit drinking (or make any other desired change). This usually makes a person feel pretty good, e.g., finally accomplishing that first trip to the gym, flossing one's teeth after dinner, attending that watercolor class. It improves mood because it creates a new sense of personal empowerment, a "Good for me, I did it" feeling. Unfortunately, sometimes with alcohol or other drugs there may be some withdrawal symptoms to contend with (see the previous chapter for withdrawal management options) that can make quitting addictions a more daunting challenge than

      making other types of life-style changes. But in most cases, people who do manage to quit drinking soon tend to feel especially good about themselves—there is an element of *relief* beyond the basic sense of accomplishment.

5.   Unfortunately, arriving at the Action phase is not sufficient for lasting behavior change. Witness the great rise in gym memberships in January followed by a membership exodus by March. Recall the smoker who states "I can quit whenever I want...I've done it hundreds of times." In general, it takes several months of sustained effort for a change to become an established part of one's behavioral repertoire. This is known as the *Maintenance* phase of behavior change. It is a time when you can no longer imagine not continuing the change you have made because it has become inherently rewarding and a part of your very identity. I will discuss more detail and cover specific strategies for how to avoid failures and succeed at this stage in Chapters 17 and 18 on relapse prevention.

6.   To arrive and stay in the *maintenance stage* is the goal of any behavior change attempt. This takes considerable perseverance, so it is important to keep in mind that most healthy behavior changes become easier across time. Positive changes eventually become inherently rewarding and enjoyably self-sustaining. Ultimately, a change can become an integral part of one's very identity, e.g., "*I am* a non-smoker" or "*I am* a runner." Helpful strategies include monitoring progress, setting up a self-reward system, and not falling victim to the *abstinence violation effect* at any slips in progress. This is when, following a slip-up in progress, one says, "Well I've blown it now so what the heck" and then fails to restart his or her behavior change.

I will talk more about this is in Chapter 18. For now, it can be helpful just to recognize what stage you are in, consider how long you really want to stay at this stage, and how you might move ahead.

Stages of Readiness to Change

Pre-contemplation → Contemplation → Preparation →
Action → Maintenance

Where are you?
Where do you want to be?
What will you do?
When will you start?

Phases of Recovery

Contrary to popular assumption, there are no set stages of addiction that all alcohol-dependent persons go through. The textbook offering is that first there is experimental use, then regular use, then abusive use with associated costs accruing, and then addictive use. However, many people do not cleanly follow this pattern. For example, some alcoholics are addicted from the moment they first try alcohol. In truth, alcohol dependence develops in different people at different rates. Some go from experimental use to addictive use in a matter of days. Some take decades to establish an identifiable dependence on alcohol. Many seem to move up and down the scale from times of non-use, to regular use, to dependent use.

Counterintuitively, unlike stages of addiction, scholars have observed clear and recognizable phases of *recovery*. In a framework that is somewhat different from the stages of readiness to change just described, Terrence Gorski, author of *Staying Sober: A Guide for Relapse Prevention* (1986) and other books, conceptualizes these phases of recovery in a nicely comprehendible way. As a result of my experience and observations, I have put some of my own spin on these phases over the years.

The majority of alcoholics probably never make it to the first phase of recovery, which means they never recognize the extent of the problem. Of those who do, only a few go on to the second phase, and fewer still beyond that. Each phase has specific risks for relapse. These phases are not lock-step or mutually exclusive. An individual may be involved in several stages at once or slide back and forth between

51

phases. Some individuals move through the first three phases virtually overnight, but for most, this takes years or decades. The last three phases are rarely, if ever, completed in a short time, and it can take as little as a year or as many as 10 or 15 years to achieve a truly balanced living in maintenance recovery.

Recovery is no day-hike. It is a trek, a journey of a lifetime, for most people that make it. But if you can envision recovery as a method of travel rather than as a destination, it can be an amazing experience. Daunting? Yes, but also exciting and liberating.

Phase 1: Recognition

Even though it is difficult to know how many alcoholics ever get on the road to recovery in the first place, estimates are that it may be less than three out of ten, with the majority living shorter, less happy lives, often never fully recognizing the problem. For those who do, the first phase of recovery begins with that moment of recognition when they realize that indeed there is a problem. What distinguishes who will or will not arrive at this initial *recognition phase* is not known. We can only speculate that it involves a mix of the biological, social, psychological, and/or spiritual aspects of each individual. It seems to have nothing to do with basic intelligence or will power, or a person's inherent goodness.

Alcoholism is an insidious illness that does not discriminate for race, socioeconomic status, or intelligence. It strikes people from all walks of life, and in the long run it takes away for good the majority of people it affects. As a dire effect of alcohol dependence, the drinker is rarely able to comprehend the extent of the problem. This phenomenon is known as "denial." It comes from the subconscious mind hoodwinking the conscious mind with a barrage of defense mechanisms to allow continued or resumed drinking. The drinker unwittingly uses rationalizations, justifications, minimizations and other defense mechanisms, to support drinking. I will discuss this fully in Chapter 6, on the psychology of addiction.

For a fortunate minority, any single event or series of events can cause the break in defense mechanisms that is necessary for the drinker to recognize the problem and to want to do something about it, at least briefly. A person may become suddenly or gradually aware of the problem. Perhaps recognition will come with one too many hangovers, or a regrettable evening that ended with social embarrassment, or one or more DUIs. Typically, there is a confrontational event. People can arrive at the recognition stage as a result of surviving a disaster, such as a car crash, or experiencing something much less dramatic, such as a child saying "Oh Daddy, you don't need that beer." For some drinkers it might be as simple as that, for others it could be some combination of failed jobs, divorces, DUIs, and health crises.

Whatever the situation may be, this initial recognition is the beginning of a possible recovery. And, of course, it is just a beginning. Rarely does a person suddenly experience that first recognition and immediately stop drinking for good. I have never had a client present for the first time at my office and say, "You know, I've been thinking about how important alcohol has become to me emotionally and socially, and so I've decided to quit drinking for good before something bad happens in my life as a result of my drinking."

Rather than attempting to quit, the recognition phase is characterized by attempts to merely limit or otherwise control the quantity and/or frequency of alcohol use. It begins when a person literally or figuratively wakes up one morning and says, "Damn! I overdid it again. I guess I have a problem here. I've never realized this before. Now that I know my drinking can be a problem, I'll just control it. With my superior will power and intellect, I'll just stop overdoing it."

Unfortunately, this does not put an end to the defense mechanisms. The mind—at least subconsciously—still wants the option to do what it has come to know makes it feel good. People sometimes stay in this phase of trying to control their drinking for years, and often are fooled because at times they *do* seem to control it ("I don't drink every day"; "I don't get drunk every time I drink"; "Sometimes I just have one or two, so I can't be an alcoholic"). Tragically, millions of people have died with these mistaken beliefs. Some alcoholics drink every day or get drunk every time they drink, but most do not.

Phase 2: The First Attempt to Quit

After many years with the hope that they can control their drinking, for an anguished few individuals, the punishing effects of alcohol sufficiently outweigh the benefits, and he or she recognizes the need for total abstinence. This second recognition, however, tends to be insufficient to establish lasting sobriety. The person's internal dialogue goes something like this: "Well, okay, I can't seem to control it, so I probably need to quit drinking entirely." He or she may even announce this to a partner: "Honey, you don't have to worry anymore; I'll just quit…but I don't need to change anything else about my life."

This kind of thinking, again, can go on for years, with repeated internal and external excuses for repeated relapses. In this phase, I rarely see anyone go for more than a week without drinking again. The defense mechanisms continue. Patterns of living and associations do not change. People do not know what to do with the emotions that they have usually handled with alcohol. They slip when Steve and Mary drop by, when it rains, when it shines, when it's a holiday, when it's a weekend, when someone is having a birthday. This was wonderfully noted years ago by the famous recovery speaker Father Martin, who used to wind up his description of this type of self-deception by telling his audiences that even a dog's birthday can become a reason to drink.

Phase 3: Stabilization

The third phase begins with the recognition that some form of help is needed—an educated strategy or system to follow that may or may not involve participation in a treatment program or AA. This ends the pretreatment phases and allows for the person to initiate a truly meaningful recovery. It appears, though, that only a minority of alcoholics ever arrive at this stage. It tends to occur only after years of repeated failures to control or abstain from drinking, and at a point at which one's defenses are overwhelmed.

This is seldom a truly "voluntary" process. Usually it takes a serious threat to health, marriage, job, or freedom to reach this phase. Probably 90 percent of persons in outpatient treatment programs are there by legal mandate, usually DUI. Thus, the vast majority of outpatient treatment programs are designed to meet state requirements for DUI diversion programs.

This phase may involve counseling, treatment programs, serious self-help support group participation, or expanding one's knowledge base through books, reading online, or other approaches. Regardless, this *stabilization phase* is about the mechanics of how not to drink. The task here is to gain *basic abstaining skills,* including where not to go, who not to be with, how to say no, what aisles of the grocery to avoid, how to deal with episodes of the continuing urges to drink, and where to find support. In AA, this is summed up by the adage that, to stay sober, you must "change your playgrounds and playmates."

In my own observation, these changes are truly important. As noted in Part 5, much of relapse prevention has to be learned the hard way. Steve, for example, discovers that, despite his best intentions, he can't play pool at Southside Bar anymore without risking relapse. And Mary can't continue to hang out in the afternoon with her neighbor Susie, who is an active alcoholic.

The stabilization phase can be relatively brief. Although some people do not get through this phase at all, many become quite comfortable in their new patterns of abstinence within several weeks.

Phase 4: Emotional Recovery

Even after people recognize the problem (Phase 1), that they cannot effectively limit their drinking (Phase 2), and that they need some form of help and/or accurate information and a strategy for abstaining (Phase 3), relapses remain the rule rather than the exception. After Phase 3, the stabilization phase, approximately 90 percent of relapses are attributable to the challenge of emotional/psychological recovery rather than merely physical recovery. Again, the body's de-habituation is rather rapid, but the mind's de-habituation can take weeks, months, or longer. Literally, what do you do with worry, depression, frustration, anger, and other uncomfortable emotions without your usual medication? Thus, this phase is about *emotional recovery.*

Remember—emotional dysregulation is the defining feature of addictions. The substance becomes the emotional manager insidiously, across time, compromising the mind's ability to be its own emotional manager. Research by Dr. Alan Marlatt indicates that most relapses fall under three categories: (1) bad moods, (2) interpersonal conflict, or (3) social pressure. But what does interpersonal conflict or social pressure cause? A bad mood. So I conclude that 90 percent of slips are attributable to negative moods being poorly managed. Much of recovery is involved directly or indirectly with emotional management—how to deal with emotions without the medication of alcohol or other drugs.

Important features of this are more carefully discussed in Part 5, on relapse prevention .

In this phase of emotional recovery a person has much to learn. With limited time, in a rush to introduce people to the AA recovery system, and with a general lack of knowledge about the psychological aspects of addiction and recovery, it should not be surprising that treatment programs do not spend nearly enough time on this vital aspect of recovery.

Emotional recovery means getting back, or in many cases gaining for the first time, reasonable control over one's emotions. *Alexithymia* is a term that has been used to describe active addict's eventual loss of ability to accurately identify and label their internal experience or feelings, let alone to cope with them. It is critical to understand this term, and to understand it well. Chapter 6 covers the concept of alexithymia in detail.

The good news is that most people who stay with their recovery effort actually become excellent emotional managers—far better than the average person ever will. Never challenged, many people without alcohol use problems, never come to understand the dynamics of their own emotions and subsequently do not cope as well as they could when faced with life's inevitable larger challenges.

Phase 5: Managing Major Life Challenges

This phase involves consistent and persistent follow-through and reworking of recovery plans. Even after a person has recognized the problem, that he or she needs to quit drinking, has begun working a recovery plan, and becomes an excellent day-to-day emotional manager, relapse can occur in the face of *major stressors*; family crisis, career or health crises, untreated *mental health problems*, or unresolved *family of origin issues.*

Major stressors can occur any time, but they seem to happen when we are least prepared to deal with them. Recovering people often have difficulty recognizing when they are under serious stress. This is complicated in that what may be stressful for one person may not be at all stressful for another. Generally, we can agree that major stressors include things such as divorce, the departure or death of a loved one, a health failure, or a job/career crisis. During such events, it is crucial that recovering people recognize and accept that they are in fact experiencing an emotionally challenging time. Awareness of when we are experiencing stress is the first defense.

Consider my client, Robert, who returned to our recovery support group after a three-week absence. He acknowledged that he had relapsed. We inquired as to what had happened. He told us that his wife, as we had guessed might happen, left him. Then his son broke his leg and Robert traveled to Eastern Washington to help with the grandchildren. Then his car broke down on his way home. He subsequently lost a job opportunity. At that point, he drank. We asked him, "Bob, did you realize you were under a lot of stress?" Bob slapped his aching forehead. Indeed, he had not realized how much stress he was under and was therefore all the more vulnerable to relapse.

You can't escape major stressors or times when everything seems to conspire against you. Yet, if you can get through one or two such episodes sober, subsequent episodes become easier and easier to handle. The more you face problems sober, the better you will become at handling them. Yes! Recovery has very real benefits.

Recovery often is hampered in Phase 5, as in earlier phases, by emotional or psychiatric problems that have not been fully addressed. Chemical dependency itself causes significant emotional problems. Depression and anxiety are the well known psychological sequelae, or associated features, of alcoholism. The longer the mind uses the substance to cope, the less able it is to cope alcohol-free. The majority of persons entering treatment programs have signs and symptoms of mood disorders, but for most the symptoms all but disappear after several weeks of sobriety.

Just as in the rest of the population, however, the alcohol dependent/recovering population has its share of persons with additional emotional or psychiatric problems. When this occurs it is termed *dual diagnosis*—chemical dependency plus an independent depressive illness, anxiety disorder, or other psychiatric problem. These problems must be addressed and treated effectively if recovery is to last. With professional help to identify and treat dual diagnosis problems, people can make dramatic progress in both their mental health and their sobriety.

Another threat to lasting recovery relates to *family of origin issues*. Dealing with the effects of growing up in a dysfunctional family, child abuse, or other trauma can overwhelm the resources of a person who is new in recovery. Generally, professionals agree that exploring these long-term issues is best delayed until a person is stabilized in recovery for a year or so. In some cases, however, these issues must be dealt with to establish initial recovery. Again, in most cases, with professional help, outcomes tend to be positive. Many support systems are available now for adult children of alcoholics, co-dependents, survivors of child abuse, and can become part of a person's recovery plan.

Phase 6: Balanced Living

With years of persistence, faith, hope, and working on recovery, people eventually tend to achieve a balanced life. Many report that their lives have not only been saved but also broadly enriched by the experience of recovery. These individuals are self-actualized, largely at peace with themselves, in touch with their feelings, and have genuine and authentic relationships with others. They achieve *balanced living* with work, play, relationships, leisure, and spirituality, in accord with the needs of their real selves. Even in this phase, however, recovering people tend to maintain a certain vigilance (as opposed to hypervigilance) about their recovery, because if they do not they are still at risk of reactivating a life-threatening disease.

The Hero in You

In concluding this chapter, I leave you with one additional thought: Overcoming addictions takes courage, and the people who overcome their alcohol dependence are heroes. I know a firefighter who got his name in the paper because he pulled a boy out of a blazing house. I know another fellow who got a job as a greeter at a local big-box store for minimum wage. Who is the hero? Okay, certainly the firefighter's work is greatly appreciated, but in this story the store greeter is also a hero. The firefighter did a great deed and deserved everybody's appreciation. Yet, he himself said it was nothing, that it was routine. He had been a firefighter for many years, knew what he was doing, had a team supporting him, and had not felt seriously frightened.

The store greeter was a war veteran. He was chair-bound and had a forty-year history of profound alcoholism. He had lost his wife, alienated his children, lost a couple of possible careers, and, more than anything else, had lost all of his self respect and confidence. He had met the criteria for posttraumatic stress, depression, and social anxiety disorders. For him, sobering up took a long time. When he got that job, it seemed to me to be a Herculean feat. It took everything he had. Over the years I have learned that *heroism cannot be measured by the apparent scope of a deed but, rather, by the distance between any task achieved and a person's initial confidence to do it.*

Sometimes I run across something I like in the most unlikely place. Here is a quote from Steven Spielberg's 1991 animated film *Fievel Goes West—An American Tale.* It is a metaphor about a young person's search for a positive identity in the story of a little mouse traveling across the country in the days of the Old West. The old sheriff (in the magnificent voice of Jimmy Stewart) offers Fievel advice as he mounts his horse to continue his westward journey at the end of the movie:

> Just remember, Fievel, I don't know what's out there beyond those hills. But if you ride yonder—head up, eyes steady, heart open—I think one day you'll find that *you're* the hero you've been looking for.

I wish the same for you—and success in all of your heroic efforts.

Recommended Reading for Chapter 3

Addiction and Change: How Addictions Develop and Addicted People Recover, by Carlo DiClement.

Passages Through Recovery: An Action Plan for Preventing Relapse, by Terence Gorski.

Part 2

What Happened to You?

Chapter 4

A Drug Called Alcohol

Problem:	*Misconceptions about the true nature of alcohol dependence can seriously impede recovery.*
Solution:	*Forewarned is forearmed; learn about:*
	• What alcohol is, where it came from and how it spread
	• Health, societal, and economic costs of alcoholism
	• The advance of conflicting beliefs about alcohol dependence
	• Why alcoholism is considered a disease
	• The nature versus nurture debate
	• The wisdom of the broader bio/psycho/social model

What Alcohol Is

Alcohol, known chemically as *ethanol*, is a rapidly absorbable carbohydrate molecule, with no nutritive value. Once ingested and metabolized, alcohol functions as a *central nervous system depressant*. This doesn't mean that alcohol causes you to feel depressed. That only happens over time with repeated overuse. The term "central nervous system depressant" means that it interferes with normal brain functioning, depressing it in the sense that it suppresses the transmission of nerve cell firings—the way the nervous system communicates with itself to manage our thinking, walking, and talking. Reaction time and thought processes slow down. Physical aches and pains and the intensity of unpleasant emotions are reduced appreciably, and the world seems like a better place.

Remember, ethanol at first acts as a stimulant, effects our judgment and lowers inhibitions. Conversation becomes easier and memory is briefly enhanced. Social drinkers begin to notice the depressant effects on the central nervous system after one to three drinks (See the discussion on the loss-of-control phenomenon in Chapter 2 for more about this effect). Alcoholics seem to only become more energized with each additional drink they imbibe and do not get the negative effects until too late.

Young people typically assume that there are different types of alcohol because there are so many different types of beverages. In reality, though, the ethanol molecule is the same in beer, wine, and hard liquor.

Beer and wine are the result of *fermentation*. This involves a simple naturally occurring process as yeast breaks down sugars into carbon dioxide and ethanol. You can witness this phenomenon simply by leaving a container of raw apple cider sitting around for a few days. It will undergo fermentation because of exposure to natural yeast molecules that exist in our atmosphere. The result is called hard cider. If you let it go too long it will turn into vinegar.

As noted, the amount of alcohol in beer and wine is limited because once the alcohol concentration rises to a certain level, the yeast is destroyed and fermentation stops. In the production of beer, grains such as wheat or barley are used for fermentation. With wine, grapes are used. Actually, just about anything that grows can be used. For instance, wine can be made from dandelions or from walnuts.

Hard liquors, such as vodka, whiskey, gin, and tequila, are produced by human intervention in a process known as *distillation*. This requires boiling the alcohol away from its sugar bath and thereby condensing it.

Where Alcohol Came From and How It Spread

Did you ever wonder how beverage alcohol came to be in the world? Historians have found that beer and wine have been around for at least the past 7,000 years. Egyptians were mass-producing wine by the beginning of the fourth millennium B.C. They even used additives to preserve the wine, as well as labels on containers to identify the date, type of wine, and vineyard of origin.

Cultural anthropologists believe that fermented alcohol was discovered much earlier in human history. Just imagine a band of hunter/gatherers on the African savanna thousands of years ago leaving berries or juice in a satchel too long, then finding the taste not half bad, imbibing it, and discovering intoxication. This must have happened many thousands of years ago, before humans even advanced to tribal societies with the dawn of the agricultural revolution. We do know, however, that Persian alchemists did not discover how to *distill* alcohol until around 800 A.D.

Historically, alcohol has persistently worked its way into nearly all societies and civilizations. The effects have been consistent and predictable in terms of human suffering—with broken families, increased healthcare costs, antisocial behavior and crime, loss of life, and in compromised productivity. Typically, the longer that alcohol is part of a culture, the more that culture has attempted to limit, control, or ultimately abolish it. Witness the Middle East, "the cradle of civilization"—where alcohol use is now forbidden.

Populations around the northern rim of the Mediterranean (Greece, Italy, southern France and Spain) do not have the problems with alcohol that northern Europeans have. One theory to account for this holds that alcohol has existed much longer in those Mediterranean cultures and that it has done its killing through a long process of evolutionary selection. That is, across the past 3,000 years, those who had problems with alcohol did not live as long, did not reproduce as many children, or take adequate care of the children they did have. Thus, their genetic material was not passed on to their offspring. At the same time, those who did not over-imbibe lived longer, took better care of their children, and passed along their genetic material.

Indeed, the northern rim of the Mediterranean has few treatment centers, yet people there probably drink as much or more than people in any other part of the world. These regions traditionally include wine with meals. Even children drink wine at meals with their families. As teenagers, then, they are familiar with alcohol and disinclined to do the irresponsible drinking that American teenagers do.

The theory maintains that alcohol has not been available in northern European cultures for as many centuries as in southern European cultures. So the farther north we look the more we see blatant alcohol use-related problems, and the more treatment centers we find. Scandinavian countries and Russia have high rates of alcoholism. The worst-case scenario seems to be that of the American Indians, whose lives and populations were decimated by the introduction of alcohol when Europeans first arrived. Tragically, Native Americans continue to struggle with high rates of alcoholism. I feel a great sadness when I realize what alcohol has done to the pure systems of these beautiful indigenous peoples. In keeping with the above theory, it will take a few thousand years for alcohol use among American Indians to finish selecting out.

Of course, the above theory can be questioned, other influences might account for the higher rates of alcoholism in northern cultures. For one thing, it's more difficult to grow grapes in northern climates, so northerners may be more likely to drink hard liquor. With the significantly higher percentage of ethanol per volume in hard liquor, intoxication may be more difficult to avoid than when imbibing wine or beer. In addition, perhaps because winters are colder and darker in the north, with a dearth of outdoor as well as other indoor activities, alcohol use became a lot more appealing.

In America, of course, alcohol was brought by the very earliest European explorers. By this time people already understood that alcohol was associated with a lot of family, societal, and economic problems. In the United States, from colonial times, there have been persistent efforts to control the gender and ages of who's allowed to drink and limits on when and where people can drink—called *temperance* movements and laws. This practice continues, with different states and counties having various laws concerning the age at which one can legally drink, as well as laws about drinking and driving, when taverns can be open, and who can go in. In Wisconsin, for example young children sit in bars alongside their parents, but not so in Washington.

Also, there have been periodic attempts to ban alcohol altogether. This is known as prohibition. The most well known example was the federal prohibition against alcohol enacted in 1920. Lasting 14 years, the law was repealed in 1934, as it seemed to create more trouble than it was worth. Interestingly, Alcoholics Anonymous was founded the very next year.

Prohibition failed while organized crime ran rampant, involved in smuggling and controlling booze. Some people now question whether prohibition was really a bad idea or just poorly managed. One outcome was an increase in temperance laws controlling the use of alcohol. Another outcome, however, seems to have been a public perception that because the law was repealed, alcohol is a perfectly safe and normal part of life. The perception even went beyond this, with alcoholic beverage advertising promoting the belief that drinking alcohol is the most sophisticated way to live. By the 1950s, martini lunches, home bars, the cocktail hour, and beer barbecues, became equated with successful living, and teenage drinking became an excepted "rite-of-passage."

Health, Societal, and Economic Costs of Alcoholism

Consider the following costs of alcoholism.

Costs to Health

- Conservatively, 14% of adults in the United States suffer from alcoholism.
- Hundreds of thousands succumb to alcohol-related deaths each year.
- Alcoholism is the second leading cause of death, next to cancer.

    - 40,000 deaths per year are attributed to cirrhosis of the liver.
    - Alcohol use is highly implicated in heart disease.
    - Alcohol use compromises the immune systems, which increases the vulnerability to all diseases including AIDS.
    - 50% of emergency room presentations are related to alcohol use.

- Fetal alcohol syndrome is the leading cause of learning and other cognitive disabilities, costing billions of dollars in health care, special education, low productivity, and expanded welfare rolls.

Costs to Society

Alcohol is involved in:

- The majority of cases of child abuse, spouse abuse, and domestic violence;
- 40% of all rapes;
- 64% of homicides;
- 50% of fatal traffic crashes; and
- 80% of suicides.

Economic Costs

The economic costs of alcoholism were estimated to be $185 billion in 1998 alone (National Institutes of Health, 1998). These costs result from: lower industrial productivity, higher health care costs, crime costs, prison costs, and treatment costs.

The Advance of Conflicting Beliefs about Alcohol Addiction

Historically, different beliefs have evolved to account for the devastation of alcoholism. Of these, here are several of the most prominent.

The Moral View

The moral view, probably the oldest and most frustratingly unenlightened point of view, holds that the afflicted individual is evil and morally deficient. This is the epitome of *blaming the victim* and merely represents the observer's own psychological defense against what otherwise is too difficult and painful to comprehend.

The Criminal View

In the criminal view, drunkenness is simply a crime, and if we set up sufficient punishments, it will go away. The underlying opinion is that the person lacks good judgment and getting drunk is an act of *willful misconduct.*

The Poor Willpower View

This is a spin-off of the old "moral deficiency" view. The observer deals with his or her frustration/fear by simplistically believing that alcoholics merely lack willpower—that if alcoholics had any will-power they would pick themselves up by their boot-straps and stop drinking.

The Psychological Problem Point of View

Here we are getting more sophisticated—but unfortunately incomplete. The strictest psychological view proposes that alcoholism is not at all biogenetic but, rather, that (a) the person has an underlying *personality problem*, or (b) the person has a learned *behavioral problem*.

In response to the first point, despite many years of research, an "alcoholic personality" has not been identified that could predict who will become alcoholic. The confusion arises when studies identify personality traits that are common to some alcoholics, such as social introversion. But the studies are invalidated by the use of measures taken *after* the fact—thus not accounting for the possibility that after years of drinking, alcoholic's personalities could be affected in some predictable ways, such as feeling more socially inept when sober.

In the second view, behavioral learning dynamics are indeed involved in alcohol use problems. Reinforcements and punishments tend to shape our behaviors. We all learn to increase behaviors that tend to make us feel good and to decrease behaviors that make us feel bad. Unfortunately, this point of view leaves out biogenetic factors and a host of cultural and other psychological factors that may contribute to drinking problems. It also tends to lead back to blaming the victim. Yes, profound behavioral features are at play in alcoholism, but this model does not adequately explain why, in the same learning environment, some people become alcoholics and some do not.

The Disease Concept

From time-to-time historically, medical professionals have recognized that the alcoholic is not necessarily demonstrating willful misconduct, poor willpower, or any prior psychological problems, but instead is the victim of a disease process. By the 1950s, all major medical associations including the American Medical Association had officially recognized alcoholism as a disease. From this perspective, great strides have been made in understanding and treating those afflicted with alcohol dependency.

For most people, the "alcohol as a disease" question is understandably confusing—even maddening. After all, one can't catch an alcoholism *germ*, so how can alcoholism really be a disease? Isn't it just a result of poor choices and bad behavior? Also, if alcoholics are victims, what are we to do with the hurt their behavior causes others? And what about self-responsibility?

In the first place a *germ* is not required for something to be a disease. All that is necessary is a physical and/or mental deteriorating *process* going on in the body and/or mind. There is no germ for diabetes, heart disease, cancer, schizophrenia, or for countless other serious diseases, yet they clearly are understood as diseases. We accept that individuals largely inherit the way the body metabolizes sugar, breaks down cholesterol, fends off cancer, or reacts to psychological stress. Similarly, people may inherit the way they metabolize alcohol, which causes profound physically and mentally deteriorating changes if they drink. What is unique about the disease process of alcoholism is its direct effect on the brains of alcoholics, and the thinking, emotional, and behavioral problems that predictably result.

Accepting the above argument, which holds that alcoholism is a disease, still leaves the question of why so many alcoholics continue to drink even after years of obvious costs to their health, relationships, work, and other life areas. If it is a disease, why do some people seem to choose to continue drinking when a total cure is so simple—just stop drinking. Surely individuals with any other major disease would quickly embrace such a simple cure. Well, in reality, people with other diseases often fail to follow prescribed behavior changes that could cure them. In fact, the record for alcoholics' adhering to treatment recommendations is no worse than for most other diseases. People with high blood pressure and diabetics are notorious for not following prescribed medical advice and not making important life-style changes, such as avoiding fatty foods, quitting smoking, and exercising. As an example, it has been found that 90 percent of diabetics do not follow their medical regimens. Chapter 7 provides more information on this topic in describing the *medical model* that underlies standard treatment and AA.

For those who are simply uncomfortable with the word "disease," an acceptable alternative term is "condition"—as long as by the use of this somewhat less harsh expression, one does not minimize his or her drinking problem and what it may take to overcome it.

Nature versus Nurture in the Development of Alcoholism

The question commonly arises as to whether alcohol problems are primarily inherited genetically or are simply learned misbehaviors. It has long been noticed that alcoholism seems to run in families. One argument to explain this phenomenon is that children who are brought up by excessive drinkers are likely to become excessive drinkers themselves because of the emotional challenge of growing up in such a household. In the process, they vicariously learn that alcohol use is the way to manage personal and interpersonal problems. This is the so-called *nurture,* or learning, model of addictive disease.

Another model purports that genetically set biological factors are what cause alcoholism. This is the *nature* or genetic difference model. Early research conducted in Denmark claimed that infants of alcoholic parentage, although adopted out and raised by non-alcoholic parents, were still four times more likely to become alcoholic than were children of non-alcoholic parents, even though they had never known their alcoholic parents. This research, by Donald Goodwin (Goodwin et al., 1973) continues to be cited in treatment centers as evidence of a fundamental biological cause of alcoholism. Unfortunately, this research was badly controlled and poorly interpreted. Subsequently, many scholars have concluded that any genetic differences between alcoholics and non-alcoholics are far less profound than the early research proclaimed (Fingarette, 1988; Lester, 1988).

Similarly, early research demonstrated higher alcoholism concordance between identical twins than between fraternal twins or ordinary siblings: If one member of a pair was an alcoholic, the other was likely to be an alcoholic beyond the co-occurrence ratio of alcoholism among ordinary brothers or sisters, even when raised apart. This was interpreted as evidence of a predominately genetic basis for alcoholism. Further research, however, has found that while inherited biological differences are at play, factors of learning appear to account for the lion's share of the variance (Kaprio et al., 1987).

Another line of research is referred to as *genetic marker* research. Because of millions of possible combinations, it is difficult to identify specific genes or sets of genes responsible for different diseases like alcoholism. Therefore, researchers look at different genetic "markers" that may implicate genetic differences between groups of people. One bit of research that treatment centers continue touting found a difference between alcoholics and non-alcoholics in the gene that controls the Dopamine D-2 receptor site in the brain (Blum et al., 1990). Here again, better-controlled studies have been unable to substantiate any real difference. Large-scale research associated with the Human Genome Project has not found any connection between the D-2 receptor and risk for alcoholism. More likely, it appears that probably no single gene but, rather, sets of genes may render one person somewhat more vulnerable than another person to alcohol use problems (Reich et al., 1998; Thombs, 1999).

Additional research has investigated metabolic differences in hormonal and brain activity that could identify who is at risk for alcoholism. A research problem has been that to simply study metabolic differences between alcoholics and non-alcoholics would provide inconclusive results. This is because any differences found could have been caused by the effects of alcohol on the body from years of drinking rather than from any preexisting differences. Therefore, researchers have studied differences between *sons* of alcoholics and *sons* of non-alcoholics (young men before they have started regular drinking), simply to rule-out the effects of years of drinking alcohol.

In some remarkable studies by Dr. Mark Schuckit, young men were brought into the laboratory and given alcohol. Immediately upon imbibing, those who were sons of alcoholics had three different brainwave responses compared to the sons of non-alcoholics. They also had a more rapid fall-off in cortisol and prolactin, two hormones necessary for breaking down acetaldehyde. Although they were left with higher levels of acetaldehyde, they subjectively reported feeling less intoxicated drink-for-drink than did sons of non-alcoholics. To determine this, the young men were placed in girdles attached to guide wires that could measure body sway. After a couple of drinks, the sons of non-alcoholics were measurably swaying and reporting that they were feeling really intoxicated. Not so for sons of alcoholics. They were more stable on their feet and did not report feeling as intoxicated—they seemed to have a natural tolerance (Schuckit, 1984, 1985).

A Progressive Disease?

The classic medical model holds that alcohol abuse/dependence is an invariably progressive disease—that it always gets worse if not arrested. In this mainstream concept the problem is fundamentally metabolic, under genetic control, and therefore *can only worsen* as one ages (Milam & Ketcham, 1983). A variation of the progressive disease concept is offered by Vernon Johnson (1980). His position is that advancement of alcohol dependence is not so much a physiological progression as it is a psychological progression.

These scholars have done excellent work in describing important and useful aspects about the physiological and psychological processes involved in alcohol dependence. The inevitability of *progression* of the disease, however, has not been found to be true. To the contrary, it is well documented that many abusive/dependent drinkers move away from problem drinking as they age (Miller-Tutzauer, Leonard, & Windle, 1991; Peele, 1985). This is known in research as *maturing out.* The empirical studies indicate that most of the problematic drinking among young people, which is so prevalent in Western culture, is more a function of emotional and social immaturity than a progressive metabolic disease (Gotham et al., 1997).

A "Chronic" Disease?

The disease model maintains that alcoholism can only be arrested but not cured. In AA, alcoholics are never "recovered" but, instead, forever "recovering" or "in recovery" as long as they don't drink. Here again, research flies in the face of folklore. As cited in the introduction to this book, research shows that many people who have had alcohol dependence problems never drink again. If a person's sobriety continues uninterrupted for two or three decades, perhaps we could say that he or she has recovered, rather than being merely in remission.

That many problem drinkers, especially young problem drinkers, advance or return to non-problematic drinking is also well documented. As pointed-out in Chapter 2, however, many factors may preclude a person's success with social drinking. The longer one has been involved with alcohol, the more problems that have accumulated, the older one is, the more emotionally unstable one is, and the extent to which one may be metabolically susceptible, the more one is gambling with his or her life in attempting to limit drinking rather than totally abstaining. Much scholarly and not so scholarly debate has been directed to this issue (Thombs, 1999).

The Bio/Psycho/Social Model

Under the scrutiny of objective reasoning, the theories of moral bankruptcy, defective willpower, and willful misconduct simply do not hold up. Whether progressive or chronic, or from nature or from nurture, we can accept that addiction strikes people as a disease (or condition, if you prefer). The theory that genetic inheritance is the sole and inevitable cause of this disease/condition, however, is not well supported in research or in clinical experience. How am I to explain that four times in my career I have met identical twins in which one of each pair had serious alcohol dependence problems and the other had a long history of light social drinking? Identical twins are monozygotic; they share the exact same genes. Clearly, genetic make-up is not the only factor involved. Nevertheless, the preponderance of research evidence does point to a genetic role that cannot be ignored. So the practical way to understand the problem is to say that genetic inheritance establishes a susceptibility or propensity toward alcohol dependence contingent on other social and/or psychological factors for each person.

Thus, to understand this disease/condition, we have to apply an even broader model, called the *bio/psycho/social* model. This most contemporary understanding of addiction does not attempt to supplant the disease model but, rather, to expand it. The bio/psycho/social model recognizes that, in addition to genetic factors, addictive disease processes have significant sociocultural and psychological influences that contribute to establishing and maintaining dependence. With this broader model, we can understand the addiction process for each person involving a unique blend of:

- inherited physical susceptibility and biological adaptations,
- psychological processes, and
- social/cultural factors

Standard treatment programs accept the bio/psycho/social model of addiction and have added a fourth dimension of *spiritual factors*. This is an important and useful addition for many people, unless it leads back to the moral bankruptcy view of alcoholism and blaming the victim.

If you can accept this broader bio/psycho/social understanding of alcohol dependence problems, I hope you can more easily accept that it has happened *to* you rather than being some mysterious fault of your own, and that you can approach your recovery from a pragmatic rather than a self-recriminating point of view. Just like discovering that you have any other condition or disease to contend with, it probably is not your fault. What you want to do is focus on overcoming it, not on blaming yourself.

Chapter 5

Physical Addiction to Alcohol: Process and Effects

Problem:	*Failure to understand the biology and consequences of alcohol dependence leads to massive health problems.*
Solution:	*Know your enemy: Learn all you can about the biology of alcohol dependence and the true effects of alcohol on your body.*

The Biology of Alcohol Dependence

Many drinkers have no idea how addiction to alcohol happens and how alcohol effects the brain and the rest of the body. Perhaps most people don't really want to know, and I can't blame them. The reality of alcohol's effects are not pleasant. Still, you really do need to know. Knowing can increase your motivation to quit drinking. To begin with, it helps to understand how habituation to alcohol happens.

Habituation

The nervous system has two divisions—the central nervous system and the peripheral nervous system. The *central nervous system* (CNS) consists of the brain and spinal column. The brain directs movement and manages language, memories, thinking, emotions, self-awareness, judgment, and other cognitive actions. The *peripheral nervous system* (PNS) is a network of microscopic fibers that transport messages throughout the body, which allows for feeling, movement, and a host of metabolic processes including heartbeat, digestion, and breathing.

With alcohol use, important adaptations take place throughout the body—of which changes within the brain are most important. Each individual has about a trillion brain cells to start with. How we breathe, move, and think depends on how these cells communicate with one another, which takes place in part through an electrical circuit system. Cells "fire" one to the next, relaying information on feeling, thinking, and moving. Each nerve cell has a cell body and long arms called *axons*, which end in finger-like tentacles called *dendrites* that reach out toward the next cell in a communication network.

Interestingly, the nerve cells do not directly touch each other. There is a microscopic gap between cells called the *synapse*. The message to fire from one cell to the next depends on tiny molecular chemicals crossing the gap. Called *neurotransmitters,* they are released from the dendrites of one cell, cross the gap, and are picked up at receptor sites on the next cell, thereby relaying their messages. Despite the millions of cells involved in a single communication, messages are sent and received at incredible speeds—up to 70 yards per second. Dozens of types of neurotransmitters send different messages between cells. Among other functions, some neurotransmitters are associated with feelings of well-being and relaxation, some with excitation or pain.

As discussed in Chapters 2 and 4, alcohol is in a class of drugs known as *central nervous system depressants*. This class includes all the opioids such as opium and heroin, and pain medications such as Oxycontin, Percocet, and Vicodin. The class also includes a host of anti-anxiety drugs such as Valium, Librium, and Xanax. Like these other drugs, alcohol disrupts the normal activities of neurotransmitters such that the functions of inhibitory (calming/relaxing) and excitory neurotransmitters are off-set. Alcohol *enhances* the effects of neurotransmitters associated with relaxation and emotional wellbeing. These include GABA, glycine, adenosine, dopamine, and serotonin. At the same time, alcohol *inhibits* the effects of excitory transmitters like glutamate and aspartate. The drinker calms down and feels good. However, millions of years of evolution have assured that our brains constantly seek homeostasis—a chemical balance. So, as drinking continues across time, one's neurochemistry adapts to alcohol's effects and habituation occurs, commonly called "tolerance"—one needs more alcohol to get the same effect. The brain has amped-up its excitory neurotransmitters system to compensate for alcohol's suppressing effects and it has toned down use of its inhibitory neurotransmitter system because alcohol is now doing the job. So, if one stops drinking, his or her brain's ability to relax on its own will be compromised. Calming transmitters are weak at doing their job and the excitory transmitter system, accustomed to fighting a resistance, is now hyperactive. Like a dam suddenly bursting, the person is flooded with arousal and anxiety, often with shaking and sleeplessness.

But do not despair. Mother Nature/God has made us so well that the brain again seeks homeostasis and, in the absence of alcohol, slowly but surely rebuilds a healthy excitory/relaxation/feel good neurotransmitter balance. This dehabituation takes only a few days.

The reverse happens when people stop taking a stimulant-class drug such as cocaine or methamphetamine; they feel slowed down, depressed, and may sleep for a few days, as their brains are suddenly under-stimulated by their excitory transmitter systems that had been artificially stimulated, and are now overwhelmed by their sedating neurotransmitter systems.

In addition to what is happening at the brain-cell level, a person's relative biogenetic propensity contributes to the addiction process. As discussed previously, individuals who are so disposed habituate more rapidly and experience positive sensations, rendering them more susceptible to alcohol dependence. As mentioned in Chapter 4, research with sons of alcoholics indicates that they have a natural, built-in tolerance.

The effects on the brain and the rest of the nervous system may vary from person to person but are largely a function of the amount of alcohol a person imbibes per occasion. Different beverages have different levels of alcohol.

Drink Equivalencies

Of several types of alcohol, *ethyl alcohol* (ethanol) is the type that is present in all drinks—wine, beer, and hard liquors. Regardless of its "clothing," or form, ethyl alcohol has to get in the bloodstream to achieve its effects. Each of the following contains about the same amount of ethyl alcohol and is considered one drink:

One glass of wine (5 oz)

One beer (12 oz)[1]

One mixed drink (with 1.0–1.5 oz liquor)

It takes about 20 minutes for alcohol to be distributed throughout the body—somewhat faster if consumed on an empty stomach, somewhat slower on a full stomach. The body takes about an hour to process and eliminate one drink. The intoxicating effect, and damage caused, depends on the level of alcohol present in a person's overall volume of blood.

Blood Alcohol Content

The proportionate amount of alcohol in a person's bloodstream is referred to as the *blood alcohol concentration* (*BAC*). A BAC of .10 means that 1/10 of 1 percent of a person's total volume of blood consists of alcohol. The average person will die of acute alcohol poisoning if his or her BAC reaches ½ of 1 percent (.50 BAC)—about six times the legal limit for driving. Many people die each year at lower alcohol levels, but most people vomit and pass out before they reach this point. BAC will be higher or lower depending on the following.

The quantity of alcohol consumed

The rate of consumption

The faster one drinks, the higher is the potential "spike" in the BAC as the liver cannot keep pace—it can only metabolize about one dink per hour.

Body weight

Larger people tend to have lower BACs drink-for-drink than smaller people do. Bigger people simply have larger volumes of blood. For example, if a 200-pound man and a 130-pound man each consume four

---

[1] Some of the new "ice" beers and microbrewery beers have twice the alcohol of regular beer.

drinks in an hour; the smaller man could reach .10 BAC while the larger man might reach only half that level—.05 BAC.

Gender

Women tend to develop higher BACs than men do, even for the same body weight. This is thought to be attributable to a generally higher body-fat ratio in women versus men, and to differences in hormones between men and women involved in the metabolism of alcohol. Studies have shown, for instance, that women's BACs tend to be higher during their menstrual periods.

Mood

Alcohol may enter the bloodstream at different rates because mood can affect rate of metabolism. For example, when a person is angry or anxious, metabolism can be faster than when that person is depressed.

Carbonation

Those tiny bubbles in champagne, beer, and other carbonated beverages speed alcohol into the bloodstream (the carbon dioxide carries alcohol more rapidly through the walls of the stomach and intestine).

Metabolization

Alcohol is a poison that kills if consumed in large enough quantities. Even in the small, palatable amounts that people typically drink, it is an irritant to all body organs. Once consumed, the body works to eliminate alcohol. In effective metabolization, the liver enzyme alcohol dehydrogenase breaks down ethanol into acetaldehyde. This is further broken down to acetic acid, and then to carbon dioxide and water, and is eliminated through urine, perspiration, and respiration. Once in the body, alcohol has both short-term and long-term effects on all organs and systems, including the central nervous system.

Damaging Physical Effects

Once ingested, alcohol causes a variety of harmful effects throughout the body.

Mouth and Esophagus

Drinking pure alcohol has been described as not a taste but, rather, a sensation—something like drinking ground glass! On its way to the stomach, trace amounts of alcohol are absorbed directly into the bloodstream through the tongue. Over time, alcohol can lead to *esophageal varices* (varicose veins along the esophagus), which can cause death from hemorrhaging. Another risk associated with excessive drinking is *cancer of the esophagus.*

Stomach

About 20 percent of alcohol consumed penetrates the stomach wall into the bloodstream. Short-term effects include *gastritis*, a sometimes painful irritation of the stomach lining. Long-term effects include *ulcers* and possibly *stomach cancer.*

Small Intestines

About 80 percent of alcohol enters the bloodstream through the small intestines. Once in the bloodstream, it is transported to all parts of the body immediately.

Liver

The liver is the body's filtering system, responsible for the metabolism of any toxic substance, including alcohol. The liver also manages the release of blood sugar (glucose). As a pure carbohydrate, alcohol initially increases blood sugar. However, because the liver responds to alcohol as a toxin, it prioritizes breaking down (metabolizing) the alcohol and soon stops releasing glucose. This then results in a lowering of blood glucose levels. Excessive alcohol use across time can damage the body's ability to regulate and metabolize blood sugar.

Alcohol's first metabolite, acetaldehyde, is a close cousin to formaldehyde. The medication Antabuse (disulfiram) keeps acetaldehyde from breaking down further. That's why a person who drinks while taking Antabuse will become violently ill—too much acetaldehyde accumulates quickly.

If too much alcohol is consumed over long periods, a variety of problems eventually occur in the liver. *Fatty liver* is an enlargement of the liver caused when the liver cannot successfully process the increased fat accumulation that comes from excessive drinking. An inflammation known as *alcoholic hepatitis* can occur, causing fever, pain, and jaundice. Only abstinence and good nutrition can reverse fatty liver and alcoholic hepatitis.

With repeated alcohol insult, liver cells begin to die and scar. This irreversible damage, called *cirrhosis*, results in death to thousands each year. Once a certain amount of the liver (about 50 percent) is scarred, the victim rapidly reaches a point of no return and will die without a liver transplant. Cirrhosis is said to be the fourth leading disease cause of death in the USA, 90 percent of which is caused by alcoholism and the remaining 10 percent caused mostly by hepatitis.

I often see people with end-stage cirrhosis, who are seeing me as part of many things they must do to get on the list for liver transplantation. Because good livers are not readily available, doctors don't want to waste a transplant on someone who is not sober and working on a credible program of recovery. Liver transplant boards in various regions of the country want to approve livers for the healthiest people, those most likely to take good care of the new liver and to live a long time. Alcoholics can get on transplantation lists, but only after proving at least one year of sobriety, quitting smoking, and being within body weight limits. I'm sorry to say that over the years, most of the people I have seen who need a new liver, although they are sober, do not make the list, or they get on the list too late. These are people I have come to know and care for. When the appointments at my clinic stop for good, we miss them.

Pancreas

The job of the pancreas is to secrete appropriate amounts of insulin to balance blood sugar. Excessive drinking causes *pancreatitis* and *hypoglycemia*. Part of the reason that alcoholics have radical ups and downs in mood and energy is thought to be that the alcohol-affected pancreas causes erratic changes in blood sugar levels. As with the liver, after a certain amount of damage, only a transplant can save the victim.

Muscles

Alcohol contains a substance that causes red blood cells to clump together. This "blood sludging" phenomenon clogs up tiny capillaries that supply oxygen and nutrients to all body organs, including all muscles. Because of this deprivation, muscle cells throughout the body begin to *atrophy*, a process in which muscle cells shrivel and age prematurely. This effect is noticeable in adult over-drinkers, who may appear heavy from the excessive fat in the midsection while their arms and legs appear weak and spindly as a result of wasting of muscle tissue.

Regular alcohol use also reduces a man's ability to produce *testosterone*, the male hormone that produces larger, firmer muscles, body and facial hair, and a deeper voice, among other male characteristics. In many male heavy drinkers, this suppression of testosterone allows the small amount of estrogen in men to have greater sway. Thus, the drinking man can develop in time what are called *secondary feminine characteristics*, with poorer muscle tone, less muscle mass and fleshier bellies and breasts. The good news is that muscle cells (unlike brain or liver cells) can recover. This requires abstinence, good nutrition, and regular rigorous exercise; the muscle cells plump up again in a process known as *hypertrophy*. Rigorous regular exercise is a powerful fountain of youth for muscle cells.

Heart and Blood Vessels

Also due in part to the blood sludging effect of alcohol, excessive drinking—in some individuals even moderate drinking—significantly weakens the heart muscle. The resulting cardiomyopathy (a weak and under-responsive heartbeat) is not entirely reversible. In addition, alcohol is a common cause of *hypertension*, or high blood pressure. Fortunately, after an initial rise in blood pressure during withdrawal, we frequently see a significant drop in blood pressure early in sobriety. In some cases people are able to discontinue the blood pressure medications they had needed when they were actively alcoholic.

Still another problem associated with alcohol is premature *arteriosclerosis*—hardening of the arteries. This is because excessive drinking diminishes the liver's ability to metabolize cholesterol appropriately.

Immune System

The body's ability to fend-off illness and disease is seriously jeopardized by the effects of alcohol. Excessive drinking increases vulnerability to many diseases to which people are exposed—everything from colds and flu to tuberculosis and AIDS. This is because:

- alcohol in the blood destroys many vitamins, including vitamin C, on contact;
- consuming only two drinks is enough to destroy all of the disease-fighting blood platelets produced in the body in one day.
- Alcohol leads to malabsorption syndrome—the inability of the body to utilize sources of nutrition even when normal food is ingested. All alcoholics have some level of malnutrition.

Nervous System

Alcohol affects the entire nervous system. In the peripheral nervous system, a long-term effect of drinking is *polyneuropathy*, which causes numbing and tingling in the hands and feet. *Cortical atrophy* occurs in the central nervous system in late-stage alcoholics, as evidenced by losses in brain cortex functioning. Over many years, decreased oxygen and nutrients cause brain cells to die irreplaceably in sufficient numbers to cause losses in senses of touch, taste, hearing, sight, and smell, coordination in body movement, reasoning, and memory. In autopsies of chronic alcoholics, physicians say they can visibly note entire convolutions of the brain shrunken from loss of tissue.

Specific brain effects include Wernicke/Korsakoff syndrome, commonly referred to as "wet brain." As alcoholics become malnourished, they can develop Wernicke's encephalopathy, a brain disorder that is caused in part by a thiamine (B1) deficiency. Symptoms of Wernicke's include loss of muscle coordination, confusion, and vision problems. Wernicke's can be followed by Korsakoff psychosis which is an even more serious form of brain damage resulting in loss of memory functions, hallucinations, and death.

Experiential Effects

As mentioned, the drinker experiences alcohol in small amounts as a stimulant due to an initial increase in glucose, and feelings of well-being and disinhibition. The initial stimulating effects soon are overshadowed by the sedative and toxic effects—slowing of mental and physiological processes, dizziness, nausea, sweating. That's why nonalcoholics tend to slow down automatically and stop drinking after one to three drinks. Alcoholics can drink more than this due to habituation—increased tolerance.

If the person continues to drink and BAC increases, mental sluggishness and declining physical coordination can be noticed in an unsteady gait and slurred speech. As the BAC rises to more than .20, nonalcoholic drinkers are likely to pass out. This is fortunate (assuming they aren't driving) because if they continue to drink, the BAC can reach a level high enough to paralyze the centers in the brain that control life-essential involuntary functions such as breathing and heartbeat.

Passouts

Unlike going to sleep, passing out means literally becoming unconscious when and where the person did not intend to do so. Different individuals will pass out at different levels of alcohol intoxication, but generally between .20 and .35 BAC. Younger, less experienced drinkers tend to pass out at lower levels, whereas a severe alcoholic may be walking and talking at .35 BAC or even higher. Usually, a passout will save the individual from death simply because he or she cannot drink once unconscious. A person sometimes dies, though, as a result of falls or car crashes, and sometimes this happens because of imbibing just prior to passing out. Even after passing out, alcohol can continue to enter the bloodstream, raising BAC to fatal levels. Here again, there are no magic numbers. Novice drinkers have died at BACs below .30, and others not until over .50 BAC.

Blackouts

A blackout is the complete loss of ability to place into long-term memory any perceptions occurring while intoxicated. Those affected do not "forget" anything. Whatever they did while intoxicated simply was never recorded in their long-term memories. Typically, the individual awakens in the morning wondering how he or she got home and feeling frightened. At other times a person will not be able to recall limited portions of an evening of drinking and be distressed and embarrassed at what friends say he or she said or did while intoxicated. If a person eventually recalls most of the evening, it is referred to as a *grayout*, which does not represent a true blackout.

The loss of a person's orientation to time and place while in a blackout is specifically referred to as *alcohol intoxication delirium.* Impressively, in a blackout, although memory, judgment, and sometimes orientation to place and time are seriously impaired, motor functions are relatively spared. This means that an alcoholic in a blackout can handle change, have basic conversations, and drive a car—albeit seriously impaired. The ability to move and talk while in a blackout is no indication that all is okay with the brain. It is not. Perception, sequencing of thoughts, and judgment are severely impaired. This occasionally leads to disastrous events such as car crashes, assaults, and killings, without intent as we know it, as the individual in a blackout tragically misinterprets his or her situation and other's intentions. Many alcoholics have been killed in blackouts, and many alcoholics are in prison for crimes of which they have no memory.

The blackout is not just a late-stage alcoholism phenomenon. Blackouts can occur in the early and middle stages of alcoholism. Many non-alcoholics report that during their high school or college experimental drinking, they had a blackout and/or passout. At an early age, a blackout or two does not necessarily represent alcohol dependence or alcoholism, but blackouts continuing into a person's 20s or 30s usually do. Most, but not all, alcoholics have experienced blackouts.

Among the many tales of alcoholic blackout, a dear client once called my clinic at about 10:00 on a Monday morning. He was distressed because he was in a strange room. I asked him how he got there, and he replied, "Never mind *how* I got here, I don't even know *where* I am!" I asked him to look out the window, and he discovered that he was in a motel. In fact, he was in Spokane, Washington—and my clinic was in Eugene, Oregon at the time.

Another time, a man came in on an urgent appointment stating that he was done drinking—ready to quit alcohol forever. In a blackout over the weekend, he had hand-painted his brand new pick-up truck with yellow house paint!

On a considerably more alarming level, an airline pilot referred for treatment told me a frightening account. He had piloted complete round-trip flights while so intoxicated that he had absolutely no memory of the trips.

Reverse Tolerance

Chronic alcoholics sometimes experience *reverse tolerance.* Most people have known or at least have heard about a person who gets plastered on one drink. This usually is because the person's liver is damaged so severely that it is unable to break down acetaldehyde, which then continues to circulate in the blood in a high concentration, producing severe intoxication with a small amount of alcohol.

Acute Withdrawal

As discussed in Chapter 1, once tolerance is established, different individuals experience withdrawal somewhat differently. Some people have only emotional sensations—usually a mixed anxiety/depression syndrome. By way of review, in acute withdrawal, a person can experience:

- depression
- anxiety
- insomnia
- perspiration
- increased pulse rate
- nausea or vomiting
- hand tremor
- seizures (in the more severe cases)
- DTs (in the more severe cases)

Beyond hangover effects, withdrawal typically begins the next day or evening after last imbibing alcohol. In hospital detoxification units, withdrawal commonly is seen before all the alcohol has been eliminated from a person's body. That is, a person may initiate detoxification with a BAC of .35 and begin symptoms of withdrawal, feeling shaky and emotionally distressed, when their BAC drops to .15. Such individuals are treated with special medications to ease the effects of withdrawal and offset the increasing risk of permanent diminutions in cognitive abilities with each successive withdrawal. Indeed, unlike withdrawal from heroin—although emotionally distressing—withdrawal from alcohol can be damaging and sometimes fatal.

Post-Acute Withdrawal Syndrome

Post-acute withdrawal syndrome (PAWS) refers to continuing emotional, cognitive, and/or behavioral disturbances, which may appear in some persons at any point after stabilization from acute withdrawal. Captured in the term "dry drunk," it is typified by a return of moods and behaviors formerly associated with the person's drinking: Irritability, blaming others, or even becoming overly self-confident. The importance of post-acute withdrawal syndrome, of course, is its role in relapse. PAWS is thought to involve the return of denial and is understood to originate subconsciously in the part of the mind that wants to drink again. It is a set-up for relapse.

Delirium Tremens—The DTs

Delirium tremens, the *DTs,* is a dangerous phenomenon, as discussed in Chapter 1 regarding assessment of withdrawal risks. DTs, which tend to occur in later-stage chronic alcoholics, involve the onset of hallucinations with severe mental agony several days after detoxification.

Longevity

As mentioned in Chapter 2, several decades of research support that for most people regular drinking of small amounts of alcohol—a *maximum* of two drinks per day for men and one drink for women—likely promotes good overall health. This low level of drinking is associated with a host of health benefits including reduced risk of cardiovascular disease, dementia, diabetes, arthritis, and several types of cancer. However, it is critically import to know that drinking beyond these limits has the reverse effect, ultimately resulting in severe problems in all aspects of health. And controversy remains about whether light/moderate drinkers really outlive teetotalers. A major experimental design flaw has been discovered in much of this research. It is called *selection bias.* The flaw has been in the reason behind the teetotalers' abstinence. In many cases, it was because they had to abstain to better manage other diseases they had. They had comparatively shorter lives because they died of other diseases, not because they did not drink. So reanalysis of the research indicates that teetotalers outlive drinkers at any level (Fillmore et al., 2004).

Even with this information about the genetic vulnerability and the insidious physical addiction process, it can seem difficult to understand why alcohol-dependent people have such a hard time quitting. Once we accept that some people may be biogenetically prone to metabolize substances in a way that makes them more susceptible, it still does not fully explain why they don't just quit once they know they have a problem. Before we retreat to the old moralistic, judgmental model of blaming the victim for weak willpower or willful misconduct, we have to understand *psychological* aspects of the addiction process, discussed in the next chapter.

Chapter 6

The Psychology of Addiction

Problem:	*Months after quitting drinking, physical craving is not what causes relapse. It's what do you do about depression, anxiety, or frustration without your usual medication—alcohol.*
Solution:	*Strengthen your resolve for a lasting recovery by learning about the profound role of psychology in addiction.*

Mere physical addiction is not the major hurdle in recovery from alcohol dependence. Hollywood depictions, naïveté, myth, and legend have led the general population to believe that *physical withdrawal* is the biggest obstacle that drinkers have to overcome before they can quit for good, and that once the alcoholic goes through physical withdrawal, everything will be fine. But things are not fine after physical withdrawal. Long after the body has de-habituated, the mind continues to struggle.

Although I don't believe in a pure mind/body dualism (the body and mind are inextricably connected), it is useful to consider them separately to better understand addiction and recovery. Functionally, there are two addictions and two withdrawals, one *physical* and one *psychological*. People do habituate physically to alcohol and consequently suffer some withdrawal problems, *and* they also habituate mentally, which presents a different kind of withdrawal problem. The physical withdrawal process is relatively brief, whereas psychological recovery can take many weeks or months.

As stressed in Chapter 2, dealing with self-assessment, emotional dysregulation is the lynchpin in an array of costs associated with alcohol abuse and dependence. Excessive drinking over many years causes an increase in depression, anxiety, and irritability. This is counterintuitive for drinkers because, when drinking, they feel emotionally better, not worse. Subconsciously, the mind has found a fast track to feeling good that it quickly comes to prefer over other methods, so drinkers lose the capacity to process feelings in healthier ways. They lose the ability to label feelings accurately and fail to use negative emotions as signaling systems for making positive changes. Thus, the drinker becomes emotionally handicapped, usually without knowing it. The life domains that are affected across time by excessive drinking vary from person to person. One person may have had an alcohol-related health crisis, while another might be completely healthy but has failed at relationships. Someone else may be fired from his or her job but maintains a great marriage. No matter what areas of life are affected or spared, emotional regulation is always compromised. Subsequently, the inability to cope with negative emotions is the single largest cause of relapse.

As I have said, once stabilized in early recovery, probably 90 percent of relapses are a result of negative emotional states that the newly recovering person has not yet figured out how to manage. Imagine that you have a badly broken arm with a cast running from shoulder to fingertips. When the cast is removed three months later, you're astounded and gasp, "What happened to my arm, Doc?" The arm has shriveled to half the size of your other arm. The muscles have atrophied from lack of use. "Don't worry," says the doctor, "it's perfectly normal. In a few months it will be just like your other arm again."

Excessive drinking over several months or years puts a cast over one's emotional management system, artificially propping it up, and it withers for lack of functioning on its own. It will recover but, just like the broken arm, it is weakened and the person will have to learn how to take special care to avoid relapse.

Emotional recovery is the single most important area of recovery. Yet, most people don't realize this. They are more concerned about money, jobs, families, and an array of immediate problems that confront them as they stop drinking. Then they are surprised to discover that they begin drinking again when they are overwhelmed, not with external challenges—we all have those—but with anxiety, depression, and/or anger. This emotional instability is part of post-acute withdrawal syndrome (PAWS)—a very real and predictable process within the recovering person.

You Are Not to Blame!

Before we look at the psychological addiction process and how you actually can prosper emotionally in recovery, let's dispel one huge misunderstanding: To clear the slate for emotional recovery, you have to suspend the natural human tendency to blame ourselves or others for what we don't really understand. Alcoholics commonly blame themselves for their problem, and their family members usually blame them as well. People naturally assume that because only the alcoholic can be *responsible* for the problem and for recovery, the alcoholic, therefore, is the one who is to *blame*.

This is a non-equation. Indeed, the alcoholic must be held responsible and accountable for the damage done and is the only one who can be responsible for getting well. Yet, because alcoholics are not at fault for the problem itself, they can't, in all fairness, be blamed. People simply do not consciously seek to become chemically dependent. I have never met a person I thought was *to blame* for his or her alcohol use problem. Moreover, the attitude of blame is both wrong and unhelpful to those with substance abuse problems.

Many people are naive regarding the influence of genetic predisposition, physical habituation, and the misery of withdrawal. Fortunately, once educated, most alcoholics and family members appreciate the role of genetic risk factors and the biology of habituation and withdrawal in the development and maintenance of addiction problems. But confusion and blame abound as most people remain completely in the dark about the dynamics of *psychological* dependence. They then continue to blame the person for getting addicted, for lying and covering up, for not seeking help, and for continuing to "choose" to have relapses. Only when we truly understand the psychological addiction process can we see that, although individuals with substance use problems indeed must take responsibility for the problem and their recovery, they are not to blame.

We tend to assume that all of our behaviors are under our conscious control. Therefore, we naively assume that people who over-drink simply lack willpower, or are engaging in *willful misconduct*. Actually, the psychological addiction process circumvents willpower as we know it, and willful misconduct is about the least frequent reason for excessive drinking. I have never met a person who went to his or her high school guidance counselor and said, "I really admire alcoholics. How can I become one and ruin my life?"

True, a young person occasionally will drink because he or she thinks it is glamorous. Perhaps we could consider this willful misconduct. Also, there is the phenomenon of *revenge drinking*, in which a person who's angry with a parent or a spouse acts out with a sort of a passive/aggressive "I'll show you" attitude. This, too, could be considered willful misconduct. But by far-and-away, forces out of a person's conscious control are what drive excessive drinking.

In my practice, I have seen countless bright and successful people who are unnecessarily self-disparaging because they fail to realize that *responsibility does not equal blame*. Added to this, they think they should be able to quit drinking readily. I'm talking about alcoholic doctors, lawyers, professors—people with obviously high IQs, strong willpower, and the best of intentions. They have become so successful at controlling their lives that they assume they should be able to quit drinking easily. Then they become terribly frustrated when they cannot quit. What they are initially unable to understand is that *IQ, willpower, and goodness of person are functions of the conscious mind, whereas the addiction is ensconced in the subconscious and runs the show from there.*

Defense mechanisms that are otherwise healthy hijack the conscious mind and allow drinking to continue. These defense mechanisms include rationalization, minimization, justification, intellectualization, projection, anger, humor, and/or flat-out denial. Why does this happen? The underlying cause is emotional distress—anxiety, fear, and depression.

Your Good Mind Hijacked

The subconscious mind operates on the *pleasure principle*: It seeks pleasure and to avoid pain at every moment. It does not track the passage of time, it cannot delay gratification, it has absolutely no morals, and is not afraid of destruction. Some people wonder if their excessive drinking is a subconscious attempt to commit suicide. In therapy, we sometimes do "parts work," in which we ask clients to turn their thoughts inward and imagine that they have two parts—a part that doesn't want to drink and a part that does. We have them ask the part that wants to drink, "Why do you want me to drink?" They frequently are surprised by the response. The part that wants them to drink is not trying to hurt them. To the contrary, it is trying to make them feel better—to keep them from feeling anxious, fearful, or depressed. Then we help the person convince the side that wants to drink to use other methods to avoid negative feelings that may be more healthy than drinking.

So give yourself a break. You didn't acquire this problem because of lack of willpower, IQ points, or good intention. It's like a popular old episode of *Star Trek*. Sent by an alien force, a tiny earwig-like robot bores its way through the hull of the Enterprise while the crew sleeps. It drops on Captain Kirk's head and crawls into his ear. The next morning Kirk isn't the same. He and the crew are not aware that he now is secretly under the control of aliens on a mission to sabotage the ship. The crew members see that their captain is acting difficult and strange, but they don't catch on until nearly too late, and only after a lot of damage has been done. They're angry with their captain for a while, but when the reality of his predicament is revealed, they do not see cause to blame him. Like the drinker, his mind was hijacked.

Consider this example. A man has been feeling increasingly tired at work. Others wonder if he is slacking off. One day he is driving home and runs off the road, smashing into somebody's front porch. He's taken to a hospital where, although not seriously injured, is told that he had a diabetic seizure while driving. From that point, the man must learn all about diabetes, make significant adjustments in his diet, monitor his blood sugar, and work with insulin daily. He struggles to learn and apply these new health maintenance strategies. Does he get it right from the start? Of course not. He has to practice, stumble along for a while, and learn many lessons through trial and error. Family members say, "Honey, don't eat that doughnut," and "Have you checked your blood sugar this morning?" Everyone—family, friends, coworkers—all expect him to be *responsible* for managing his diabetes, *but no one blames him for having a faulty pancreas.*

The trouble with understanding addiction is that we see no smoking gun, i.e., no faulty panaceas to blame, and fail to comprehend the psychological addiction process. I strongly believe that *alcohol invades the mind no less that tuberculosis invades the lungs.* Just as the innocent passenger on the airplane unknowingly contracts tuberculosis, so too, does the drinker innocently contract alcohol addiction.

Even if people stop blaming alcohol-dependent persons for the problem, they will continue to blame them for relapses. This is equally counterproductive and unjustifiable. Alcohol and other drug dependencies are known in medicine as "diseases of relapse." Other diseases of relapse include hypertension and diabetes. Hypertensives notoriously have difficulty managing their blood pressure. They don't consistently stick to their low sodium/low cholesterol diet. They fail to exercise as advised, don't take enough time off work, skip their medications, and repeatedly wind up in their doctors' offices. Similarly, as previously mentioned, 90 percent of diabetics don't follow their medical regimens, and they pay a high price in compromised health and shortened life (Meichenbaum & Turk, 1987).

Behavior patterns are hard to change. Everything from weight loss to academic success takes hard work, study, and practice. Interesting new research shows what it takes to master anything—from playing piano or playing golf, to building a successful business or mastering a science. In his book *Outliers: The Story of Success*, Malcolm Gladwell (2008) calls it the "10,000 hour rule." Pretty much across the board, this is the average amount of practice time needed to master anything.

The Normalcy of Self-Protection

To mitigate the blame-and-shame problem, I sometimes lead a group exercise with family members. It focuses on the tendency to blame-and-shame drinkers because they are so evasive, even deceitful, regarding their drinking. I ask the group members to imagine in the safety of their own minds something about themselves that may embarrass them or make them feel ashamed, something that they would never disclose to anyone. I have them focus on just one thing, then guide them through a process of getting in touch with the event or situation by asking them to consider what it is or was, or what they did, when it was, where it was, and who else may have been involved. Then I ask them all to share that shameful embarrassing experience with the person sitting next to them.

The facial expressions say it all. Everybody chokes. Then I say, "Don't worry—I'm not really going to ask you to do that. But what happened?" The group members then volunteer that when I directed them to tell their secrets, their minds raced for something safer to share, to the extent that many admit to making up something. This is the deployment of a type of denial in the normal mind—in this case to actually tell a lie—to protect themselves from embarrassment and recrimination. This is where the addict lives, in a place of fear and shame. They are doing only what anybody would do—hiding a painful, frightening secret. As the anxiety exercise demonstrates, denial and lying are common defenses that people deploy to protect themselves from humiliation and shame and, for drinkers, to protect loss of the only thing that reliably makes them feel good—drinking.

Alexithymia

As I have emphasized repeatedly, the crippling feature of addiction is not so much the *physical* addiction but, rather, the *psychological* dependence. Without question, physical withdrawal and healing can be quite a challenge, but the *mental reliance* on alcohol is what causes relapses and extends the healing process.

I have taught groups of patients in treatment programs about the psychological aspects of addiction. Alcoholics usually have at least a vague sense that psychology might have something to do with the problem, and they are naturally curious. I begin by asking my students/patients to take a few minutes to just think about and jot down any feelings, moods, or emotions they may have had during the past year. After several minutes, I notice that they start looking at the ceiling, pensively tapping their pencils, or glancing nervously at each others' papers. I have never seen a patient write down more than three words, and even these are basic, such as "sad," "angry," "worried." Many pages remain completely blank.

These patients are suffering from *alexithymia*, the compromised ability to even label feelings, let alone to cope with them. By the time people get to an inpatient treatment program, alcohol is well established in their minds as the primary overriding emotional management system. This is indeed a serious handicap in life. As the humanist Carl Rogers (1995) cautions, we are in trouble whenever we deny to conscious awareness important emotional experience. When we are aware of our real feelings, coping with problems is a lot more accurate and productive.

With respect for the intelligence and sincerity of those in my treatment groups, I show a PowerPoint projection of 150 words that describe emotional states. You can see the lightbulbs switch on. With the stimulus of looking at words that describe feelings, people are able to make reasonable lists. I hear comments such as, "I've had *that* feeling—and, oh yes, I've had lots of that one ... and that one, too."

As a rule, people with alcohol dependence do not understand this deficit in emotional management. After all, alcohol makes them feel good, not bad. Although this usually is true, the good feelings come only while they are imbibing. In the interim, when they're sober, they feel worse and worse, thinking alcohol is about the only thing that helps. When we're young, the effects of alcohol take us from a neutral mood to feeling high. Eventually, with psychological habituation, we wind up feeling depressed and we drink just to feel normal. Drinkers usually are unable to see this. Some protest that they don't even drink at all for several days at a time during the work week. They assume that they must be managing their moods well enough without alcohol. Although they don't realize it, the dependence on alcohol as emotional manager is still there. Many weekend-only drinkers merely store up or mentally shelve their negative feelings rather than process them in any productive way during the week. They rely, consciously or subconsciously, on the weekends and alcohol use as their chief coping tool.

The Psychological Addiction Process

So how does alexithymia develop? It has to do with the psychological addiction process. This has been well described by Dr. Vernon Johnson (1980) in his book, *I'll Quit Tomorrow*. Initially a person may be biologically prone and/or psychologically prone to alcohol dependence. The latter includes anybody who has grown up in a nonvalidating environment with abusive or negligent caregivers, people with depression, anxiety, attention or learning disabilities, or an otherwise challenging early life. Also, every stage of life has its emotional challenges, and we all have some fluctuation in moods, whether from hour to hour or day to day. Some people seem to stay in a positive mood most of the time, and others tend to be unhappy most of the time.

Imagine a person whose mood overall on a weekly average is neutral. Let us imagine a teenage boy—although the below description can happen at any stage of life and the gender is irrelevant. In adolescence we are not yet ready to understand our own feelings, and we have to figure out how to relate to a rapidly changing body, new social expectations, and school responsibilities. If this young person, who may be genetically predisposed to addiction already, begins to experiment with alcohol, the initial effect usually is a shift in mood toward the positive. He finds himself less inhibited, perceives that he is socially successful, and initially there is no overall psychological cost. Next week his mood is still neutral. He feels that he is on to a good thing and learns that he can alter his mood by using the substance. Therefore, he is innocently likely to seek it out again, and eventually he learns that, if he consumes enough of the substance, he can blast himself all the way into a euphoric state of intoxication.

This learning, according to educators, is the strongest type of learning. It is *experiential*, not merely intellectual. It's like learning to drive a car. No amount of textbook learning can compare to actually getting behind the wheel and driving. Even if our experimental drinker consumes enough alcohol to get sick, the initial experiences usually have no big emotional cost. Over time, however, there certainly will be emotional costs, of which the person is initially unaware.

The line between social drinking and dependent drinking moves so incrementally that the individual does not recognize when he or she is beyond the pale until it is too late. Like sailing from one ocean into another without any visual reference point, a whole sea change occurs before one realizes that the line has been crossed. With all of the challenges of adolescence, it is easy to understand how a person may begin to find life's challenges a little easier to negotiate when intoxicated—challenges such as overcoming social self-consciousness, managing academic responsibility, and coping with the rushing tides of adolescent emotions.

As our hypothetical young drinker begins to drink more regularly, he begins to pay a psychological price. Instead of drifting back to neutral after substance use, he becomes incrementally unhappier. At a time when he should be starting to better understand his own feelings, manage responsibilities, overcome youthful self-consciousness, and relate more confidently to adults and peers, the substance slowly becomes his mood and social manager, and he does not learn better methods of coping with life's challenges. While intoxicated, our young man easily can overcome a bad mood and feel socially confident as if he were James Bond, but because this is *state-dependent* learning, he will not be any better off emotionally or at socializing when sober. Thus, with drinking comes an arrest in the natural development of emotional learning and social skills, leaving the person with increasing deficits in these vitally important areas of life. In time, our young person will feel depressed and will drink, if only on weekends, just to come back up to normal.

This example holds true for people who begin to use alcohol more regularly in their adult lives even if they didn't have alcohol-use problems in their high school or college years. Unfortunately, the drinker would have to be super-human to understand what is happening, as psychological defense mechanisms deny to awareness of the extent of the problem.

When a person arrives at a place where alcohol use has established itself as a primary, if not *the* primary, emotional and social manager, his or her mind subconsciously will do the most natural thing that any mind would do: Attempt to protect itself from feeling emotional pain. The person's otherwise normal mind *automatically*, subconsciously, uses any number of defense mechanisms to facilitate the use of the one thing it knows will make it feel good. Here's a short list, and there are others.

- Rationalization
- Minimization
- Justification
- Intellectualization
- Denial
- Projection
- Anger
- Humor
- Positive anticipation

In general, defense mechanisms are normal and necessary for everyday living. After spending too much money on a golf club, I might try to *justify*, *rationalize*, or *intellectualize* the purchase in my mind to avoid feeling too badly about it. In an interpersonal conflict, I might mentally *project* faults of my own onto the other person to avoid personal embarrassment or shame. When I read about the world's atrocities in the morning paper, I shudder and turn to the comics. This is a healthy use of *denial*—I simply cannot carry to the office the anguish over the woes of the world and be helpful to my psychotherapy clients.

We need defense mechanisms to get through ordinary life. They can be conjured-up consciously but usually emerge subconsciously so we are seldom aware that we are using them. In psychotherapy, we worry only about people whose defenses are either overblown or too weak. With addictions, however, these otherwise natural and necessary defense mechanisms are deployed in the service of something that eventually will destroy the person. Thus, the person (read: victim) unwittingly finds himself or herself using minimization, rationalization, intellectualization, projection, humor, anger, and other defense mechanisms to allow and protect the substance use. Examples are:

- I drink only after 6 o'clock p.m. (rationalization).
- I drink only beer, not hard stuff (minimization).
- It's my parents'/spouse's/boss's fault (projection).
- Certain proteins in beer are good for you (intellectualization).
- I don't drink more than anyone else. It's not a problem, and I can handle it (denial).

The insidious problem is the subconscious level at which defense mechanisms operate. We get angry at drinkers for using these, but the process is not under their conscious control. Actually, a wall of defenses eventually surrounds the person to such an extent that friends, coworkers, and family members often are confused about the person they are dealing with. The worst part is that the drinker is the last to know. Again, this is exactly what makes addiction recovery so difficult. Willpower, intelligence, and good intentions are functions of the conscious mind. The addiction is ensconced in the subconscious. The conscious mind is hijacked and held hostage.

I liken this to tuberculosis. This germ is a parasite. The human lung is the host. The parasite cannot exist without the host, so it feeds on it slowly, postponing but eventually killing it.

In our example, the young drinker experiences an *emotional arrest.* Countless times, I've seen middle-aged and older people who, once they stop drinking, may be intelligent, worldly, and have a good fund of knowledge but emotionally are about seventeen again. The emotional arrest can occur at any age. It begins whenever the use of alcohol becomes regular.

Psychological addiction is an insidious process that involves the slow but profound takeover of healthy emotional knowledge and coping. Thus, it makes sense that we must pay close attention to emotional management for recovery to be successful.

Social and Cultural Factors

Social and cultural factors influence the make-up of our personalities and contribute strongly to alcohol use problems. No matter how biologically or psychologically susceptible a person is to dependence on alcohol, it obviously is not going to happen if the individual never drinks alcohol. It has been said that a person can be born an alcoholic and it just takes eventual drinking to activate the addiction. This is only partially true. As we have seen, individuals indeed can be born with a biological propensity to become active alcoholics and experience the ravaging effects of alcoholism if they ever drink. Unfortunately, ours is a drinking culture. It is legal to drink. More than 70 percent of adults in the United States drink alcohol. Drinking is heavily advertised. Surveys year after year show that by the time young people are seniors in high school, 90 percent have tried alcohol.

In the past several decades, nation-wide movements have been initiated to discourage youngsters from drinking. These programs advocate *zero tolerance* and are attempts by schools, police, and parent groups to set a new standard about youth and substance use. The hope is that young people will be better protected if they do not start drinking until they are older—and hopefully wiser. Although highly celebrated, annual surveys show only minimal declines in the self-reported drinking behavior of high school students (Johnston et al., 2009). The power of peer influence in a culture that glamorizes drinking provides a more compelling reason to drink than all the forces condemning it.

Recognizing a distinction between physical and psychological addiction helps us understand what otherwise seems so confounding about alcohol dependence. Self-blame vaporizes with awareness of the psychological addiction process against the backdrop of a drinking culture. This is why Chapter 11, Emotional Recovery, is probably the most important chapter in this book. Part 5, dealing with relapse prevention, also focuses on psychological and social aspects of recovery and is important to read.

Recommended Reading for Chapter 6

I'll quit tomorrow: A practical guild to alcoholism treatment, by Vernon Johnson.

Chapter 7

The Backward-Gazing Model

Problem:	Misunderstanding the pros and cons of the major systems of recovery can lead you in the wrong recovery direction.
Solution:	Learn the strengths and limitations of what standard treatment programs, AA, and the medical models have to offer.

Those in charge of treatment programs genuinely want to offer something of value and to do a good job, and they are staffed with sincere and caring individuals. Millions benefit from their assistance. For millions more, the 12-step program of Alcoholics Anonymous is a powerful and enduring resource. I am grateful for these well-established helping systems. However, it has also become abundantly clear that there are problems with these systems and that they are not for everyone. As we have seen, recovery can take *many* routes, including by your own design.

What's Up with Standard Treatment Programs?

There really isn't such a thing as rehabilitation (rehab) centers. This expression is popularly used, and that's fine. But professionals tend to avoid the term because rehabilitation is for criminals and alcohol dependence is not a crime. It is a disease, illness, disorder, condition, or whatever you might like to call it, but not an act of willful misconduct or crime. Treatment is what is needed, so that term is preferred rather than rehab.

Another important distinction needs to be made between *detoxification* (*detox*) and *treatment.* When someone says, "I went to detox" or, "I went to a dry-out" or, "I went to treatment," it's difficult to discern whether he or she went to a detoxification center, a treatment program, or both. *Detoxification* and *treatment* are not the same thing. They represent two distinctly different tasks or experiences in early recovery.

Detox

Detoxification is what the body goes through for repair after a person quits drinking. This physical withdrawal generally lasts from several days to a week, depending on the individual and his or her pattern of drinking. In general, the symptoms can include feeling overly alert, agitated, anxious, and physically nauseous—opposite from the effects of alcohol while it is being used. As discussed in Chapter 1, withdrawing from alcohol can be dangerous.

What a person experiences or does in attempting to manage withdrawal is called *detoxification,* or simply *detox.* These two terms often are used interchangeably with *withdrawal* or *withdrawal management.*

Detoxification centers are of a couple of major types; Social detoxification centers and hospital-based detoxification units. At social detoxification centers, individuals may be medically screened, and if their withdrawal indicates a risk, they are referred to emergency rooms and/or inpatient detoxification units. As a rule, outpatient treatment programs aren't involved with detoxification. In contrast, many hospital-based inpatient treatment centers have attached detoxification units.

Residential treatment centers in general do not do detoxification management. To be clear, detoxification has to do with the safe physical withdrawal management of substance dependent patients. People are not allowed to participate in treatment programs unless they have been sufficiently detoxified. At many treatment centers, individuals who arrive intoxicated or in withdrawal are sent to a hospital or social detox center.

Treatment

Treatment comes after detoxification—if detoxification was necessary in the first place. Treatment programs last much longer than detoxification services and are provided at inpatient or outpatient settings. In either case, treatment programs impart knowledge about addiction and recovery using curriculum-driven, group-based approaches. Information is typically delivered in units covering the history of alcohol and other drugs; the evolution of society's perceptions of substance use problems; assessment processes; the disease model; physical effects; the physical addiction process; life costs; stages of recovery; introduction to 12-step programs; and relapse prevention strategies.

Outpatient programs are almost always DUI programs. In fact, the rapid and wide proliferation of outpatient treatment programs correlates directly with the advent and application of DUI laws throughout the United States beginning in the 1970s. Enactment of DUI laws has been called a full employment bill for substance abuse counselors. At present, at least 90 percent of participants in outpatient treatment programs are there by court mandate, mostly DUI.

What is called *intensive* outpatient treatment, or "I/OP," usually involves three group meetings per week at two to three hours per meeting for two or three months. During this time, the attendees receive information about addiction and recovery and are encouraged to share and process how this information applies in each of their lives. Thus, treatment programs run on an educative curriculum but also are involved in a kind of group therapy. After about three months of the intensive component, most outpatient treatment programs step the attendees down to a once-per-week aftercare (or continuing care) support group meeting for the remainder of one or two years of total program participation.

Inpatient treatment programs and the curricula they offer are not tied directly to DUI laws. Although inpatient treatment programs do serve the mandated population, they have a higher proportion of non-mandated patients than outpatient programs do. Technically, an inpatient treatment program is hospital-based. If it is not, it is referred to as a residential treatment program. Inpatient and residential treatment programs typically have a 21- to 28-day length of stay, but this varies considerably. Length of stay usually is shorter at an inpatient treatment program than at a residential center because of the higher costs associated with a hospital stay. When I directed inpatient programs, I had to turn over a full 50 percent of the program's monthly income to the hospitals for indirect costs.

There are also what are called *"day" treatment programs*. These usually are offered by hospital-based inpatient treatment programs as a step down following an inpatient stay, or as an alternative to inpatient treatment. Day treatment programs usually involve patients' living in their own home or in a temporary apartment and coming to the hospital for some number of hours daily to participate in group-based and individual treatment.

The Group-Based Approach

Whatever the mode of treatment (outpatient, day treatment, inpatient, or residential), all of these programs rely on a classroom or group-based venue for presenting and processing information. In fact, many proponents of this approach believe that a person has not been through proper treatment if not systematically educated in a group program, focused on the 12-step system of AA, and staffed by counselors who are themselves in recovery. There is little evidence to support this model of treatment delivery, however, and several reasons militate against the wholesale application of the group-based approach.

Staffing

Treatment programs usually are staffed by counselors who themselves are in recovery. Obviously, this can be a good thing, as they have a special empathy for what alcoholics go through and know how challenging recovery can be. Most states, however, require that certified substance abuse counselors complete only a handful of addictions courses, usually offered at community colleges, and do not even require completion of an associate's degree. Thus, sometimes these counselors will press their counselees to get recovery just the way they did themselves without too much awareness or appreciation of other routes that might be better for a given person.

These counselors also tend to have a hard time appreciating individual differences or understanding the psychological issues involved in addiction and recovery. Too often, they don't possess a sufficiently broad knowledge base or experience with counseling and therapy techniques. They can be too narrow regarding options, and too demanding of their clients. This sometimes stems from their own *reaction formation*—a psychiatric term describing a person's rigid overcompensation for unresolved shame and guilt feelings. These persons strive to become the polar opposite of what they fear they are or were, to escape guilt and shame. In the process, they become too judgmental and demanding of others to assuage their deep feelings of failure and guilt.

Another common problem is that counselors can over-identify with clients and behave in ways that violate the boundaries of the doctor/patient relationship. Having taught ethics courses and seminars, I know of countless such violations in the substance abuse treatment field, in which patients are emotionally harmed and centers get sued. In the simplest terms, a counselor who forms a business relationship, a friendship, a romantic relationship, or otherwise consorts with his or her client outside of the office, violates the fiduciary relationship (paid-for relationship of trust) with the client, and tends to cause the client confusion and emotional damage.

Also, counselors in recovery are often critical of counselors who have not had addiction problems. But is being a recovering alcoholic really so necessary to be a good counselor? Must a person have died to be a good hospice counselor? Even in 12-step-based treatment programs, research finds no superior benefit to clients treated by counselors themselves in recovery versus non-recovering counselors (Project MATCH Research Group, 1998). Indeed, other factors are more important for being an effective helper than whether one has walked the exact same mile in the exact same shoes as the one needing help. When I directed treatment programs, I made sure that we had a mix of recovering and non-recovering staff members. Non-recovering counselors, I have found, are quite capable of genuine empathy toward people who have substance use problems. These staff members often bring higher academic degrees, particularly in the field of psychology. They maintain a broader view of recovery possibilities and can stay somewhat detached from their clients in a healthy way.

Psychological issues are profoundly involved in the establishment, maintenance, and recovery from substance use problems. The more counselors know about psychology, the better. If we construe alcohol

107

dependence as a disease, again, the most distinguishing feature is that it is not merely a disease of the body but also a disease of the mind. In short, those who are intending to go to a treatment program might first ask about the credentials of the counseling staff and the philosophy of recovery.

Even better, read Anne Fletcher's new book *Inside Rehab* (2013). This is a very well researched, comprehensive and considered look at addictions treatment in the United States, and a very helpful guild for people considering treatment options.

The Questionable Value of Peer Feedback and Support

Another underlying rationale supporting the group treatment approach is that the social aspect of groups will enhance learning through peer feedback and support—that not just knowledge but also group dynamics will help people recover from substance use problems. But the venue for learning and what exactly is taught are not always the best. Research on group-based therapy—something that had a heyday in the late 1960s—indicated that probably less than half of people who participated in encounter group therapy thought they had benefited from the experience. Three in seven reported that they actually found the experience to be negative or detrimental. Apparently, only groups composed of mutually supportive, uninhibited, voluntary participants with good ego strength produce psychological benefits.

In a series of studies on self-help groups, Lieberman (1979) found that even when groups seemed to have that positive component of "give and take" support, many participants evidenced no psychological improvements whatsoever at follow-up. That research was based on *voluntary* participation.

Now consider that at least 90 percent of people in standard treatment programs are there by court mandate. This is not conducive to trustful learning with the already iffy proposition that group-based treatment will help people. Individuals do not feel safe when their participation in the group is reported to probation officers or they may be judged negatively by group participants who obviously are unhappy, even hostile, about being there. In such an environment of mistrust, the potential for learning is compromised significantly and the attendees participate perfunctorily at best. Their resistance often shows.

Unfortunately, research on education-focused addictions treatment groups indicates that this commonly used approach actually has the lowest benefit to participants compared with any other treatment approach (Miller, Wilbourne & Hettema, 2003).

Normal Human Reactance

Sometimes resistance or defensiveness is a sign of denial of an alcohol use problem, but sometimes it is not. My own research on 350 individuals entering a DUI program pointed to a tendency among counselors to place clients in more intensive, or higher levels of treatment if they seem defensive or resistant (Portman, 1987). Although counselors have a tendency to perceive resistance as denial of an alcohol use problem, in many cases what they are seeing is *normal human reactance*. Most of us tend to try to protect ourselves, to hold our cards a little tight, when we perceive that our lives may be controlled and our freedoms threatened or lost.

After facilitating, witnessing, and supervising countless recovery treatment groups, I have seen first-hand that many attendees feel unsafe, stay guarded, are hurt by noxious confrontations, are flat unable to offer appropriate feedback or support to other group members—and fail to benefit from the experience. This is especially true in adolescent treatment groups. Teens are naturally at a socially awkward, self-conscious, self-centered time of life. In their fanciful struggle to find a positive identity, they can be anything but compassionately supportive of one another. Of particular concern is the power of negative peer influence and the tendency of teenagers to model one-another's inappropriate behaviors, to the extent that, as research suggests, adolescent treatment groups may do more harm than good (Dishion, McCord & Poulin, 1999).

Non-Mandated Versus Mandated Groups

Further, counselors tend not to realize how mistrusting or otherwise unhappy the group participants are, because most people do not want to risk complaining. Just because someone agrees to participate does not mean that he or she feels comfortable or safe. This was proven to me when we opened a side group for only non-mandated clients at a treatment center in Eugene, Oregon. Indeed, these groups were more enjoyable to lead. The participants were more motivated, more supportive of one another, and learned faster than those in mandated groups. The counselors all wanted to lead that group.

An interesting thing happened, though. The counselors sadly reported that, although they were thrilled with the first group they led, only half the original people showed up for the second meeting. It seems that after a few years of leading mandated client treatment groups, the counselors assumed they were good group leaders. In truth, no matter how dull, sloppy, or otherwise poor their presentations were, the participants had to show up and participate or risk being dropped from their diversion agreements with their probation officers and the court. They were a captive audience. What the counselors learned is that, to motivate non-mandated clients to return, they had to be a lot more knowledgeable, sensitive, and entertaining than they had been for mandated groups.

Narrow Curricula and Lagging Changes

Known and acknowledged or not, treatment programs all adhere to the time-honored epistemological assumption shared across most cultures that *knowledge is a good thing* and will help people make better choices and live better lives. This is not always true, however. For example, if a terribly disenfranchised young man learns how to make a bomb, is this knowledge a good thing for him or anybody else? Sure, this is a far-out example, but common assumptions shouldn't be taken for granted. As mentioned above, research on the delivery of addiction and recovery information in standard treatment groups fails to show much benefit (Miller, et al, 2003). Yet I do believe that knowledge is a good thing and the more one knows about addiction and recovery the greater their odds of successful abstinence. But compared to group-delivered information, individual tutoring and/or private study may be more beneficial for most people. Just imagine the benefit you might get from individual instruction in golf, skiing, tennis, or anything else, compared with group lessons.

The relevancy and accuracy of the information taught in treatment programs is also questionable. Changes in the curricula delivered in organized treatment programs come slowly. Perhaps unlike any other area of medicine, treatment in the addictions field lags behind research by about 25 years. Part of the problem is that treatment programs are strongly wed to the AA model. Referred to as the Hazelden model of treatment, it was with a strong AA focus that this archetypal Minnesota-based treatment center got its start 60 years ago. Although Hazelden has long-since expanded its approach and offerings, most programs have not.

AA, of course, makes an explicit point of not changing at all. Those for whom it works believe that that AA was established by divine intervention and must not be tampered with. AA adheres to the axiom, "If it isn't broken, don't fix it." This is fine for AA, but what about new discoveries and changes that might improve the odds of successful treatment program participation and recovery for greater numbers of people? And, if most treatment programs adhere to the 12-step model, what distinguishes treatment programs from AA, or is treatment, indeed, merely an expensive introduction to AA?

An Office-Based, Individual Approach

Ultimately, the reason that group-based treatment is so prevalent has to do with dollars and cents—group delivery of information is much more financially expedient for treatment centers. But is this mode best for everyone? Alternatively, an office-based approach—counseling with a private specialist—is highly individualized. I have found that many people working with a private specialist are more relaxed and mentally flexible, and they learn more and faster by far than they would have or did in group-based treatment programs. This is so because, with a private counselor, individuals have less need to stay defended, their specific needs are targeted, and the experience is more relevant to their lives.

The role of the private counselor is more like that of a personal trainer, life coach, or therapist, helping each person to identify his or her own recovery strategies and to achieve those individual goals. And, of course, because clients are the ones who are in charge and do the actual work, they have personal ownership in their recovery. This is no different from, say, individual versus group ski or golf lessons. Individual attention works better for most students, but the pro makes more money conducting group lessons. Paradoxically, though, group-based substance abuse treatment has become considerably more expensive than individual office-based treatment for the client.

What's Up with Alcoholics Anonymous?

At the end of prohibition (1920–1934) a couple of truly remarkable individuals founded Alcoholics Anonymous. AA is decidedly worth looking into. My position is, "Don't knock it too hard until you've tried it, or at least studied up on it a bit." AA literature is everywhere—on the Internet, in bookstores, and at meetings. The "Bible" of AA is devotedly referred to as the "Big Book" (*Alcoholics Anonymous: The Story of How Many Thousands of Men and Women Have Recovered from Alcoholism*, 2001). Partially updated from time to time, it's a remarkable achievement. For those who are interested in a fault-finding alternative, however, try *The Small Book*, by Jack Trimpey (1995). Jack is the founder of *Rational Recovery*, the first major alternative to AA.

AA, as you may know already, is the grandfather of self-help groups. There is no charge to attend and no mandate to speak for those who do attend. The only listed requirement for attendance is a desire to be sober. Those who attend aren't punished if they relapse and then come back. Although many people have told me that they did feel punished when returning to AA after a relapse, the idea is to keep coming back until it works, and then continue to attend whether one feels the need or not.

The meetings used to be reliably anonymous. Because alcoholics are greatly misunderstood by a naively stigmatizing public, they face prejudice, and they often bear the brunt of a lot of blaming and shaming. Thus, the anonymity has been valuable. This component was compromised, however, with the advent of DUI laws and diversion programs. Many people attending meetings are there merely to comply with probation stipulations and treatment program requirements, and do not necessarily give a fig about anonymity. AA members tend to tolerate this because even mandated attendance eventually helps some people. Indeed, the person chairing a given meeting may well have been there originally by mandate.

Potentially Helpful Components of Alcoholics Anonymous

Alcoholics Anonymous has perhaps four components that are thought to be helpful. A brief discussion of each of these follows.

The Higher Power

Acknowledgement of powerlessness over the alcohol addiction and turning one's recovery over to a Higher Power is the most fundamental component of AA membership. This feature is understandably difficult for many people. We are accustomed to believing that we have free will and free choice, and that we are responsible human beings who can and should control just about everything about our lives. It seems to us that we can choose our friends, design our careers, choose where we live, and so forth. Should quitting drinking be any different? Isn't it just another behavior like playing tennis or flossing teeth?

We can decide to do these things whenever they become important to us. But if you really study addiction, you will see that dependent substance use defies choice as we know it and certainly is not an act of willful misconduct. The Higher Power component of AA, of course, comes from the program's Christian conceptual origins. This has been appreciably expanded over the years such that, for most AA members, any higher power is acceptable, from Buddha to a seagull—whatever works. For many people however, this premise is still difficult. It seems to run counter to the humanistic concept of self-actualization (Maslow, 1971). Many Americans relish individualism and find a great sense of accomplishment, reward, and even safety, in doing things on our own.

Interestingly, although state divisions of alcohol and substance abuse and courts throughout the country acknowledge that mandating a person to attend AA meetings is illegal, this has become common practice. Wherever anyone has legally challenged this requirement, however, judges invariably rule in favor of the individual because, when they review AA materials, they cannot help but define the organization as a religious one.

Need I remind anyone that our country is founded on a clear separation of church and state. This is a bedrock feature of our democracy, long safeguarded in our Constitution. Treatment programs and probation officers get around this by stating that, technically, a person "volunteers" to participate in court diversion agreements that include participation in AA. People with DUIs, for example, are free to elect not to participate in an offered diversion program, but they will face stiffer penalties and a conviction on their record.

Nevertheless, natural selection seems to have favored humans with a mental propensity to benefit from perceiving a connectedness with a superhuman agency that has an all-powerful controlling interest in our welfare. Simply put, ever since the ancient dawning of self-awareness, those who have believed in a higher power or powers probably experienced an anxiety-reducing buffer against hardships, giving them and their offspring an edge in survival. This cognitive trait—to throw one's arms up to the night sky saying, "God, Jesus, Buddha, the universe, anybody, please help me; I place my life in your hands"—is clearly a great benefit for many frightened and struggling alcoholics.

The 12 Steps

Another potentially helpful component of Alcoholics Anonymous focuses attention on "working" the 12 steps themselves. The 12 steps where conceived of and documented in the Big Book by Bill Wilson and Dr. Bob Smith, known as "Bill W. and "Dr. Bob" within AA. The 12 steps are very briefly stated but can be quiet complicated in practice. I summarize the essential features as:

- Accepting that alcohol dependence cannot be brought under control by the individual affected and subsequently turning one's life over to a greater power.
- Identifying the mistakes of one's past and admitting inherent personal flaws to oneself, God, and others
- Looking to one's higher power to remove personal flaws
- Identifying and making amends to any persons negatively affected by one's drinking
- Continuing to help other alcoholics gain sobriety

The 12 steps can be found on the Internet and in myriad books and articles on recovery. The steps have been adapted for use in other addiction support systems such as Narcotics Anonymous, Gamblers Anonymous, and many others.

The 12 steps are also augmented by the 12 Traditions. These are a set of recovery practice principles stressing the importance of group fellowship, anonymity, and the non-professional singular purpose of AA.

The curriculum of the AA program consists of working-through the 12 steps. Although these may seem simple, they aren't easy to do well and generally take years to complete adequately, in which case the person is advised to start over again. Treatment programs usually get people started on the 12 steps because treatment programs in this country are based on the AA model and work to get people introduced to that program. Inpatient treatment programs focus predominantly on helping people complete the first two or three steps. To do a first step well, people have to spend a considerable number of hours thinking about and writing down how alcohol may have affected their lives in all areas of functioning, including education, health, work, relationships, leisure activities, and so on, across all periods of their lives. In most cases, the process is thought to help individuals break through the fog of denial that has been part of their addiction. This is not to be rushed.

When I was directing treatment programs, I was impressed by the occasional patient who bounced into my office after only three days at the center saying, "Well, Dr. Portman, I finished the 12 steps. Now what should I do?" With great respect for the person's good intentions and with an appreciation for a little thing called the "pink cloud" phenomenon (feeling great relief at having successfully quit drinking and now irrationally optimistic about how wonderful life is going to be), I would steer the person back to his or her individual counselor to review the first step and perhaps to begin again. The 12 steps are certainly practical and practicable, and working them provides a positive focus of attention. But are the 12 steps divine? Think about it. Could you make up your own steps of any number with items of importance to you? Of course, you could.

Fellowship

A third major component of the AA program that seems to benefit many individuals is the sense of fellowship. Time and time again, individuals have reported to me a huge feeling of relief and gratitude for the acceptance offered in AA meetings by people who showed compassion for the newcomer's experience from the very first meeting.

Again, don't knock this until you've tried it. Moreover, proclaiming in front of a group what one intends to do can provide a powerful incentive to follow through.

Sponsorship

A fourth major component of AA participation is sponsorship. It is highly recommended within the program, at some sooner-rather-than-later point in attendance, that new members identify a regular member who will take them under his or her wing and help them negotiate the 12 steps and stay sober.

Interestingly, of the four components—a Higher Power, the 12 steps, fellowship, and sponsorship—recent research indicates that sponsorship may be the component that correlates most highly with lasting sobriety. It can truly make a huge difference, especially for some who may not have experienced before in their lives anyone who is so caring and available to them. Regardless of whether you participate in AA or not, having someone in your life who cares about you and supports what you are doing is an important ingredient for recovery.

Clearly, millions have been helped by AA. As pointed out by addiction scholars (Miller, Forcehimes & Zweben, 2011) there is beacoup research supporting a moderate positive correlation between AA attendance and lasting sobriety. However, meta-analysis research has indicated that *forced* (court or treatment program mandated) AA attendance produces worse outcomes than no AA or treatment attendance at all (Kownacki & Shadish, 1999). In net sum, for people who voluntarily attend, *and* participate with reasonable sincerity, AA tends to work. It is especially beneficial for those lacking abstinence-supportive social networks, and for those inclined to appreciate the presence and role of a higher power in their lives.

However, while AA attendance and involvement moderately predicts abstinence, abstinence does not predict AA attendance (McKellar, Stewart & Humphreys, 2003). That is, many prior active alcohol addicts achieve abstinence without AA. Clearly, of those who attend AA, *and* of those who try other means, some get sober and some do not. The prior cited National Epidemiologic Survey on Alcohol and related Conditions (Dawson, et al, 2005) found that 7 out of 10 people in recovery had never been to AA or a treatment program. Again, AA is great and/or necessary for some, but not so great or necessary for everyone, and is toxic to a few.

My position is to try it, and if you have a positive experience, that's wonderful. AA is not for everyone, but there can be a special security in the perception that one is doing something that is historically well established in the presence of others—and hopefully antithetical to active addiction.

Issues with Alcoholics Anonymous

I do wish that several aspects of AA were a little different. I'll explain.

Character Defects

One aspect of concern is the expectation that each person must acknowledge his or her "character defects." I think the expression was coined initially to avoid invoking the concept of sin—that drinkers would have to accept that they are sinners. The lesser expression "character defects," however, is still problematic. Many people have acknowledged to me a self-defeating perception of an assumed character defect. As a result, they feel depressed and less entitled than others to pursue their hopes and dreams. They harbor the misperception they are forever marked with an internal flaw stemming from their inherent badness.

If you were to visit the maternity ward of a large hospital, you might see several babies lined-up in their basinets for family viewing behind a Plexiglas window. Could you identify the ones who were born bad? Of course not. Their little self-perceptions are blank slates. Who among them will grow up feeling or behaving badly will depend on how they are raised.

Let me give you an almost worst-case scenario: When I was a young chemical dependency counselor, I saw several dozen men who were in counseling as part of a pre-release program from a state prison. To a man, they all met diagnostic criteria for antisocial personality disorder. These were society's bad actors. I lost a lot of my liberalism about crime and punishment at that time. Those guys *had* to be in prison to avoid harming us or themselves. Yet, after taking all of their life histories in detail, I realized something: Every one of them had experienced what is called total *bi-parental failure to nurture*. From infancy, they had been passed from a drug-addicted mother to an abusive uncle to neglectful foster homes, and so on. By the time they were five or six years old, they had wrongly concluded that they were made of bad stuff, and if they didn't get other people, other people would get them. As a survival strategy, they lost compassion as we know it.

If this, then, is considered to be a defect of character, even in this extreme example the trait is learned, not inherent. So what is a character defect? It is a learned set of misperceptions and misbehaviors that do not emerge from any *inherent badness* within the person. In my practice with ordinary and extraordinary people from all walks of life, the only character defect I see is that people *erroneously believe* they are defective. Indeed, all of humanistic psychology and psychotherapy therapy is designed to get people to realize their own innocence, goodness, and entitlement to a fulfilling life. I would love to see someone stand up in an AA meeting and proclaim, "My character defect is that I was taught to believe that I had one." I would further propose that the steps that have to do with "…a searching and fearless moral inventory" of character defects, be changed to a search for "misperceptions and behavioral errors" that may have occurred while one was in the throes of active alcohol addiction. In fact, a noteworthy humanistic version of the 12-steps has been proposed by R. B. Skinner (Skinner, 1987). The first two steps are: "We accept the fact that all our efforts to stop drinking have failed," and, "we believe that we must turn elsewhere for help." And in this revision there is no reference to acknowledging any sort of character defects.

In addition, the self-shaming character defect construct can contribute to too much self-depreciation in the steps about "making amends" to people who may have been harmed by the alcoholic's behaviors. Apologizing to others for alcohol-effected behaviors makes sense, and I support that effort, but within limitations and not to excess (more on this in Chapter 13: Relationships Recovery). I would also encourage, in some instances, others to make apologies to recovering alcoholics for shaming and blaming them—for treating them as criminals for having a physical and mental health disorder. While many behaviors are criminal, having an addiction in-and-of-itself cannot be a crime.

The Higher Power

Another issue that seems to cause some people problems in AA is the dogmatic insistence that one must turn one's life over to a Higher Power to succeed in recovery. As I have said, this seems to conflict with the humanistic concepts of free will and self-actualization. Again, mental health therapy largely has to do with actually building up the person's sense of self-worth, self-empowerment, and personal responsibility, not tearing it down. These positions are not necessarily incompatible. It is possible to reconcile the dilemma with the realization that, indeed, it often is unwise to be too egocentric, imagining that we can really control everything in our lives, or that we should. But this does not mean we should relinquish the sense of self-control entirely. Many successful AA members tell me that a Higher Power creates us but only intervenes as necessary, expecting us to show some modicum of self-direction; that's why the Higher Power provided us brains in the first place.

One Day at a Time

A third problem I have often encountered with individuals trying to follow the AA program as closely as they can has to do with taking everything "one day at a time." I've seen too many people far beyond the stabilization phase of recovery who are still discouraged about their lives. Sometimes I suggest things such as taking up a new pastime, making a plan to find new friends, or perhaps even making a career change. The retort I get is, "Oh, no, I was told to take things just one day at a time or I might relapse."

For some people the one-day-at-a-time adage is good for the behavior of not drinking alcohol (for example, managing urges to drink, coping with negative moods, taking care of oneself, and using available supports). Still, I don't think the founders of AA, or God, or Mother Nature intended humans to live their lives this way. Modern human life is complex. Our brains are well evolved for the survival necessity of anticipating futures, strategizing, and making plans. As a mindset to avoid drinking, you bet—one day at time. But as a strategy for managing the rest of your life? Bad choice.

Support Group Alternatives to AA

While AA is by-far-and-away the most available and attended group-based recovery system there are a few others. As Miller, Forcehimes & Zweben (2004) have observed, such groups differ based on differing values and philosophies. The AA approach is noted as ego-deflating rather than self-empowering. It values "...humility, surrendering self-control, accepting one's powerlessness, and admitting and addressing character flaws." Like traditional Protestant religion, AA is rooted in concepts of "sin, confession, repentance, humility, and salvation through grace rather than one's own merit." Here are some other options:

Smart Recovery

Self Management and Recovery Training (SMART) was an off-shoot of a popular self-help group called Rational Recovery which was vehemently oppositional towards AA. Rational Recovery's founder, Jack Trimpey, no longer supports the group approach but you can explore his approach to recovery by reading his books (Trimpey, 1995, 1996, 2010) and visiting his website https://rational.org.

SMART recovery, on the other hand, is not oppositional to AA . But it also does not have 12 steps, does not advocate the role of a higher power, and does not emphasize endless participation. It focuses on practical cognitive and behavioral strategies for recovery. See the website at www.smartrecovery.org.

SOS

SOS stands for Secular Organizations for Sobriety. As stated in the organization's General Principles, SOS is not based on any religious platform but relies on groups and printed material focused on support, accurate communication, and advancing knowledge of addiction and recovery. You can check out their website at www.sossobriety.org

Women for Sobriety

Unlike AA, while supporting one's personal spiritual development, Women for Sobriety clearly is ego-*strengthening,* and focused on personal empowerment, self-responsibility, and reinforcing an optimistic lifestyle. It has "Thirteen Statements" starting with "I have a life-threatening problem that once had me. I now take charge of my life and my disease. I accept the responsibility." Have a look at: www.womenforsobriety.org.

LifeRing

LifeRing is the new kid on the block of self-help recovery support groups. Rapidly growing in popularity, this approach does not denounce any spiritual approach but clearly focuses on personal empowerment and self-responsibly. It focuses on group discussion and support with practical personalized recovery strategies. There is also a well prepared workbook and other reading material. You can get a glimpse at www.lifering.org

Al-Anon

Al-Anon is a support group for the spouses, family members, or significant others, of alcoholics. Its position is that that alcoholism is a disease that other's cannot control. They promote "detaching with love," and group support, to focus on finding balance and fulfillment in one's own life, whether one continues or separates from the relationship with the addicted person. See for yourself: www.al-anon.alateen.org.

The brief listing I have presented here is not complete; there are other recovery support systems out there. For example there are Christian groups more unabashedly religious than AA. Having no question about who the higher power is, is refreshing to some. If you are so inclined, investigate *Alcoholics Victorious* and/or *Overcomers Outreach*. Also, many independent churches, synagogues, temples, and ashrams, often have their own local recovery groups not necessarily affiliated with national organizations.

Research on the efficacy of AA and alternative recovery support groups finds no approach to be superior to another, but that voluntary attendance and involvement in any of these groups does tend to promote lasting sobriety (Atkins & Hawdon, 2007). Thus, I really encourage giving group support a try, per your own personal preferences.

The Medical Model

Treatment programs largely evolved out of AA and the so-called medical model of treatment. As discussed in Chapter 4, by the end of the 1950s, the American Medical Association and almost all other allied medical professions had defined alcoholism as a disease. A major benefit of this approach is that individuals seem to seek help more readily if they understand that they have a disease and are not merely weak-willed or morally bankrupt.

Interestingly, putting recovery within the medical domain bolstered hospital-based treatment as the standard of care for alcoholism treatment, with an attendant increase in the hospital industry's capacity to capture patients' medical insurance benefits. As the American public is just beginning to realize, medical standards of care are all-too-often financially or legally driven rather than clinically driven. Nevertheless, let's take another look at the disease concept and the medical model.

Acts of drinking or ingesting other drugs by various methods are obviously *behaviors* that seem to be volitional. This makes it difficult for most people to think of an alcohol use problem as a disease. As discussed in Chapter 4, unlike the flu, or tuberculosis, or venereal disease, alcohol use problems aren't associated with contracting any germ, virus, or bacteria. Yet, there is no germ, virus, or bacteria, involved in heart disease, cancer, or diabetes, and we still freely label these conditions as diseases without question. This is because they are understandable *processes* that eventually cause damage to living beings. This is also true of alcoholism, but because the destructive processes involved are not so directly observable, they are difficult to appreciate.

As alcohol addiction develops, a number of predictable processes eventually break down the mind and body. Moreover, alcohol dependence actually does involve the very physical process of *habituation*, which happens at a cellular level within the nervous system. If the individual quits using alcohol, it results in de-habituation, or withdrawal—a decidedly biological phenomenon. If that was all there was to it, recovery would be easy. As most recovering people will explain to you, quitting is not really the biggest problem. In most cases, people do not have that much difficulty quitting drinking initially.

The real problem comes later. It bears repeating that this is not merely a disease of the body but of the mind as well. The body heals quickly from alcohol—to the extent that it will. But psychologically the addictive urge remains in the subconscious mind and the conscious mind takes a long time to overcome this. In an insidious process, the alcohol becomes the person's emotional manager across time and without his or her awareness, critically compromises the ability to cope emotionally. After a few weeks of sobriety stabilization, most relapses occur because of this phenomenon—the person's inability to identify and productively manage negative emotional states. Once again, what does one do with worries, fears, anxiety, depression, sorrow, guilt, anger, and so on without his or her usual medication?

This *post-acute withdrawal syndrome* (PAWS) is a very real and predictable process within the recovering person. So, although for some people it is conceptually challenging, considering alcohol use problems from a disease or medical perspective is far from unreasonable, is arguably accurate, and can be serviceable as people recognize that although like diabetics, they must be responsible for their behaviors and their wellness, they are not to blame.

Part 3

The New Model: Finding Your Pathway with the Recovery Template

Chapter 8

A Forward-Going Approach

Problem:	*Backward-gazing approaches are not appropriate for everyone, and living your life one-day-at-a-time is a script for a sad life and eventual relapse.*
Solution:	*Humans are planning animals. Learn to productively orient your recovery toward your future. Take the forward-going approach—a life areas model of recovery.*

Quitting Versus Recovery

Quitting drinking is not recovery. For most people, recovery turns out to be a major adventure far beyond the mere act of quitting. Many recovering alcoholics will tell you that quitting was relatively easy compared to the challenge of staying off alcohol for good. Quitting is like stepping through a swinging gate. But then one is left standing at the edge of a vast new frontier, with many challenges and potential rewards in the distance.

Alcoholics Anonymous and treatment programs clearly recognize that quitting is the easy part and that recovery is the hard part, but they overemphasize what I see as a backward-gazing model. It is as if recovering persons must travel on the train of life seated backward, looking at where they've been and daily recounting the "wreckage of the past." It's okay to look out the window to view your current location, living the proverbial "one day at a time," but for heaven's sake, don't look forward. No question—many people need and benefit from what this approach offers. And no wonder. Addiction can hijack the mind so horribly that for some people a daily review of the misery it caused is the only way to avoid relapse.

Looking forward without a map can be overwhelming. Like taking a covered wagon across the prairies, the journey would be exciting but also daunting and risky without a map. But what if a map could be drawn for each individual's recovery? Such a map, a template for recovery, is indeed possible.

Years ago I saw a movie called *The Stargate*. What a great metaphor for recovery! It was a science-fiction story about a huge stone arch discovered in the Egyptian desert. Once it was uplifted from the sand, it was discovered that anything that passed through it disappeared. Scientists concluded that it was a portal through which the first humans may have come to Earth from somewhere across the universe. A research expedition was formed, and the team bravely marched through the stargate. The travelers were helplessly tumbled around through a space/time warp, complete with frightening lights and sounds, at least metaphorically similar to the way dependent drinkers can feel when they quit drinking. Then they crash-landed on some planet on the other side of the universe. It was nighttime, and they were scared. They counted their fingers and toes, checked their supplies, and set up tents. In the morning, as the twin suns rose over the new, mysterious planet, they looked out across a vast new terrain. This is what early recovery can seem like. It's intimidating, but also *intriguing,* and it calls to you.

Thus, I have a different vision of recovery, and many people share it with me. I say: Turn and look forward. Let quitting drinking be a launch pad to advance your life as you never realized you could. Plan, prepare, and pursue goals in your life. In doing this, you can greatly outdistance addiction. This way tends to fill up life, and as the years pass, someday you will look back over your shoulder and only dimly see the addiction at a great and increasing distance behind you.

Finding a Model to Live By

How can you begin this positive journey of recovery? Where can you find a map? A map writes itself if you have some sense of where it is you might want to go. You need a destination. Simply put, how do you want your life to be? This brings up the question: Where can you get a model to live by?

In the renaissance of the 1960s, a whole generation questioned the establishment and sought answers to questions about the meaningfulness of life and how to find enlightenment. Even the Beatles went to India and found a guru. Many others followed their lead. Every mountaintop in India seemed to have a guru. Once seated at the feet of a guru, the visitors asked the same question: "Tell me—what is the meaning of life?" At this point the gurus hauled out a bamboo cane and whacked the poor pilgrim soundly on the head, saying:

Wrong question. It is presumptuous—it assumes there is meaning and excludes the possibility that there may been none. If there is meaning, it might not be the same for everyone. Therefore, I cannot answer that for you. Ask another question.

Eventually, some people got around to the right question which is simply: "How shall I live?"

At this, the gurus brightened up, said, "Good question," and then provided the following universal answer: "Follow your inner directives."

Similarly, a generation later, Joseph Campbell (1991) encouraged people to "follow your bliss." Initially feeling elated, young people returned to America only to become overwhelmed with the realization that they had no idea what their inner directives were. Following the rejection of their *real* selves early in childhood, they had been so busy trying to be *ideal* selves that they had become completely disconnected from what they might have wanted for themselves in life.

On a grand scale, we have been massively misled. With entire generations lacking positive identities, modern America has been fertile turf for the Madison Avenue money garden. We are the world's best-cultivated consumers, with the belief that "I own; therefore I am." I see many people who initially respond to questions about how they want to live by describing things they have or want to have—cars, cloths, toys, houses, careers.

Recovery has to be based on the needs of the *real* self—a concept carefully discussed in Chapter 11: Emotional Recovery. In the meantime, assuming that you're able to realize your own innocence and decide to liberate your real self, you may need a practical, uncontaminated view or model of human life to live by, or at least as a basis for comparison. Then you can build your unique plans for recovery the way you want it to be.

Many people today find a model to live by in dense urban settings. In these scenarios the thing to do is to live in a sanitized, high-rise metal cubicle, wear a spiffy suit, and drive a sexy new automobile to a job in another high-rise cubicle. I once lived in Montana, where a different model thrives. There, many idealize the cowboy life. They wear cowboy hats and cowboy boots and have rifle racks in the cabs of their pickup trucks. Others like the East Coast lifestyle and live in colonial houses. Still others build castle-like places after the Middle Ages. And others think the Romans or Greeks had it made and design their homes in the Mediterranean style. Some people take to the mountains hiking and biking, while others enjoy auto racing on TV. Of course, many people adhere to certain religious, quasi-religious, or pagan faiths or practices. The list goes on and on. Although many of these lifestyles have a certain appeal, they have gotten disturbingly far-a-field of how humans really evolved to live.

We must break the bonds of contemporary confusion and seek a more meaningful model. Again, Occam's razor: The simplest answer is most likely the correct one. So what are humans? We are a species of mammal. Therefore, the overarching model of human existence is available for inspection deep in our pre-history, where the bulk of human evolution took place. For most of this first million years of our existence, humans lived in bands of interconnected families. They followed the game and the seasons up and down the African continent. These were the hunter/gatherers, and what we know about them can provide insights about what may be important in human life today—insights that became obscured in modern times.

I'm going to romanticize this history to make my point, but where we went awry was the point at which someone planted some seeds and corralled some animals. This was the dawning of the agricultural revolution, and it was very, very recent in our overall evolution. The ability to manage animals and crops propelled us abruptly from band-level to *tribe-level* society. Rather suddenly, many people could live in the same place and not have to travel with the seasons. There could be permanent structures, too many people in the same place. Thus came the onset of resource exploitation and pollution. There were new divisions of labor, stratification of society, a warrior class and warfare, the invention of money, and new crimes to be committed. Most men and women became slaves to the chieftains. They could no longer hunt and gather but, rather, hoed rows of crops or built monumental structures for their rulers.

In an evolutionary wink of the eye, this stage advanced to the Industrial Revolution, and now the so-called Computer Age. And with all of this came the Age of Anxiety, with too many confusing choices amid a baffling array of possible lifestyles. Not enough time has gone by after the agricultural revolution for humans to adapt emotionally and socially to these rapid and profound changes. An obvious cost has been the loss of effective parenting. Thus, humans are not able to get two important things out of childhood—a positive identity and a clear understanding of how to live life. From this failing, most of our mood, anxiety, relationship, and substance abuse problems emerge.

Until the middle of the twenty-first century, cultural anthropologists encountered band-level societies in remote regions around the globe. None exist today that have not been contaminated by modernity. What anthropologists found, however, can be instructive in answering the question: How now shall I live? I don't buy the Hobbesian thesis that prehistoric human life was short and brutish. Short maybe, but not so brutish.

The Bushmen of the Kalahari Desert provide a good case in point. For several hundred thousand years, things did not change much. Through thousands of generations, the Bushmen's ancient relatives knew how to live in harmony with their environment, specifically in the functional areas of life that cultural anthropologists have identified and studied. The Bushmen knew how to take care of their health and fitness from the experience of countless generations. They knew what to eat and what not to eat, what to cover wounds with, and how to sleep. They were lean. Their skin was dark and clear, their eyes and teeth white. They knew what their work was—hunting and gathering, preparing food, making shelter and clothing. They knew how to manage relationships. Men and women apparently were coequal, with separate responsibilities and shared responsibilities. As often as not, a woman would be the head of a band (coequality seemed to go away when we got to *tribe-level* society, when men, so emasculated, sought self-aggrandizement by subjugating women). Regarding relationships, band-level peoples, unlike modern humans, seemingly were trusting and uninhibited. Around the campfires at night, they laughed together, or cried if they felt like it, and they generally supported one another. They knew how to bring up their children. Men apparently had a greater role than modern men seem to have in the care of infants and young children. They were astounded when told that modern people spanked their children. According to Russell Means, speaking about American Plains Indians, fathers were so bonded with their sons that they could not bear to send them into warfare, so they did not.

They also knew how to play. Paleontologist Richard Leakey (Leakey & Lewin, 1979) observed that the average band-level man and woman worked only about 30 hours a week at hunting and gathering. They spent the rest of their time eating, playing games, making music and art, dancing, conversing, or simply sitting under a shade trees chipping on spear tips. (Activities from knitting to washing our cars in the driveway may be modern equivalents. Why else do we love them so?)

The Bushmen had to have had high IQs because without television they were able to spend many hours memorizing and recounting the histories of generations before them, manufacturing clothing, tools, musical instruments, and preparing foods. I believe that the average Bushmen knew more about his environment, including animals and plants, than the average psychologist knows about psychology. The Bushmen also took care of their living environment, often returning to the same pleasing seasonal locations. And they had a sense of their existence, sleeping in the open, lying on their backs night after night, staring up at the stars and contemplating their place in the universe. They evolved a solace in believing in the interconnectedness of all things and a simple spirituality in which the sky was masculine, the earth feminine. When it rained, the sky and the earth were making love and life sprang forth.

No, obviously I'm not advocating that you get a loincloth and a spear and start chasing deer through your neighbor's backyard. I offer this example of the Bushmen's way of life to show that what really matters in human life is to find fulfillment in several naturally evolved areas. These different functional areas of human existence are clearly seen in our evolutionary past and remain the same today, just under the surface. We lose sight of this by living in buildings, driving cars, and experiencing constant bombardment from many sources about how we should define ourselves by lavish acquisitions and consumption.

We will never get back to band-level living, nor would we really want to. I have read that there are modern Bushmen, who, for a few thousand dollars, will take you into the Kalahari for a couple of weeks to experience what it must have been like, but most of us enjoy, if not depend on, our modern conveniences: solid houses, hot showers, automobiles, electricity, cell phones, computers, and the rest. What is important, however, is to cull out of anthropological findings, some pointers about how we might better live our lives today. By breaking away the confusing and confining shell of modern life, we can gain a beautiful and more reality-based conceptualization of what is important in our lives and begin to answer the question of how we each shall live.

Chapter 9

The Life Areas Model of Recovery

Problem:	*Waiting for happenstance to lead you to recovery will lead you nowhere.*
How to win:	*Build a map that works for you, and follow it to successful recovery.*

The Template for Recovery

So here we are. Why look any further? Why not capitalize on our natural evolutionary heritage to begin to answer the question of how we each shall live? Like the Bushmen of the Kalahari, we, too, must direct our attention to the functional areas of life. Doing this provides a realistic, naturally evolved model to live by, and delineates the *areas of recovery* to pursue. So, again, recovery from alcohol dependence need not be merely a sacrifice, or consist of waiting for life to get better, or be comprised of just one thing. Recovery can be a foreword-going, self-actualizing adventure, across all the important domains of our lives. This functional, anthropologically realistic model breaks out as follows, but feel free to add, delete, blend, or modify the areas as you please:

- Health and fitness
- Emotional wellness
- Relationships
- Productivity
- Leisure activities
- Living-place
- Spirituality or a philosophy to live by

The secret gift in recovery is the chance to create balance in your life by finding fulfillment in each of the life areas. In humanistic psychology, this is referred to as *self-actualization*. In this model the question of where to focus recovery becomes answerable. By delineating the naturally evolved functional areas of life, a forward-looking map or template emerges.

The following template is for conceptual purposes. You will be provided with other forms to work on specific to each area. The overall idea is to turn quitting drinking from a sacrifice to a liberation. Recovery is not just about succeeding at not drinking; it's about rising above all of the assaults against your self-esteem, inhibitions, and losses throughout all of your life. Remarkably, as discussed in Chapter 11, following this template is also the way out of depression.

The Template for Recovery

Areas of Recovery	1 Needs	3 Pathways	2 Goals
Health and fitness			
Emotional wellness			

Relationships:
    Life companion
    Family relations
    Friendships
    Co-workers			

Work/ productivity			
Leisure/ recreation			
Living place			
Spirituality or philosophy to live by			

How to Use the Template

First consider where to start. The longer a person has been involved with excessive alcohol use, the more areas of life become negatively effected. Different people experience costs or losses in different areas. Generally, recovering persons want to work first on the area where they have experienced the most cost. That is, if a woman lost her job because of drinking, it makes sense for her to start with that area of life. If your wife has moved out because of your drinking, you may feel unable to work on any other life area until you figure out how to rebuild your marriage.

Sometimes the most appropriate area of life to start working on almost leaps off the template, but going with your first instinct is not always advisable. As examples, an estranged spouse may be unwilling to cooperate for a few months, or a person needs a break from work. Then perhaps it makes sense to start with a less urgent area of your recovery, such as leisure and recreation. This is about recovery on your own terms—you get to decide where you want to start. All I recommend is that you do start somewhere, because what matters in life turns out to be not so much *what* we do, but *that* we do.

If you aren't sure about which life area to work on, I suggest the shotgun approach: First tape a copy of the above template on your refrigerator, bathroom mirror, or bedroom wall. Then, when you get up in the morning, face the template, put one hand over your eyes, and with your other hand place a finger on the template. Then uncover your eyes. You just identified the area to begin to work on. Once you have selected an area, here is my recommended action sequence:

1.   *Needs identification*

For any single area of recovery you may want to explore, always start by identifying your *needs.* To start with goals or pathways without first identifying your needs is tantamount to turning over your life to sheer happenstance.

Once you have identified a specific area you would like to work on, by obvious choice or the shotgun method, the first thing to do is to ask yourself: *Am I living the way I want to live in this area?* Assuming the answer is "no" or "I'm not sure," get a pen and notebook, sit down at your breakfast table, and start brainstorming. Use the strategies and any worksheets that may be provided for this adventure in the chapter that is specific to that area of recovery.

- Chapter 10: Health and Fitness Recovery
- Chapter 11: Emotional Recovery
- Chapter 12: Leisure/Recreational Recovery
- Chapter 13: Relationships Recovery
- Chapter 14: Career/Occupation Recovery
- Chapter 15: Living-Place Recovery
- Chapter 16: Philosophical/Spiritual Recovery

In your needs assessment, the ideas you come up with must be based on the needs of your *real self*—not the *ideal self*, not the one you thought you ought to be to gain acceptance, or to please others, or for status. Take your time. Just like Rome, your recovery cannot be built in a day. Take several days, or even a few weeks, in this needs assessment phase for any single area of recovery. This is about trying to follow your inner directives, but feel free to look outside yourself to stimulate your thinking. Look at magazines, newspapers, or television for ideas. Observe others, and talk to people about that area of life. Do not hold back. Put down on paper anything that occurs to you about your needs, and then highlight what you decide or guess may be your most important needs.

2. *Goal setting*

When you get a sense of what your *needs* might be in any single life area, set a *goal*, or goals, in that area. Realize that goals do not have to be clear; they can be vague. They can be near or far, and to set and pursue a goal, you do not have to be 100 percent invested in whether the goal is right for you, or 100 percent confident that you can even achieve it. Remember—the hunter/gatherers never knew whether they would or would not find food on any given outing, but they did have the goal.

In our case, the goal is necessary only to illuminate the pathway, because most often being on a pathway, not having arrived at the destination, is what empowers us, makes us happy, and fills up our lives. All the years I worked on earning a PhD—a terribly vague and distant goal, about which I had many doubts—I may have been overworked, but I was not depressed. I felt that I was going somewhere, and that I had some power and purpose, and I was happy. The same was true when I built my lawn shed. I had never built one before. I did not know if I had the skills, and I only sort of needed one. But the summer I built it, I was happy. I could not wait to get out of the office each afternoon to work on it, and I roared energetically into the project each weekend. Certainly, it is nice to have the lawn shed, but once it was done, so was the thrilling part.

3. *Designing the pathway*

When you've finished identifying a need and have set a goal or goals in a certain life area, you can begin to figure out the *means* to get there— your plan or *pathway* to follow. Some goals and pathways are more complex than others. If you have a goal to learn to make your own kites, signing up for Kite-Making 101 at the community college is a simple and straightforward pathway to that goal. Becoming a dentist, on the other hand, might require a pathway that is more complicated to plan and follow. For the more lofty goals, a strategy for figuring out the pathway to follow is to start by thinking of the *last* steps first.

For example, the last step on a pathway to becoming a practicing dentist might be to assign staff their hours and duties. The steps before that include: hiring and training staff members, procuring equipment and a clinic in which to practice, identifying a community in which to practice, getting licensed to practice, completing an internship, earning a DMD degree, getting into a dental school, completing an undergraduate degree majoring in biology, getting accepted to a four-year college, earning an Associate degree at a community college, getting a job as a dishwasher to earn enough money to pay for community college classes. Then it's a simple matter of plotting these tasks on an estimated timeline. With this type of plotting backward, you can know where you need to begin.

For any pathway you have planned for any life area, look at your other life areas for compatibility. It's not going to make much sense to earn a degree in dentistry if your *Living-place* plan calls for residing in a cabin by a trout stream 70 miles outside of Remoteville, Montana, population 5.

Finally, assuming your plan is *reasonably compatible* with your other anticipated areas of recovery, lay it out on a calendar and get started. As you do, you may begin to experience the refreshing sense that you're going somewhere, with a new feeling of empowerment and the dawning of self-actualization. This is a sure sign that you've begun a successful recovery.

Eight Roadblocks and How to Overcome Them

If you aren't familiar with this sort of needs/goals/means process, it may seem a bit daunting at first. To get a better start—to get off the dime—here are eight commonly encountered roadblocks and how to overcome them:

1.   Lack of faith in your real self

Generally, we have been so busy in our lives trying to be ideal selves, that our real selves remain underdeveloped. Often, one's real self has been suppressed for so long that it hasn't had much, if any, experience on its own. So every time we try to do something based on our perception of the needs of our real self, we get anxious with a kind of abandonment anxiety because we still don't trust our real self.

All you have to do to get over this hang-up is to realize that although your real self may be inexperienced, it is made of all the right stuff. It doesn't have the defects you've perceived, so if encouraged to express itself (the "you" that you were meant to be), you can trust that everything will work out for the best. Read Chapter 11 for tangible ways to do this.

2.   Not feeling entitled

Related to doubting one's real self is the feeling of not being entitled to getting what one wants in any life area. Similar to self-doubt, lacking a sense of entitlement stems from deep-seated perceptions of fault, badness, or inadequacies within. In the extreme, it means holding back from one's self the good things in life as a form of self-punishment—the perpetual carrying out of a sentence for assumed crimes of the past. When the two young protagonists in the movie *Wayne's World* finally meet their rock hero, Alice Cooper, they fall to their knees chanting, "We're not worthy … we're not worthy."

When I ask people where they got such a low sense of entitlement, they look surprised and invariably say, "I have no idea." Most of them don't ever stop and consider the question; they just assume an internal fault and live a life of perpetual self-recrimination and self-deprivation.

Studies show that 80 percent of lottery winners are back at their old jobs and lives after five years, whereas 80 percent of rich people whose businesses went bankrupt are back on top again in five years. What's the difference between these two groups of people? IQ has nothing to do with it. Lottery winners, as a group, simply don't have the same sense of entitlement that successful business people have.

My client Larry, new in recovery, told me that when he was 18, he saw a picture of the then young Clint Eastwood on the cover of *Life* magazine. The actor had just become famous for his portrayal of the laconic cowboy in the "spaghetti westerns." The story featured a picture of him sitting in his home gym overlooking the Pacific Ocean at his house in Pebble Beach. He had a couple of gym sets and barbells with free-weights. Larry was impressed. However, not until he quit drinking at age 52 did it suddenly dawn on Larry, "Oh! I can have a home gym!"

Why do so many of us assume that we aren't entitled to all the good things and activities that we see other people have and do? The answer to the question is important: People are naturally reluctant, if not afraid, to look for the answer in their childhood because they assume that they will discover their inherent badness. If they do look, however, they usually find a different truth, and this is liberating. The answer lies in early perceptual errors. We come out of childhood with the mistaken perception that fault and blame reside within us. To start developing a positive self-identity, we need to move beyond that perception. For more on this topic, read the discussion of self-validation in Chapter 11. Then begin to experiment with at least *acting as if* you're entitled to pursue any goal in any life area that you may want to work on.

3.   *Subconscious resistance*

It's natural to resist change. Often, we delay sitting down at the kitchen table to brainstorm our needs and set goals because we're instinctively suspicious of change. We know that a lot of work may be called for and we might not get what we want, so we procrastinate. This seems to be worse in our teens, and sometimes in later life. By the time we're in our early 20s, we're probably able to make major commitments, such as moving across the country or going to graduate school, more easily. Mother Nature imbues us with a burst of optimistic risk taking energy at that time of life to build the best future that will ensure survival of offspring. Also at that age we're naive concerning the actual effort and sacrifices that such changes will require. Thus, in our 20s we're able to make choices that will affect the rest of our lives, based on the most flimsy, fanciful, and fleeting images of what it will really be like.

Fortunately, when reality obliterates these images, we simply adapt. My friend Janet thought marine biology would be her dream career, so she enrolled for studies at the University of Hawaii. Soon after she got there, she realized that marine biology was nothing like she thought it would be, but she really liked Hawaii and forged a whole life around working in the resort industry on Maui. (Read about the profound role of happenstance in shaping our lives in Chapter 14.)

As we age we accumulate more and more memories and slowly lose our naiveté about making changes in our lives, and changes begin to seem more daunting. For millions of us baby-boomers, the challenge of midlife transitions is as profound as our initial metamorphosis from childhood to adulthood after leaving home at age eighteen. More and more people come into my practice saying things like, "We always imagined that after the kids left home, we'd move to Arizona. Now the whole idea scares us, and we wonder what were we thinking. The effort would be so enormous. Why was it so easy to do something like that when we were young?" If these sentiments resonate with you, I recommend Sara Davidson's (2007) book, *Leap! What Will We Do with the Rest of Our Lives?* You'll see that such changes are not only normal but tend to work out well.

To overcome resistance of any sort, stop and think about the initial question. In any specific life area of concern, *are you living the way you really want to live?* Now carefully consider where you will be or what will be happening in your life five years from now if you *don't* make the change you're considering. What will be the price of continuing to live the way you have been in this area? Remember, too, that in most situations, at any point in the process, you always can let it go and resume living the way you were. For example, if you take up painting, are you any worse off if at some point you decide you don't like painting and give it up?

4.   *The perfectionist's script for self-defeat*

People in early recovery from alcohol dependence sometimes say that they wish they could be involved in various activities. Upon closer questioning, I've often discovered an insidious little mental attitude that underlies why they do not initiate desired activities. This impediment to working the template is called the "perfectionist's script for self defeat." What happens is that persons with self-doubt and fears of failure may consider taking up a new activity or goal (play tennis, apply for a better position at work, pursue a relationship with a crush, etc), but they somehow expect themselves to do the new thing perfectly. When they realize that they may not succeed at the new activity perfectly, they refuse to attempt it at all: "Gee, I'd really like to (play tennis, get a new job, meet so-and-so), but I might not do it perfectly, and that would be embarrassing and awful, so I'm not going to do it at all."

The way out of the perfectionist's script for self-defeat is simple: Allow yourself to *strive for mediocrity*. This is a strange recommendation, I know, and you may not have to apply this get-off-the-dime strategy to everything in your life, but as a means of giving yourself permission to start something you otherwise might not start, it can be incredibly liberating. It's a lot easier to initiate something new and possibly challenging if you say, "Well, I'd just like to be an average (golfer, club member, graduate student, etc)." This strategy has allowed me to take up many things in my life that I otherwise would have shied away from, such as golf, skate-skiing, and joining Toastmasters to improve my public speaking skills and confidence. If you were to ask me if I have succeeded at becoming mediocre at these activities, I would ask you back, "What difference does that make?" All I know is that I'm having fun.

5.   *The "too lofty goal" hang-up*

Another phenomenon that holds up progress while attempting to work on any life area in recovery is the perception that one's goal is too lofty. Mary has an eleventh-grade education, but in her heart she knows she would really want to be a doctor. Her goal seems too far out of reach, so she lets it go. The way out of this trap is to first realize that, as I've said, goals don't matter as much as pathways when it comes to contentment in our lives. The chief function of the goal is merely to illuminate the pathway. The *sense of going somewhere* is what makes us feel fully alive. Therefore, in a way, it doesn't really matter how lofty one's goals may be. The only restrictions are the boundaries of one's imagination. Even a delusional goal, as long as it's not mean or harmful to anyone, can make for a full and interesting life—witness Don Quixote tilting at windmills.

Another aspect of the "too lofty goal" hang-up comes from one's sense of not being capable of achieving the goal. If your perception is that you have some inherent defectiveness that precludes you from achieving your goals, I strongly recommend that you see a therapist who can help you see otherwise. Most likely, you're suffering from a history of discouragement, lack of knowledge, inexperience, self-doubt, and/or irrational fear. These are normal feelings, and you must not mistake them for being incapable or defective. If you do, you surely will sell yourself short, miss the chance to achieve your potential, and fail to find self-actualization. I strongly recommend Susan Jeffers' book (1987) *Feel the Fear, and Do it Anyway.*

6.   *The "I can't see the pathway" bailout*

Some people fail to pursue a goal because they cannot see a *direct* pathway. Joan may think, "I would really like to be a Forest Ranger, but how could I ever do that?" Here it helps to understand that when it comes to pathways, sometimes we have to take a step or two backward. This is more than okay. It often is a necessity, and it need not stop you at all. It just makes for a more interesting journey. Thus, Joan may have to begin her quest to be a Forest Ranger by moving back into her parents' home and getting an entry-level job which will allow her to pay for classes at a community college, so she can transfer to a four-year university where she can major in Forestry. Just about any goal has a pathway, even the goal of taking a ride in a space shuttle. You merely need to set your goal, then step back, take your time, and imagine the pathways.

7.   The "I'm not 100 percent committed" poop-out

As human beings, we too often harbor the mistaken belief that we somehow should be or must be 100 percent committed before we can allow ourselves to pursue a goal. Having certainty that a goal is right for us is a wonderful thing when it happens—but it seldom does. In truth, waiting for a 100 percent commitment is a major source of procrastination. What happens is that we typically have a choice to do or not to do something. As we wait for a magical total mental commitment, we end up not making a possibly needed change. Thus, by not deciding, we're actually making a choice, by default, not to do something.

The way out of this trap is to realize that you don't have to be 100 percent invested in a goal to give yourself permission to go after it. In reality, getting going in a life area most often means setting a goal based on a reasonable hunch, or even on just a fleeting intuitive impulse, that the goal might be worthwhile. The trick is: Once you've set a goal, pursue it *as if* you were completely committed to it, relegating to the back of your mind the knowledge that the goal actually remains questionable.

8.   Just not being able to get started

Studies that have looked into how people change have shown the following stages of readiness to change (see Chapter 3 for details): pre-contemplation, contemplation, preparation, action, and maintenance. Often people fail to make the transition from the stage of just thinking about a change to the stage of taking action are failing to do one simple thing. They fail to set a start date. Indeed, something is magical about setting a date to begin a desired change. Most of us are such creatures of habit that if we merely manage to write down something on our calendars, it's actually quite likely that we will do it.

Thus, for any change you've decided you want to make, plan the steps as outlined in the Life Areas Template instructions, then write a start date on your calendar. To ensure that you actually will start on that date, also write down in advance exactly what you will be doing on that day, and make arrangements in your life ahead of time so when the day comes, nothing will stand in your way.

Sometimes, not being able to get started stems from a lack of any real faith that we will be capable of following through—so we don't get started. In the extreme, one may believe that he or she lacks willpower and is lazy. I don't believe that anyone is inherently lazy. Operationally defined, laziness is simply a learned lack of perceptions of reward. This is a natural outcome of a series of discouragements and failed attempts in one's life. If a person's efforts historically have failed to produce rewards, how can that person expect success and reward from future endeavors? In psychology, this is referred to as "learned helplessness" (Seligman, 1991). In this phenomenon, with a learned pessimistic explanatory style, a person perceives that since the past wasn't good, the future isn't likely to be good either. Thus, the person is stuck in the present. These people find that gaining the motivation to change is difficult because they operate under the perception that what they do won't matter. They feel hopeless about the future and helpless to do anything about it. These twin *perceptions* are what actually produce feelings of depression in most depressed people (as opposed to mere brain chemistry imbalance).

To overcome this sort of procrastination, you must stop thinking of yourself as lazy but, rather, as reward-challenged. The world spins on rewards. Who would keep showing up for work if paychecks stopped coming? Who would keep playing golf if they didn't at least occasionally get a good shot? Our behaviors are predominately the result of what follows them—rewards or punishments. So work at setting up rewards for yourself.

Try this: For any life area on the template in which you hope to make a change, set up something as a reward to look forward to after you initiate the first step of a planned change. The reward could be anything that pleases you: a round of golf, dinner at a favorite restaurant, going out to a movie, buying that blouse or shirt you've been wanting, or merely taking the time to sit down with a new book. You may find that you're not so lazy. You may discover the antithesis of learned helplessness, *self-efficacy*—the perception that you are likely to succeed at, enjoy, and find rewarding any specific activity or behavior change you attempt. This can open many doors for you in your life. Try it.

Roadblocks in the way of change vary from person to person and situation to situation. They all can be costly in the long run, but I suppose the two most common and ultimately sad roadblocks I see are number four, about fear of failure, and number seven, about uncertainty. Many times I have sat with older depressed clients telling me that they lament never having done or achieved something they once wanted; for example, to become a teacher, or an architect, to climb a mountain, or to sail the world, or to learn to sculpt. I ask "Why didn't you?" Most often their answers come in two forms; "I wasn't really sure it would be *right for me*," or "I was afraid I *might not succeed*." At that point—if I could without sounding critical—I sometimes want to say *"Well, are you happy now?"* With this experience, I can only encourage you to not wait to be sure that a certain goal is right for you or for a guaranty that you can succeed before you begin. You may wait forever.

I recommend that you make a copy of The Template for Recovery. Make any adjustments that suit you. Include working on it into your schedule. Part 4 includes a chapter on each area of recovery I have identified. Use any or all of them to get the best start you can at a personally meaningful and successful recovery.

Part 4

The Areas of Recovery

Chapter 10

Health and Fitness

Problem:	*Drinking has compromised your health and fitness.*
What to do:	*Learn how to build your own health and fitness recovery plan and make it a lifestyle change.*

To begin, allow me to make a somewhat arbitrary distinction between the terms "health" and "fitness." Let us say that health, on the one hand, refers to the absence or presence of all sorts of diseases and conditions such as hepatitis, arthritis, cancer, or diabetes. Fitness, on the other hand, refers to one's conditioning, weight, muscle tone, energy, strength, and stamina. For many people, Health and Fitness is the best starting point for recovery—especially when their health has been directly affected by alcohol use. This is often the case whether there has been an injury or any number of alcohol-related physical costs such as liver disease, hypertension, gout, gastritis, pancreatitis, diabetes, and esophageal vertices, among others. In the absence of any identifiable diseases, the drinker's general level of fitness usually is compromised. Muscle atrophy and overweight are common in alcoholics. Even when, as can be the case with younger drinkers, there are no as yet observable health and fitness costs, it is an important area of recovery.

Whether this is the first area to be worked on or not, the Health and Fitness area eventually must be included in everyone's personal recovery plan because it is the only truly essential area. If we had to, we could live without a successful career, a perfect marriage, or any leisure pursuits, as long as we have our health. Not everyone will agree, but to me, health and fitness form the broad foundation of a pyramid that supports all other life endeavors.

The challenge in this area is that there are so many different health and fitness problems. People who are overweight, underweight, diabetic, chair-bound, young, or old—each has different capabilities and limitations, and each will require different goals and plans. This, of course, is the beauty of a self-directed recovery using the template model. You can assess your own needs, goals, and means of getting there. You are liberated from having to do what others think you should do. Sure, seek advice everywhere, but then do as you like.

Overcoming Your Health and Fitness Discouragement

Rarely do I meet people initiating recovery who are healthy and fit. Excessive drinking *and* having optimum health is simply not possible. As drinking increases, health declines (see Chapter 4, on physical effects). Only in the rarest cases have I seen an active alcoholic who appears healthier than the average person. I once saw a university student from Kenya, who one autumn set the world record for the mile run, but his times were flagging in the spring despite massive and superhuman training. He was alcoholic. He barely noticed hangover effects from getting hammered on Saturday nights and still was able to train on Sundays. When he quit drinking, though, he soon became a world record-setter again.

Compared to that young athlete, most alcohol-dependent people are much worse off by the time they seek help. If they do not have significant illnesses already, most problem or dependent drinkers I see are at the least badly out of shape, and generally overweight. So if you find that your health and fitness have been compromised, take some solace in knowing that you are not alone. Everybody in early recovery has health and fitness issues. And a brighter thought: No matter what condition you're in, you certainly can improve, and you probably will even enjoy the process.

Health

Many people who are quitting drinking aren't merely out of shape. Indeed, many have significant health challenges such as coronary artery disease, obesity, diabetes, hepatitis, arthritis, chronic pain syndrome, or any number of problems from the library of known medical conditions and diseases. For any of you with such health problems, this clearly complicates your recovery, at least at first. But it also increases the urgency to give yourself the best chance to manage your health issues by no longer throwing fuel on the fire. Alcohol seriously compromises the body's ability to heal.

The specific management of other diseases, conditions, and syndromes, is far beyond the scope of this book. Still, I want to offer an important bit of wisdom. It can make a huge difference in how you feel about any health problems you may have. It's really about a liberating point-of-view—a realistic and optimistic way of looking at your health problems. The older I get, the more I appreciate having learned this wise axiom: The secret to a long and happy life cannot be to remain free of any health problems, for this is not the true human experience. Much more realistically, the secret is to *accept what health challenges may come and manage them well.*

Recently, while skim-boarding at Carmel beach, a large dog blind-sided me, knocking me off the board. Immediately I recognized that this was not a hostile attack. It was an exuberantly playful animal wanting to join in my sport. In what appeared to be sheer joy, the dog then went bounding after some seagulls before racing up a sand dune toward his owner's call. Watching, I noticed that the dog was missing a leg, and for a moment I was sad. Then I realized something important: *The dog didn't care.* Sure, he was missing a leg, but that day on the beach, he was nevertheless 100 percent happy.

Most of our subjective state of misery is not caused by the health issue at hand but, instead, by our own ruminating about it. This may be exacerbated by healthcare professionals who seem to expect us to recover fully from everything. In the mental health field, many clinicians think their clients should completely overcome longstanding anxiety or mood problems, thereby making clients feel worse for not being able to do so. Now there is a wonderful new psychotherapeutic approach called *Acceptance and Commitment Therapy* (Hayes, Strosahl, & Wilson, 1999). From this perspective, clients are encouraged to accept that they really do have an anxiety or mood problem and not to feel guilty about it but, rather, to commit to managing the condition as well as reasonably possible.

With health issues, take heart. Accept the health problems you have, and commit to doing the best you can to overcome or keep at bay the negative effects. Using the template for recovery is a great way to get started. First overcome your fears and inhibitions, face your health problems squarely, and learn all you can about them. Use the Internet, talk with doctors, and read books and journal articles. In short, become an expert, but stop short of expecting yourself to go to medical school— just learn what a smart layperson could learn about anything. Then set health/disease management goals, followed by your specific plans to achieve them. Get those plans on a schedule and get started. Then agree with yourself that you are doing the best a person can, and give yourself permission to let go of worrying about it. Perhaps in time, you too can become a happy dog on the beach of life.

Fitness

An almost ubiquitous outcome of excessive alcohol use is the loss of one's level, or potential level, of physical fitness. Again, drinkers get out of shape. They lose muscle tone, strength, stamina, and in many cases become overweight. Several factors contribute to the lack or loss of fitness. One is the blood-slugging phenomenon cited in Chapter 4. Alcohol causes red blood cells to clump together, clogging-up small capillaries and causing atrophy of muscle cells as they become deprived of nutrients and oxygen. One simply cannot develop or maintain healthy muscle tone and be a heavy drinker at the same time. Another factor is that, as more time is spent in obtaining and imbibing alcohol, less time is spent engaging in other activities that would burn, instead of add, calories. Leisure pursuits and exercise routines fall by the wayside. As all this happens, people become increasingly depressed and lose motivation to eat healthily and exercise regularly.

First and foremost, what you want for recovery of your health and fitness is up to you alone. Perhaps you would like to be more fit but lack the necessary motivation. Maybe you lack knowledge about how to pursue fitness or long ago gave up hope that you could become healthier and more physically fit. This is often the case with people who have other health conditions, such as being grossly overweight. They think they have such a long way to go that it doesn't seem possible. People with chronic pain conditions fear that any fitness activity will only worsen their pain. Indeed, motivating people to eat healthily and work out is easier if they aren't too far out of shape and don't have chronic pain in the first place. If you think you have too far to go or fear a worsening of pain, the remedy is to set smaller goals with gentler methods rather than giving up. Remember—this isn't about looking like Brad Pitt or Penelope Cruz; it's about being healthier—having a healthier heart, a stronger immune system, and more energy—within your capacity to do so.

Some people say that living extra long is not important to them. To me, it's not so much about living a long time but, rather, about being healthy right now. I participate regularly and passionately in a variety of outdoor activities—biking, running, rollerblading, sail-boarding, golfing, and cross-country skiing. I also work out regularly in my home gym. And I enjoy working on house and yard projects for hours on end. The point is that I truly enjoy having as much energy, strength, and endurance for these activities now in my 60s as I had in my 20s.

Some people seem to harbor a deep perception that exercise somehow will hurt them, falsely assuming that any exertion somehow might wear out their bodies. Consider this: Keeping animals in zoos healthy has always been difficult. Zebras in zoos are a case in point. They tend to struggle with a host of disease processes including heart problems, skin conditions, and fragile immune systems. But zebras in the wild are healthy. The reason can be seen in their life pattern. On the African savanna, a herd of zebras might be quietly grazing at dawn. Then one of them sees a lion in the grass and spooks. The whole herd thunders across the savanna for a couple of miles and then settles down to sedate grazing again. A couple of hours later they spook again and sprint back the other way. And so it goes all day. If zebras don't get to run, their muscles, including the heart muscle, atrophy, their respiratory systems weaken, their immune systems fail, and they become sickly.

Do you think humans are that much different? We were hunter/gatherers. We were farmers. We need to move or wither. Like the wheel beings on a distant planet in Kurt Vonnegut's novel *Venus on the Half Shell*, my motto is, "Keep rolling."

What to Do About Your Health and Fitness

If a lack of knowledge about health and fitness is what's holding you back, I certainly can empathize with you. There are so many forms of exercise and an overwhelming array of diets to choose from. I won't attempt to go into detail about any specific nutrition or exercise approach, but from everything I've studied, I've come to trust several basic understandings that I think will help you.

- In terms of losing weight, no nutritional plan or diet is right for everyone. Which plan you follow isn't as important as that you follow a plan. The entire body of nutritional research points consistently to one thing: Regardless of what you eat or do not eat, or how you exercise, it all comes down to calories in versus calories out. What we eat or how we exercise really doesn't matter. If we consume more calories than we burn, we will gain weight. If we burn more calories than we eat, we will lose weight. So it's merely a question what kind of eating helps us consume fewer calories and what sort of exercise regimen is easiest for each individual. For Sally next door, it's an all-protein diet and exercising 6 hours per week on a stationary bike. Ed is on the Mediterranean diet and jogs five times a week. Who will lose weight? Both of them—but only if they are each burning more calories than they consume.
- Exercise is good for what ails you. Research on exercise consistently shows that it offers the single best protection against everything. Regular, rigorous exercise provides near immunity against coronary/artery disease, cancers, diabetes, and premature dementia, and it slows aging. Exercise is the closest thing yet discovered to a Fountain of Youth. Some researchers think it almost doesn't matter what we eat, as long as we exercise.
- To *keep* weight off, no diet will work. That's because a diet, by definition, is merely a temporary remedy. What you need is a lifestyle change.
- Three factors seem to drive one's interest in and adherence to fitness regimens: fear, guilt, and/or reward. If you have none of these but at least intellectually want to be healthier, I suppose you could work on expanding your fear. You could read-up on the effects of not building and maintaining fitness: muscle atrophy, cardiomyopathy, weakness, low energy, depression, hypoglycemia, hypertension, compromised immune system, and all the sequelae of being overweight. Or I suppose you could see if you can generate a greater sense of guilt. Beef-up

those internal voices of your parents, grandparents, the Catholic Church, and British Admiralty, all telling you how disappointed they are with you for your lack of fitness. Although these fear and guilt strategies can work, we psychologists just don't like them. They seem so antithetical to human freedom and happiness. I recommend instead that you set up a reward system to reinforce your efforts.

Your Own Action Plan

Adapting a line from *Star Wars*: "The Template, Luke. Use the Template!" Start by using the template model introduced in Chapter 7. First, spend a set time each day brainstorming and jotting down what your own fitness *needs* might be. Fitness has three components: nutrition, exercise, and rest. Think about your needs for each. Again, this is about your own private needs, not what you think others would approve, or for status. Examples might be:

- To be less tired.
- To be able to enjoy an outdoor activity.
- Enjoy highly nutritional meals.
- To live my life at a healthy body weight.

Once you have a sense of your needs, translate them into *goals*. It is important to set target dates wherever possible. Examples might be:

- Get an average of 8 hours quality sleep per night by June 1.
- Lose 15 pounds by a March 1.
- Maintain a 15 by 20 foot garden by May 31.
- Be able to complete 5 kilometer community run on September 14th.
- Be able to prepare and enjoy at least 15 healthy and tasty meals per week by February 1.

Then set your pathway. Write down the *means* to meet your goals—the steps and timelines you will follow. Examples might be:

- Start a sleep log tonight. Study and practice the strategies of "sleep hygiene" you can learn about on the Internet. Schedule a short after nap for every afternoon.
- Initiate a weight-lifting and running regimen by Wednesday. Participate every Tuesday through Friday.
- Sign up for the free gardening seminar at the local nursery on Saturday.
- Work in the garden on Tuesday and Thursday evenings and on Saturday and Sunday afternoons.
- Enroll in the *Eating Naturally* class at the health food store on Wednesdays.
- Finish reading the *South Beach Diet* to learn about nutrition.
- Shop at the health food store once per week.

For goals that are not immediately rewarding and, therefore, not immediately self-sustaining, set up some rewards—things such as buying yourself something you want at the end of each week if you stick to your plan. Record your progress on a calendar for immediate feedback as you go along, and to establish when you get the reward.

Another strategy is to announce your plan to people close to you. There is something about telling people what we are going to do that increases our motivation to follow through. And also very motivating, once you're involved in your action plan, tell others what you do, e.g., that you lift weights 4 days a week, that you are an avid gardener, that you eat oatmeal with walnuts most mornings. Even brag a little. What you are aiming to do is change you self-perception—*I am* a non-smoker, *I am* a jogger, *I am* a gardener. When a behavior change becomes part of your identity, you've turned the corner, you've got it made.

Don't worry about whether your health and fitness goals are right or doable. As always, goals are important because they set a direction, increase motivation, and get us started, but they are changeable and generally not as important as the process. Remember—being on a pathway is the key.

Recommended Reading for Chapter 10

Living a Healthy Life with Chronic Conditions: Self-Management of Heart Disease, Fatigue, Arthritis, Worry, Diabetes, Frustration, Asthma, Pain, Emphysema, and Others (3rd edition), by Kate Lorig.

Healthy Aging, by Andrew Weil.

Younger Next Year: Live Strong, Fit and Sexy until You're 80 and Beyond, by Chris Crowley and Henry Lodge.

Chapter 11

Emotional Recovery

Problem:	*A compromised ability to manage emotions is the number one cause of recovery failure.*
What to do:	*Learn where feelings really come from.*
	Learn solid strategies for how to prosper from your moods.

Where Feelings Really Come From

To quickly review; the challenge in recovery comes not so much from physical addiction as from psychological dependence. When the substance effect takes over as one's emotional manager, alexithymia occurs. In recovery, most relapses come from compromised control over emotions. This understood, we can begin to recover emotionally by learning where feelings, moods, and emotions come from in the first place.

I have many times brought this question of where feelings come from to a room full of people—counselors in training, inpatients, outpatients, patients' family members, and others. People consistently respond to the question with the idea that different situations or events in our lives directly cause different emotions. People say feelings are caused by things like, "When I have less money in a paycheck than I expected, it makes me feel worried," or, "When someone bad-mouths me, it makes me feel hurt," or, "When it rains I get depressed," or, "If I get a flat tire it makes me angry." On and on it goes, as if external events directly affect the emotional centers of our brains. More recently, a few people in any given group will call out "brain chemistry imbalances" as the cause of negative emotions. Each of these—external situations and brain chemistry—has a role to play, but neither is usually the true culprit.

The Late, Not-So-Great, Monoamine Hypothesis of Depression

In the first place, there has been a lot of hope and billions of dollars invested in the development of drugs to alleviate emotional pain—various forms of psychosis, depression, and anxiety. The basic theory has been that low levels of, or the inability to effectively utilize, several natural brain chemicals, may be associated with mood/anxiety/psychotic problems. Especially regarding depression, the theory has focused on protein brain molecules called monoamines, including serotonin, norepinephrine and dopamine. The older tricylic antidepressants like imipramine (Tofranil), amitriptyline (Elavil), and doxepin (Sinequan), target serotonin and norepinephrine. The newer SSRIs (selective serotonin reuptake inhibitors) like fluoxetine (Prozac), sertraline (Zoloft), citalopram (Celexa), paroxetine (Paxil), and escitalopram (Lexapo), target serotonin. Bupropion (Wellbutrin) increases dopamine utilization.

Unfortunately, the whole monoamine hypothesis of depression remains highly questionable (Gitlin, 2008). Much research, primarily funded by the pharmaceutical industry, supports a moderate benefit in most moderately depressed individuals. Yet, more recent meta-analysis research, not industry-funded, on the efficacy of Paxil, Prozac, Effexor, and other antidepressant drugs finds that they have no benefit over placebos—the benefit one naturally gets from the belief that they are on a real medication, although secretly on a sugar pill (Kirsh et al., 2008; Fournier et al., 2010).Much to our relief, the studies did demonstrate that the medications at least had a positive effect on mood among severely (clinically) depressed individuals.

Clearly, more research is needed. If you are interested in this topic there are several new books out that lament the theft of psychiatry by the pharmaceutical industry and identify serious research errors and negative effects of psychiatric medications: *The Emperor's New Drugs: Exploding the Myth of Antidepressant Drugs* (Kirsch, 2011); *Anatomy of an Epidemic: Magic Bullets, Psychiatric Drugs and the Astonishing Rise of Mental Illness in America* (Whitaker, 2011); *Unhinged: The Trouble with Psychiatry—A Doctor's Revelations about a Profession in Crisis* (Carlat, 2011).

In my purview of the literature and experience with so many people on medications, the antidepressants (and anti-anxiety drugs) can be helpful, and, particularly the SSRIs, are relatively safe. Also used for treating depression are anticonvulsant drugs like Depekote and Lamictal, and antipsychotic drugs like Seroquel, Zyprexa, Abilify, and Risperal. These are a little more worrisome in terms of side effects such as; fatigue, weight gain, emotional blunting, fall risk, increased risk of diabetes, cognitive declines, liver damage, and birth defects. Fortunately, for most people with mild to moderate depression, such medications are not needed and cognitive behavior therapy will likely prove to be most effective.

Of course, the most severe depression is biological, does respond to medications, and in many cases emotional and behavioral relief is more important than possible long-term mental and physical problems. And if you have been sober for several weeks or more and have tried everything else but continue to feel seriously depressed, taking an antidepressant may be the last best thing you can do for yourself—it really may help. Still, I highly recommend that if you are on, or are considering starting, an antidepressant medication, you get a comprehensive psychosocial assessment that includes history of your family, childhood, self-perception, and real-life challenges that may account for your depression rather than a brain chemistry imbalance.

The Real Story

Let us go back to my classroom where students are grappling with the question of where feelings come from. I draw a line on a board behind me. I draw 11 hash marks along the line and number them from left to right starting with negative 5, continuing up through 0, and on out to positive 5. I label negative 5 "Depression," 0 "Neutral," and positive 5 "Euphoric."

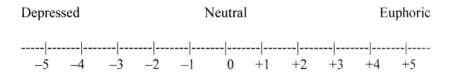

Depressed   Neutral   Euphoric

-----|-------|-------|-------|-------|-------|-------|-------|-------|-------|-----
 -5   -4   -3   -2   -1   0   +1   +2   +3   +4   +5

I then say, "Let us explore your hypothesis that situations cause feelings." I state various situations to see what emotions the group thinks they cause. I ask individuals to call out where they rate their feelings on the chart for each situation I identify. I say things like, "There is a new dress code at your work or school—you all have to dress better. How does that make you feel?" Some people call out negative numbers, but some call out positive numbers, and some are at neutral. Or I'll say, "Your grandfather is coming to stay for three weeks. How does that make you feel?" Again, people are all over the board on their emotional ratings. Some hate it, some think it is wonderful, and some are indifferent. So, I say, "What's going on here? You each heard the exact same words come out of my mouth, the exact same external stimulus. If situations cause feelings, how did we get a completely disparate range of emotions for each situation?" Well, most people get it quickly enough. They say, "Well of course Dr. Portman, we each have a different point of view about the situations you identified." Ah! So it is not *situations* (or brain chemistry imbalances) but rather *points of view* that cause emotions. Simple as it sounds, in recent times this seems to have become the million dollar suppressed secret in psychology.

Fortunately, decades of independently funded research and thousands of published studies come to this conclusion. Most of the big thinkers and top researchers agree that excessively negative emotions are by and large *perceptually* driven—not a result of external situations or brain chemistry imbalances (Beck et al., 1979; Seligman, 1991; Ellis, 1994, 1994; Meichenbaum, 1977; Burns, 1980; Yapko, 1998). Merely triggered by external situations, it is our individual interpretations, our own explanatory styles, our beliefs, the spin we put on situations, that cause our emotions to emerge. Epictitus, 500 B.C., apparently knew this; "It is not things that upset men, but the view they take of them." Shakespeare had Hamlet say, "Nothing is good nor evil, but thinking makes it so."

In addition, it is generally only *irrational* beliefs (Albert Ellis, 1961) and related thought distortions (Beck et al., 1979; Burns, 1980) that cause any seriously negative emotions. Consider this: our raw affect—the almost physical sensation of a feeling such as anxiety or anger—emanates from a small area in the center of our brains called the amygdala. When I was an undergraduate in the late 1960s, I remember seeing films in physiological psychology class, of researchers running thin wire leads into the brains of laboratory animals and sending a very weak electric current into the amygdala region. Depending on where that current hit, the critter would suddenly express behavior suggesting it was responding with an emotion. It might cower in the corner in a fear response, or rage at the cage in an anger response. Amazingly, they did these experiments on human subjects as well. Apparently, if you know where and how to run the leads, it does not hurt the subject. So here would be a lab tech sitting in front of several researchers with several wires going into his skull. A researcher would press a button sending an electric impulse into the fellow's amygdala and suddenly the guy would start crying. They would say, "What's wrong?" And he would say, "I don't know, everything just seems so sad." The researcher would press another button sending a current into an adjacent area of the amygdala and the fellow, midsentence, would start laughing. They would say, "What's so funny?" And he would respond, "Everything! Look at your ridiculous tie, ha, ha, ha."

Here is the important point. The amygdala is blind to the outside world. It has only a very primitive connection to the visual, auditory, olfactory, or kinesthetic pathways and is therefore unaware of whether it is a sunny or cloudy day, whether your bank account is full or drained, or of anything else. Flat tires, cloudy days, words heard over a telephone, are innocuous and generally incapable of causing moods in and of themselves. So, since we do not have wire leads running into our brains, where does the amygdala get its information for coming up with an emotion in response to anything? The answer is that it is housed in the temporal lobes—the seat of language—and has learned to react to our internal dialogue. Some thoughts are "hotter" in this regard than others are. Suppose in childhood a parent shouts, "Omigod you broke it," and then hits you with a belt. Thereafter, your amygdala might issue a fear emotion whenever you yourself think or say "Omigod," even when there is no real threat—like being late for work, an offense for which no one is likely to assault you. What you get is *emotional overage*—emotional responding in excess of what is really proportionate to the situation.

For example, if late for a meeting, you might think, "Damn, what if I'm late? That would be awful! I am always late. Something is definitely wrong with me. That car should not be where I usually park. I can't stand it. This ruins my day." These thoughts are riddled with irrational "awfullizing", catastrophizing, exaggerating, personal put-downs, demands, and flat-out denial of matter in the universe (the car in the space you wanted really does exist). These irrational thoughts flood you with excessive negative emotions like anxiety, anger, and depression. More rationally, one might say, "So what if I am late? No big deal; I am usually quite punctual and the meeting always starts late anyway. I will remember to leave earlier next time in case parking is a problem again. This is annoying but really not awful, and I'm not going to let it ruin my day." There is not much for the amygdala to go off on here, and you will not feel so bad. Plus, these thoughts are actually rational—you don't have to distort anything to feel better.

Thus, with humans, emotions come predominately from our thinking. Animals' emotions are more primitive—pretty much a case of stimulus/response in a one-to-one dynamic. The deer in my backyard hear the dog bark. Flooded with fear, they run. With humans, however, there is the stimulus, then cognitive processing, and then emotional response. This is the A-B-C of our emotions as described by Dr. Albert Ellis over 50 years ago, with *A* representing any activating event, *B* standing for our beliefs about the activating event, and *C*, our emotional consequence. It automatically seems to us that *A* causes *C*, but most often it is *B*, our irrational beliefs.

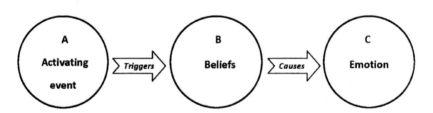

So where do these irrational thought distortions come from? Our brains are like computers. Every time one of the computers at my office freezes up, I am certain the hard drive has crashed. As a result, I support a small army of computer geeks. When they come in it is always the same story; "No, Dr. Portman, the hard drive is fine. You just have this program crossing that program." There is really extremely little variance in the hard drives coming off computer assembly lines. Faulty programming is the culprit affecting our computer's functioning. And contrary to what the pharmaceutical industry wants us to believe, variation in the hard drive of our brains isn't that great either. More likely than not, your brain is fine. The problem is usually in the programming—specifically, how we each learn across time to *interpret* the circumstances of our lives.

And so who are the programmers? I'll give you three guesses and the first two don't count. Right! More than others, in most of our lives it is our parents. In his book *The Four Agreements*, Don Miguel Ruiz (2001) writes that our parents unwittingly "domesticate" us by the use of reward and punishment. We learn how to interpret our experience accordingly. In his book *Learned Optimism*, Martin Seligman (1991), a 40-year depression researcher, gives wonderful examples of how we learn to pessimistically interpret external events. One of Seligman's examples is that of a toddler holding Mom's hand while Mom is pushing a shopping cart across the grocery store parking lot. Fumbling with the keys to open the trunk, the cart bumps the car. Mom and the little girl see the resulting scratch. Mom gasps, "Oh no! Is that a scratch?" The little girl looks at Mom and then at the scratch. Mom reaches down, touches the scratch, and shrieks, "Oh ... my ... God, it *is* scratched. That'll cost a fortune. Your father will be furious. Quick, get in the car, we've got to get home." Thus, the little girl learns that a mere scratch in a piece of metal needs to be interpreted as the end of the freaking world as we know it. Now imagine thousands of like incidents throughout childhood. We learn to awfullize, exaggerate, catastrophize, and condemn ourselves and others, about neutral, or at the most, inconvenient, situations. In fact, most situations are innocuous. Scratches on objects, rain clouds, flat tires, words heard or read, are not in and of themselves capable of causing human emotions. Many years ago, one of my wise graduate advisors, Dr. Jerry Kranzler (University of Oregon), told me, "Chris, I only have two rules in life. The first is don't sweat the small stuff." I said, "Okay Jerry, I'll bite, what's the second rule?" His response: "It's *all* small stuff."

Core Beliefs and Negative Schema

Before we turn attention to how to actually *prosper* from your negative feelings, we need to take the question of where feelings come from to one more level. The A-B-C model of emotions has a deeper level. According to mood expert Dr. Albert Ellis (1994), in addition to spinning out irrational beliefs about day-to-day situations, we each harbor what he calls "core beliefs." Learned in childhood, they are partly under the radar of conscious awareness. Core beliefs are deeply held perceptions of ourselves in relation to the world and everybody in it. I'll discus some examples of this in the next section.

Other scholars have identified the same phenomenon. Dr. Jeffrey Young (2003) calls our learned self-defeating perceptions "negative schema." What happens is (A) we learn erroneous negative schema in childhood, and then (B) we develop coping strategies such as avoidance, surrendering and serving, or many forms of overcompensating, which later become self-defeating. In childhood, we are very naive, and our universe is finite, so we are innocently egocentric. If a parent is not there for us, we assume it is because we are unimportant. If a parent is punitive, we assume we are bad inside. If a parent is demanding with high expectations we cannot reach, we assume we are defective.

In response to such negative core beliefs or schema, we develop coping strategies. For example, if a little boy has a critical and demanding father, he is likely to buy in and come to believe he is inherently flawed, thus harboring schema of *defectiveness*. If he sees his father's car in the driveway after school, he might hang out at the park for a while. This is an *avoidance* strategy.

Avoiding an abusive parent is actually a good strategy at first; what else is a child to do? Across time, however, avoidance is not such good strategy. This is the kid in the fourth grade standing by the doorway while the others are out to recess. The teacher says, "Josh, why don't you go out and play with the others?" Josh responds, "I don't think they like me." His avoidance strategy, at first useful, is beginning to have a cost—as a life pattern he will miss out on potentially nurturing relationships. As an extreme example, I recall that, well into the 1960s, occasionally a Japanese WWII soldier would be discovered living in a jungle on some remote island in the South Pacific. When such a fellow was asked why he was hiding out so long after the war, he would respond that he was not sure the war was over. He would explain that 20 years earlier, as Americans advanced on the beach he was supposed to guard, he ran off. Then, fearing he would be shot by his own superiors for abandoning his post, he just lost himself in the jungle, afraid to ever come out. Nice avoidance strategy, except that the life, family, and career, he could have had was sacrificed. Because of more subtle, but nonetheless profound, avoidance strategies, who among us has also missed out, in terms of relationships, occupations, and all sorts of life endeavors?

Due to our maladaptive coping strategies, schemas are self-perpetuating. Our avoidance strategy kid eventually builds up his courage and goes to the high school football game because he really longs to connect (humans have evolved a very deep and abiding interconnection need for very healthy reasons). However, due to fear of rejection, he sits apart from the others on the bleachers. The others see him as either aloof or disturbed and leave him alone, thus confirming his belief that he is rejectable. Young calls this *schema perpetuation*. Due to the effects of our eventually maladaptive coping strategies, negative self-perceptions are reinforced and become self-defeating.

Imagine a troubled married couple who air a lot of their emotional misery in front of their young daughter. The girl may come to feel responsible for her parents' feelings and, unable to help, develop schema of defectiveness as a result. As a coping strategy, she may *surrender and serve*, rather than avoid. She may try to help her parents: "Look Mommy, you don't have to worry, I've done the dishes [or fed little brother, been good, took out the trash, etc]." At first this may actually help, as the little girl gets some level of relief, e.g., a less frenetic parent. However, she develops schema of seeing herself as a second-class citizen and a coping strategy to surrender and serve. This will result in giving over too much power to others in her life, such as employers, co-workers, and perhaps her husband. This is great for everyone being served, but for the individual it becomes a lifetime of self-sacrificing.

Other responses to negative schema include different forms of *overcompensation*. Some children attempt to overcome their negative self-perceptions and buoy up flagging self-esteem by external yardsticks of achievement, such as earning top grades or excelling at sports. This is probably what is going on in the case of a girl who attempts suicide because she got a B instead of an A in a class, wrecking her 4.0 GPA. Or it is the boy who locks himself in the basement for a week, overwhelmed with a sense of failure and shame because he dropped the ball in the end zone, losing the football game. In cases of abuse, some children may adapt by becoming bullies themselves. Again, these coping strategies are initially helpful but terribly costly across time.

Emotional Overage

For any potentially aversive situation such as a flat tire, a money shortfall, or a rainy weekend, there is an amount of emotional responding that is appropriate and proportionate. Let us say someone spoke disparagingly about you. This would upset most of us perhaps 2 or 3 points out on a 10-point scale of emotional distress. But what if you find yourself at about 8 or 9 points out? Everything beyond the pale of what is proportionate to the situation I call *emotional overage.*

In the chart example below, for some unnamed situation in someone's life, all emotional responding past 2 points actually has nothing to do with the current situation. The current situation has merely retriggered an old pattern of perceptions and attendant emotional responding learned in childhood. This is what accounts for emotional overage, per situation, in our adult lives.

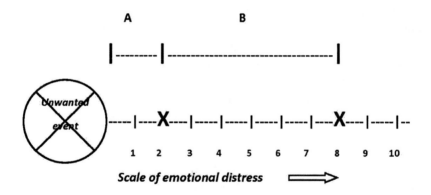

A = Emotional responding proportionate
         to the situation

B = Emotional overage, disproportionate
         to the situation

Here is how this happens. Many times, I have seen middle-aged people referred for treatment of panic, depression, substance abuse, or other problems. After taking a life history, I sometimes risk asking if they think the abuse, neglect, or related deficiencies in childhood could have anything to do with their emotional problems now. Sometimes people respond with, "No way! I left home when I was 17. How could anything from way back then affect me now?" I back off, and say, "I see what you mean." But then I explain that the *conscious* mind fools us. It demarcates the passage of the years, all of our birthdays, places we have lived, and the history of our involvments. So it does not seem that experiences from way back in our past could affect us now. However, we learn our unique emotional response patterns in childhood, and the *subconscious* mind does not track the passage of time. As far as it is concerned, what happened then might as well have been this morning. Current situations with different places and people subconsciously remind us in some way of childhood experiences and simply retrigger old perceptions and feelings without our awareness.

What Is Meant by Abandonment

In the recovery field, the concept of abandonment is very important. This is because for many people, abandonment issues from childhood both drive the addiction in the first place and then, if not reconciled, sabotage recovery. In treatment, the phenomenon is referred to as *family of origin issues*. It is considered unwise to encourage a person to work on their family of origin issues in the first year of recovery because these deep personal issues can be so destabilizing. Better to establish an abstinence-supportive lifestyle before delving into any family of origin/abandonment issues. On the other hand, many people will never get a year of sobriety unless the abandonment issues are addressed and reasonably resolved.

Some years ago, I saw a Nature channel documentary on Thomson's gazelles. They are a small deerlike animal of the African savannah that spend a lot of time running from the lions that feed on them. An amazing thing happens at birth. When the little gazelle plops to the ground, it gets on its feet in about 20 seconds and starts following its mother around. They are born fully developed because millions of years of lion predation have selected out any genetic traits related to a less mature birth. This is pretty much true throughout the animal kingdom. Humans, however, after thousands of years of indoor living, are born fetuses. We are physically, profoundly immature at birth. We need to be climate controlled, swaddled, held, fed, and cleaned, for many months before we ever get on our feet. Even the worst of parents work to meet the fragile physical needs of their children. Failing to do this would be disastrous; children would grow up crippled, if surviving at all.

Here is my point: adult human life is mentally and emotionally very complicated compared to that of other animals. In infancy and early childhood, we are just as *emotionally* fragile as we are *physically* fragile. In childhood, it is just as important to get a positive identity as it is to be physically healthy. And this too often is where even the best-intentioned parents go wrong. Human little ones need, and are entitled to, just as much emotional nurturing as physical nurturing. Failure in this nurturing results in negative self-perception, dysfunctional coping, depression, anxiety, relationship struggles, and substance abuse problems later in life.

In our first year of life, our self-perception is pretty much a blank slate—a soft clay tablet ready for its first impressions. We do not know whether we are a good thing or a bad thing, capable or incapable, lovable or unlovable. This *tabula rasa,* or soft clay tablet, is written on by our parents' interactions with us. Imagine a child with parents who cooperate affectionately with each other and toward the child are consistently available, affectionate, prizing, and reassuring. This type of parental behavior creates a sense of security about others in the world and validates the child as a worthwhile, capable, and lovable human being. By the time this child hits the school system, his or her whole worldview is, "I am made of good stuff. Wherever I go, people will like me, and good things will happen." For people with this experience, the world is indeed their proverbial oyster. If someone does not like them, they attribute the problem to the other person, or apologize for an error if they made one and commit to doing better, without self-condemnation. If something planned does not work out, they chalk it off to experience and move on. When this kid tries alcohol, it will not make much difference in how he feels because he already feels good and he will not take to it.

Now imagine a child whose parents do not get along and toward the child are not consistently available and not affectionate, but rather critical, demeaning, or physically abusive. How is this little human going to get a positive self-image? This is what we mean by the term *abandonment.* We do not mean the parents drop off their child on a street corner in a strange city and drive away. We mean that by their unavailability or meanness, they are abandoning the child's opportunity to get a positive identity.

There are two parts to this abandonment. The first is the parent's disparaging treatment, such as shouting, "What's wrong with you? Why can't you be more like your sister?" It is as if the parent is saying, "I see your real self and it's not good enough for me. You had better be like somebody else if you want to get along with me and everybody else in this world." Scores of troubled adults that I have seen have expressed impressively clear memories of being told they were stupid, or being given a disparaging nickname, or being hit, yelled at, or left alone too much. These are abandonments, and they take a toll.

The second part of abandonment is when the child internally perceives that he or she is defective. With this erroneous perception, the child abandons and tries to push back his or her real self in a process known as *psychic splitting*. In order to avoid rejection, the child takes off on a trajectory ever striving to become a more ideal self and leaves the real self in the dust. In effect, we say, "My real self is obviously not good enough. I had better hide that back and try to be different so I won't get picked on or rejected." Thus, we abandon ourselves. Unfortunately, self-rejection and ever striving to be an ideal self takes an enormous amount of energy and only generates more anxiety and depression, pancaked now on top of the self-esteem problem. When we try alcohol or other drugs, it will make an appreciable difference in how we feel and we will take to it like ducks take to water.

Emotional Arrest

Across many years as a therapist for people with mental health and/or substance use problems, I have always started with a broad assessment—an organized diagnostic clinical interview. I start with questions about the incidences of substance use and mental health problems in the person's extended family history (grandparents, aunts, uncles, cousins, and parents). I ask all about any health, social, learning, behavioral, or emotional challenges in their childhoods. I carefully ask how their parents got along, how each parent treated them, and how they got along with any siblings. I inquire about how they did socially, athletically, and academically in school, about any and all challenges in their young adult lives, and the history of any substance use. Across thousands of such interviews, I cannot escape the profound and persistent straight-line, linear correlation between the level of challenges (emotional neglect, abuses, etc.) in childhood and the level of emotional and substance use problems in adult life. The greater the challenges to self-worth in childhood, the greater the emotional, relationship, and/or substance use problems later on. Of course, there are a few exceptions—"outliers" they are called in research. What seems to happen in these exceptional individuals are subtle validating influences from a relative or significant person, despite other neglect or abuse, that prevent the person from internalizing fault. They manage to maintain a sense that they are made of good and entitled stuff and that fault and blame lie outside of them. To be clear, however, these cases are far less common than the high incidence of children who are led to self-rejection.

From this pool of negative self-perceptions, the ability to understand our own feelings becomes impaired. Up to about 12 years of age, we pretty much live in our conscious minds only. This is called the *concrete phase* of cognitive development. We have no comprehension of subconscious processes at work within us. Then we hit puberty. Our brains grow and we begin to struggle with strange moods, feelings, urges, yearnings, and desires. At first, young teens may try to ignore these internal signals, but begin to wonder if something is wrong within themselves. So they try not to let anyone know and put on a facade of okay-ness for others to see. With boys, it's a false bravado. No way are they going to let anyone know they have these strange feelings, perhaps crying at night, sexual feelings, anger, etc. They all get stuffed. If I ask a 16-year-old boy, "So why did you punch out that kid in the hallway?" he will say something like, "That kid said [this, that, and the other thing] about me and my girlfriend." Then, baiting him, because I already know what his response will be, I say, "Gee, that must have really hurt your feelings." Of course, being 16, he responds, "What? No! It pissed me off." He just cannot go there—that it hurt his feelings by threatening his youthful sense of masculinity. On the other hand, a client only about age 24 can easily say, "My supervisor at work told me everything I was doing wrong, right in front of all my co-workers. I felt so embarrassed, it really hurt my feelings, and then I got mad."

So what happens between early adolescence and adulthood? We learn to understand our feelings and accept them as normal. We are able to get a very important dialogue going between our conscious and subconscious emotional mind. Here is the very important point: If one becomes overinvolved with alcohol, or another drug such as marijuana, the substance becomes the emotional manager, arresting normal emotional maturation and the ability to identify and cope with feelings. When this happens the person fails to comprehend any distinction between his or her conscious and subconscious mind, and thus has no useful communication between them. Conscious and subconscious mind remain melded together as one, and the person is then ruled by his or her emotions without knowing it. Perhaps you know people like this.

The emotional arrest among alcoholics is very real and results in the alexithymia phenomenon described in Chapter 6. Countless times I have seen people in my clinical practice who, for example, quit drinking at, say, 40 years of age. What I see is a person with good intelligence, perhaps worldly with a broad fund of knowledge, but emotionally 17 again. The beginning of regular substance use, at whatever age, marks the onset of emotional arrest and resulting alexithymia—a compromised capacity to correctly identify feelings, let alone to cope with them in mature and productive ways. Fortunately, after quitting alcohol or other drug use, the ability to recognize and manage emotions effectively recovers, albeit at different rates of time for different people. Failure to do this, of course, becomes the greatest risk factor for relapse.

Primary verses Secondary Feelings

Related to the phenomenon of alexithymia (the inability to recognize emotional experience) we can sometimes recognize a feeling that can be the wrong one to respond to. That is, we sometimes act-out based on a *secondary* feeling and fail to recognize a more *primary* feeling beneath it. For example, it is often said that anger is a secondary emotion. Indeed, humans are hardwired for anger because of its survival value. If a lion pops its head up in the grass, falling down on the path in a puddle of fear will result in you becoming the lion's lunch. Because you would cease to exist, your trait of passively responding in hurt-type feelings would drop out of the gene pool. On the other hand, if you generate enough rage to raise up a spear and fight, you might survive, and your trait to get angry would pass on to your children. However, in modern times, we do not have lions jumping at us. Yet we continue to respond with anger to situations that are not all that threatening. The reason is that anger feels better than hurt. When we have hurt-type feelings like fear, loss, or belittlement, we feel vulnerable. To escape this, we usher ourselves up to anger. Anger provides a sense of taking control, thus freeing us from the awful feeling of vulnerability.

Unfortunately, with alcohol dependence, the deployment of anger is also reinforced by the effect of drinking. Anger insidiously gives one license to drink.

So when I see an angry person I see a person responding to some hurt-type feeling that they are usually not aware of. Even in the example of road-rage, a fellow classically believes that the other driver's honking directly causes his anger. It usually takes considerable discussion for the guy to realize that at first his feelings where hurt—that the other driver's honking made him feel belittled, shamed, and inferior as a driver and as a man—then he got mad. This is the same phenomenon that happened to the kid who punched the other boy at school after his manhood was challenged, and the women who got drunk when she assumed she should be excited that her husband was coming home when in fact she was scared.

The threat to recovery comes when one is unaware of important primary feelings. Acknowledging or buying in to only our secondary feelings, such as anger or superficial happiness, can insidiously become justifications to drink.

Fear Containment, Alcohol, and Life Transitions

A good part of emotional recovery is about managing anxiety and fear. According to existentialists such as Irvin Yalom (1980), death anxiety is the ultimate core feeling. I disagree. I think that since we cannot really know what death is, we cannot really fear it. Fearing it is another red herring, a decoy or distraction. Because we see that people die, it provides a convenient place to focus our fears. What we are really afraid of is more obscure and difficult to comprehend, so we tend to not realize it. What we really fear is abandonment—something we all *have* experienced. Any toddler or young child who suddenly cannot find its mother in the crowd at the department store or at the farmer's market knows how terrible this feels. Screeching out loud is a common reaction.

Either way, with both death anxiety and abandonment anxiety, the older I have become, and the more people I have seen in therapy, the more I realize that one's ability to contain fear is the first imperative for a happy life—in order to enjoy life, we must first be able to manage our fears. When we are little, we are fearful of many things—strangers, the dark, barking dogs, being alone, heights, and loud noises, to name a few. Around age five or so, we learn about death, and what the hell do we do with that? These natural fears have survival value, but if they are unrelenting, and in the absence of consistent reassurance, they can become emotionally overwhelming. In a healthy family, with available, protective, and reassuring parents, by the time we are 10 or 12 we have fears pretty well contained. We are on top of the world, with lots of familiar things to identify with. Our home and family, friends, school, and community and all of our activities surround us and act as defense shields, protecting our more fragile real selves. These external defenses cover and contain our fears like a dome above us.

Then we hit puberty. Our brains grow, we gain a whole new self-consciousness, and all of our defense shields seem to blow away, exposing our more fragile real selves, and our fears run wild again. I can remember coming home after a day of struggling to survive in a tough urban junior high school I had transferred to, and fixing myself a bowl of vanilla pudding, trying to recapture the feeling of a more secure time in childhood. How do we cope with new feelings, urges, and drives, a rapidly changing body, and relating to peers, teachers, and parents in the strange new paradigm of early adolescence? Fortunately, in most cases, by the time we are seniors in high school we are back on top again. Our fears are well contained by an umbrella of defenses—the things we identify with such as our high school, peer group, sports, hometown, home and family, etc.

Then we hit a major life transition. For many, it is that Buddhistic time of groundlessness between childhood and independent adult living known as *college*. I once had a counseling internship at a college and learned that every fall, on every campus in the country, the counseling centers are filled with freshmen. They say they made a big mistake. College is not what they thought it would be. They are crying in their dormitory rooms at night, and vis-à-vis their roommates, they had not known that the college admitted lower primates. They do not have their defense shields in place and their more fragile selves are exposed. Everything that defined them is now 500 miles away—their home, friends, familiar community, etc.—and they are experiencing abandonment anxiety—a fearful, lonely, identity crisis. At this point wise counselors say, "Okay. I hear you. Why don't you go ahead and pack your bags, but come see me again next week." They lead them along this way for a while until, guess what? The student decides at least to complete the first term. They just need time to develop new shields. Soon, the campus, classes, instructors, and new friends move in to fill the void and fears are once more contained. Not-so-wise counselors misdiagnose them as bipolar, get them on Prozac, and enroll them in depression research studies.

In any case, after college, we get busy building the big front bulwarks that will define us and contain our fears for the next three decades. We establish our own careers, homes, families, friends, and leisure pursuits. Of course, for most people this does not go all that smoothly, but this is what we try to create and what we live to accomplish, whether we manage to do so with any consistency or not.

After several decades we hit the next major transitional period of our lives—the infamous *midlife crisis,* or transition. This is when the kids grow up, the careers wind down or terminate, marriages are challenged or fail, and health issues appear. Somewhere between the ages of 45 and 60, give or take, our defense shields begin to erode or blow apart again. In treatment programs and my private practice, I have seen many adults who have lost everything: their jobs, their marriages, their homes, their money, their health. When we lose too many shields too fast, it can be overwhelming, and we get what is called *midlife crisis*, something beyond the somewhat gentler midlife transition. In either case, for a while, we are thrown into a time of renewed self-doubt, desperately wish things would be different, and suffer with wanting to go back to the prior chapters of our lives. Men race back to the old defenses, throwing themselves headlong into their old sports, buying motorcycles, getting 30-year-old trophy brides, whatever desperate act it may take. Woman get facelifts (okay, so do men), leave their husbands, earn trophy master's degrees, and so forth. Some of these *external* adjustments are actually healthy, some go sideways.

The battle of midlife transition, however, is not won by external changes, but ultimately by *internal* changes—it is about finally doing the work of self-acceptance we thought we had done when we were at the top of our game in our 30s and 40s. It is really a time of revaluing. A changing of the guard is called for. What was important in our young adult lives may not be what will be important to us now. We need to restructure our values and build more realistic definitions of ourselves, and this is normal.

Alcohol use tends to forestall needed life transitions. Health, careers, relationships, interests, finances, and/or other areas of life can be woefully in need of changes. Then, like a damn bursting, when alcohol use stops, one can be rapidly overwhelmed with a rushing flood of long held back discontentment and problems in various areas of life. One can feel very ill equipped to deal with these changes. If you quit drinking and find yourself in a phase of life where fear-containing affiliations that helped to define you have broken down, take heart. You are actually well designed to get through it. Everybody does. Be patient and have compassion for yourself. The climb at times seems very rough and fearful, but all you have to do is keep going. In time, you will arrive at a new and more comfortable plateau. Sara Davidson's book *Leap! What to Do with the Rest of Our Lives* (2007) is particularly reassuring in this regard. She describes dozens of people she knows who have successfully negotiated major midlife changes. Again, I refer you to the life areas template. This is a great self-empowering way to organize your transitions.

Even if you do not feel that you had to suffer any emotionally damaging challenges in your childhood and believe that you are emotionally okay, learning as much as you can about emotional management can make the difference between successful abstinence and relapse. The renowned social/psychological theorist Alfred Adler pointed out in the early part of the last century that when we are small children, we actually *are* inferior (though not defective) temporarily, in the sense that we must rely on the big people to meet all of our needs. Even under optimum circumstances, with healthy, available parents, we grow up physically, but psychically we never quite shake those feelings of inferiority. Growing through a healthy childhood usually involves at least some questioning of one's own worth and potential. We all compensate by testing ourselves against various challenges such as sports, grades, socially, etc. Actually, this is how the world turns. This is how degrees get earned, organizations formed, bridges built, and so on. Adler was only concerned with the defense mechanism he called *overcompensation*, in which the person's feelings of inferiority are too strong and deeply seated. Rather than the mere question of his or her relative worth, he or she perceives a clear deficit, does psychic self-splitting, and struggles for years trying to be a more ideal self, to avoid detection and rejection. Incidentally, the expression *feelings of inferiority* took on a pejorative patina and by the 1960s was casually replaced with the expression *feelings of inadequacy*. This was later replaced with the very popular *low self-esteem*. Roughly equivalent terms include *negative self-perception* or *negative identity*, but it is all about the same. In any case, emotions, superficial or core, play a huge make-it-or-break-it role in recovery.

How to Prosper from Your Moods

Now for the fun part. Out of all of this, I have put together a set of interrelated strategies for you to use in the challenge of emotional recovery. They potentiate each other, so I hope you will try them all. Here is how to begin emotional recovery.

Strategy Number One: Learn to identify your feelings, without fear or judgment

Never underestimate or fail to capitalize on the positive intentions of negative emotions. When I mention this, people are often quite surprised. How could emotions like anguish, depression, or fear be a good thing? Those starting recovery tend to be especially distressed at their own feelings. This is in part due to the emotional rebound phenomenon of post-acute withdrawal—sort of like how pain goes up for a while when stopping a regularly used pain medication. Moreover, people have generally suffered emotionally during their active addiction years and are naturally hoping that they will not have any more significant emotional vicissitudes once they get into recovery. They are then very disappointed and feel like failures when mood swings actually seem to intensify at some point after quitting drinking. This often happens after a few weeks of "*pink cloud,*" during which a person feels wonderful about successfully quitting drinking, relieved that after all their fears about quitting it wasn't so bad. Then they discover that they are faced with all the life problems they had before they quit—the mean partner, the lousy job, financial loses, the overweight, or whatever. Emotions flood. Welcome my friend, to normal living.

Then again, would you really want to be an emotional flatliner? Remember Carl Rodgers' crucial insight: We are in trouble when we deny to awareness significant emotional material. Lack of awareness of one's own feelings becomes especially dangerous when it can lead to relapse on alcohol. I had a client who pulled into a liquor store and got drunk prior to picking her husband up at the airport. Her husband's career frequently took him out of town. I asked this woman how she had been feeling when she left home for the airport. She immediately said, "Excited," explaining that she had not seen her husband for a week. I said, "Hmm! Didn't you tell me your husband was often critical and angry, and that you had not finished several things he expected you to get done before he got home?" She appeared stunned for a moment. Then her eyes opened wide and she exclaimed, "You are right [although I had not told her *what* she was feeling]! I wasn't excited, I was scared!" This is alexithymia (described in chapter 6) at work, and a huge cause of relapse. If she had realized her fear earlier in the week, she may not have imbibed. She may have had a chance to explore the basis of her fear, realize the iniquitous relationship she had with her husband, and gotten some help.

In addition to being unaware of their true feelings, recovering alcoholics seem to be terribly afraid of them as well. It is important to reverse this *affectaphobia* because the feelings will come, indeed at times in torrents, and *you need them*. Do not try to run from or suppress your feelings. Welcome them. Go to them. Mother Nature has evolved emotions in all mammals for very good reasons. Imagine a child born with a faulty nervous system such that she or he cannot feel pain. This actually happens in something like 1 in 50 million births. Such children have to wear pads and helmets until they are old enough to not jab themselves with things or jump off walls. The ability to feel physical pain has evolved simply to keep us from damaging our bodies by jumping off cliffs or putting our hands in fire, etc. The same is true of painful emotions. They have evolved to direct and protect our emotional wellbeing. The rabbit sees the shadow of the hawk, feels fear, and scoots under a bush. Negative emotions have survival value. Negative feelings are the mental equivalent of pain receptors. *Emotions, like fear or depression, are Mother Nature's signaling systems, telling us when we may be in harm's way and need to move, or that we are not getting our needs met and may need to make some changes in our lives.*

Without feelings, we would never know how to redirect and live our lives. I recall a client who worked at a local pulp mill. At his assessment, as we hunted for costs associated with his drinking, we at first passed too quickly over the life area of work. He had said, "No I've never been late for or missed work due to my drinking—18 years on the job without a problem." Later, I thought, "Wait a minute; some costs come more from what does not happen in one's life rather than from what does." So I said to the fellow, "Didn't you tell me that you hated your job?" He responded, "Oh yeah! I sit under a dripping conveyor belt in a raincoat, turning a valve in the dark for eight hours per shift; but then I just go home, drink my six-pack, and forget about it." Thus medicated, he was unable to experience depression sharply enough to act on it. Once he quit drinking, he became acutely aware of his feelings about his self-sacrificing job, went out to the local technical college, retooled as an electrician, and made a much-needed career change.

What to Do

Learning to listen to your feelings is essential for recovery. Start by reminding yourself to regularly check and identify your emotional status. This is the ancient peaceful meditation practice referred to as *mindful meditation*. This is the practice of simply *noticing* your feelings *without judging* them. It is best if you can identify *core* rather than superficial feelings, but accept whatever comes. If you are anything like most people, this may take some practice. It is a good idea to keep a three-by-five card with you to track your feelings every hour (set your watch to beep hourly to remind yourself) or at least as frequently as possible. Try this for several days or a week or two. Use the feelings list below, and see if you can add some of your own.

Common Feelings List

Abandoned	Detached	Impatient	Rejected
Adamant	Determined	Indifferent	Relaxed
Admiration	Devastated	Insecure	Resentful
Amused	Dissatisfied	Insulted	Respectful
Anguish	Disappointed	Interested	Restless
Annoyed	Discounted	Irritated	Romantic
Anticipatory	Discouraged	Itchy	Sad
Anxious	Disgusted	Jealous	Satisfied
Apathetic	Doubtful	Jittery	Scared

Apprehensive	Dumb	Joyful	Secure
Ashamed	Edgy	Jumpy	Sexual
Asinine	Euphoric	Lonely	Shame
Astonished	Elated	Lost	Shy
Beat	Enraged	Loving	Sorrowful
Belittled	Embarrassed	Mad	Strong
Berated	Empathic	Nervous	Stubborn
Bold	Energetic	Oppositional	Sullen
Bothered	Enthusiastic	Oppressed	Surprised
Bored	Euphoric	Optimistic	Sympathetic
Brilliant	Excited	Overwhelmed	Thrilled
Broken	Fantastic	Painful	Timid
Burned out	Fearful	Panicky	Tired
Callous	Friendly	Peaceful	Torn
Cautious	Frightened	Perplexed	Traumatized
Cheerful	Frustrated	Pity	Uneasy
Cold	Glad	Pitiful	Unhappy
Confident	Grateful	Playful	Upset
Confused	Grief stricken	Pleased	Warm
Cool	Grouchy	Proud	Weak

Curious	Guilty	Put-down	Weird
Defeated	Happy	Puzzled	Wired
Delighted	Humble	Rage	Worried
Depressed	Humiliated	Ragged	Worthless
Desperate	Hurt	Rapturous	Wounded

Strategy Number Two: Learn to change how you feel by changing how you think

Understanding that thoughts, far more commonly than situations or faulty brain chemistry, drive feelings, and that irrational thoughts produce our excessively negative feelings, gives us an edge for regaining healthy emotional management in recovery. Looking again to the people who have spent their professional careers studying emotional management, we find what is called cognitive/behavior therapy (Beck et al., 1979; Seligman, 1991; Ellis & Harper, 1975, 1994; Meichenbaum, 1977; Burns, 1990; Yapko, 1998). Abundant research shows that cognitive/behavior therapy is a very effective approach for understanding and managing emotions. I feel that it is the best approach for most people and most emotional problems. Few treatment programs really teach this, even though the sizable majority of relapses are related to compromised emotional management.

Albert Ellis advocated use of an A-B-C worksheet as a powerful way to understand where our moods come from and how to change them at our discretion. Other cognitive behaviorists have similar work sheets for helping us identify and dispute our thinking errors (Burns, 1990; Seligman, 1991). Here is a modified A-B-C worksheet and how to use it.

ABC Worksheet

A Activating event	B Beliefs	C Consequence Emotionally
Note the activating event or situation that you are upsetting yourself about (e.g., being rejected, criticized, or failing).	List your self-talk. What are you saying to yourself about the situation?	What self-defeating feelings are you experiencing?
	D: Check for cognitive distortions and _Dispute_, challenge, attack refute each of the above statements one at a time as follows: - Is there any rational support for this idea? - Does any evidence exist for the truth of the idea? - What evidence exists for the falseness of the idea? - What is the worst thing that could happen to me? - What good things might occur?	Based on more rational thoughts how do you feel now? Disappointed perhaps, but not seriously distressed. Maybe pretty good.

Here is how to use the worksheet:

1. Dr. Ellis recommends starting with column *C,* Emotional Consequence, on the far right of the sheet. Simply jot down the feeling or feelings with which you are struggling. Use the Common Feelings List above if that helps.

2. Identify the situation related to your negative feelings. Briefly describe the situation in column *A* Activating Event—what you think is causing your negative feelings. This part is usually easy. Here are some examples. The underlined parts of the following statements are the *activating events*:

    *   I feel angry learning that the room rate is higher than I was told.
    *   I lost my wallet, and then I got depressed.
    *   When I saw the bill, I got scared.
    *   When he was late getting home, I got worried.
    *   When she broke up with me, I felt crushed.

    Sometimes we do not recognize a specific situation associated with a mood. Although conditions such as low blood sugar or hormone shifts could be the culprit, it is most likely that the mood is related to a more global situation like not having a job, having an unsatisfying job, not having a mate, being with an unloving partner, etc.

3. Identify the thoughts that drive your feelings. Very carefully, in the center column labeled *B* Beliefs, try to identify your thoughts about the activating event. Literally, what do you hear yourself saying to yourself, in simple exclamatory sentences? Ask yourself what the activating situation *means* to you. These thoughts often happen so fast that we usually do not realize that we have them. Aaron Beck (Beck et al., 1979) calls them *automatic thoughts*. Therefore, it can take some practice to explore your beliefs about the situation. Take your time and write down, without initially judging, every thought you can think of related to the activating event.

4. In the lower center column (*D,* for Disputation), check all of the beliefs you have written down in column *B* for their rationality, and

dispute them. You are looking for exaggerations, awfullizing, catastrophizing, personal put-downs, childish demands with words like "should" or "should not," "must" or "must not," or "ought." Beyond identification of your irrational beliefs, emotional relief will come with your ability to successfully *dispute* them. All the scholars I have mentioned agree that *effective disputation* of your irrational beliefs is the essential component in the ability to change how you feel. Challenge each of your beliefs for rationality with questions like, "What evidence exists to support the belief? What evidence militates against the belief?"

Doctors Beck, Ellis, and Burns, have identified very useful lists of common thinking errors. Call them automatic thoughts, irrational beliefs, or cognitive distortions, they all cause disproportionate emotional reactions. Here are some that I find important for emotional recovery from alcohol dependence:

Error: Believing that you must produce or perform perfectly at everything you attempt in order to like yourself and be happy.

Truth: This belief is patently wrong. Performing perfectly at everything is humanly impossible, and your goodness of person is inherently yours and not contingent on external productivity or performance.

Error: If people treat me unfairly my only possible emotional response is to be totally distraught.

Truth: Actually you have a choice to try to correct unfair treatment from others or walk away from it. Whether you are terribly upset is up to you and you alone. Thinking otherwise becomes a convenient excuse to drink.

Error: If anything goes wrong with my plans and wishes, my only option is to drink.

Truth: Frustrated plans are a normal part of living. Many folks early in recovery are greatly disappointed to discover this and quickly realize how alcohol has been their chief coping mechanism. All you need to do is live through a few disappointments without drinking and you will come to realize that they will not kill you, and that every disappointment opens a host of new opportunities.

Error: If there is anything in the future that *could* go wrong I must dwell on it because it is so *likely* to happen.

Truth: Just because something is possible does not mean it is imminent or that you have to ruminate endlessly about it. People worry desperately about things that could happen with tests, grades, jobs, relationships, diseases, earthquakes and tsunamis, when the most dangerous thing they will ever do is drive from home from the mall.

Related thinking errors include taking things too personally, thinking in black and white, over-generalizing, exaggerating negatives, and minimizing positives. I encourage you to read David Burns' checklist of common cognitive distortions published in *The Feeling Good Handbook.* (Burns, 1989).

As you analyze your beliefs in column *B*, also look for what Albert Ellis called irrational "core beliefs." Again, these are different long held erroneous understandings that each of us hold about ourselves and our accomplishments [or lack of] in the world in relation to everyone else. These beliefs often lurk just under the surface of our conscious awareness and cause excessive emotional responding beyond the pale of not only what the various disappointments of daily living call for, but color all of our choices, relationships, and moods. For example, with feelings of inadequacy as a teenager, I believed that I had to be completely successful at everything I did in order to consider myself a worthwhile human being—successful in sports, academics, with girls, etc. When at 18 years of age I read the second item on Dr. Ellis's list of 11 common irrational beliefs, I was instantly relieved of this enormous emotional burden. The rational truth is, of course, that the goodness and worth of a person is not contingent on succeeding at anything. You don't have to be good at a damn thing in order to consider yourself a worthwhile human being.

Dr. Ellis's list of irrational core beliefs (Ellis & Harper, 1975) includes believing that one is not worthwhile as a person if not loved and approved by other people, the belief that making mistakes is terrible, and that one cannot control his or her emotions.

If you do the worksheet several times, you will get the hang of it and begin to train your mind to more regularly identify and distinguish irrational from rational beliefs. Don't worry; you will always have both positive and negative emotions. In fact, as I have said, you would not want to be without negative emotions. This cognitive self-therapy is only about reducing emotional *overage*—to not feel worse or for a longer time than the situation really calls for.

Strategy Number Three: The faster-than-a-martini mood adjuster

Once the A-B-C model is understood, here is a really quick and simple but powerful way to tone down emotional overage. When a potentially aversive thing happens, mentally do two ratings. First, rate how bad you feel on a 10-point scale. Then make a second rating on the same scale, this time with the question: *How bad is it really?* This generally brings the emotion down to something more realistic and proportionate to the situation, whatever it may be.

Strategy Number Four: Self-validation

Identify your negative schema, change your maladaptive coping patterns, and change how you feel. Referring back to the phases of recovery (Chapter 3), we see that following the stabilization phase comes the critical phase of emotional recovery. By using strategies like mindful acceptance of one's emotions and cognitive self-therapy, after a few months most people in recovery can get to be very good at managing the emotional ups and downs of day-to-day living—actually, better than many people who never had a substance use problem. There is certainly something about challenges in life that make us more intelligent and aware. But what about our deeper, often subconsciously held, negative core beliefs or schema? And what about the subsequent coping strategies of avoidance, overserving, and overcompensating that have dogged us across the decades of our lives? Here different strategies can be helpful.

If, for example, you feel that you may suffer from a deeply held perception that you are not as inherently good as other people, I recommend that you talk with a professional counselor. Even the most ardent individualists, high in self-efficacy and with internal locus of control, have few reservations about getting help when they want it. They feel entitled to it. They will see the best doctors, lawyers, or therapists they can find, confident that they are capable of weighing information for themselves and that they would never allow anyone to control them or their choices. I recommend seeing qualified professionals such as licensed psychologists or master's-level therapists for help with these deeper issues. I trust you will question this straight-to-the-shoulder advice from me because of the fact that I myself am a psychologist. Nevertheless, I recommend that you seek professional counseling for the deeper issues of your life because it is so difficult to independently understand what lies in our subconscious minds. Recall again your Psych 101 class and the concept of defense mechanisms of the ego. Simply put, we are often too wrapped up in our own mental defenses, such as minimization, suppression, denial, and rationalization, well honed over many years, to be able to independently understand why we feel the way we feel in different life situations.

Nevertheless, here is what you can try on your own. In recent years, I have been excited about the contemporary therapy approach of Dr. Jeffrey Young and his colleagues. Referred to as *schema therapy*, it is, I feel, the furthest advancement in psychotherapy to date. It builds on psychodynamic, humanistic, and cognitive/behavioral concepts, providing a way of getting at deeply held erroneous self-perceptions and changing them. To do this really well, a couple of years of therapy with a schema therapist are recommended. However, it is entirely possible to gain this type of self-knowledge on your own. Dr. Young, in fact, has written an excellent self-help book on the topic called *Reinventing your life: The breakthrough program to end negative behavior ... and feel great again* (Young & Klosko, 1994). The experience can be profoundly liberating—in many cases the secret gift in recovery.

Central to emotional recovery is the work on one's self-acceptance. I have found over many years working with thousands of people with alcohol use problems, that most people struggle with this challenge. Emotional challenges in childhood seem to underlie most alcohol abuse/addiction problems. Again, it is not so much what does or does not happen to us in childhood that counts but how the experiences weigh-in on our self-perceptions, e.g., Dad hits me therefore *I am bad inside*; Mom is gone a lot, therefore *I am unimportant*; etc. As therapists, scholars, and researchers take thousands of life histories, we realize that most people's mood, anxiety, relationship, and substance use problems all come from this same source. When I work with people, I completely accept whatever happened or did not happen in their childhoods and acknowledge that neither they nor I can, or necessarily should, change those facts. All I want to do is help them rule out of the equation irrational self-blame. That part causes emotional overage. That part is wrong and unfair, and overcoming it is emotionally liberating.

At the height of its empire, it was said that all roads led to Rome. The "Rome" of human emotional misery has been referred to as the *error in the locus of fault and blame*. Based on the way we are treated, we can come out of childhood with the abiding misperception that fault and/or blame reside within us. This is the heart of the perceptual error. In truth, the fault was outside us. It typically resides in the behaviors of parents or others who, in some cases with the best of intentions, failed to facilitate our gaining the most important thing in childhood—a positive identity.

The first task for recovery from this involves an honest and brave searching for and identifying one's negative schema. It is about answering the question, What negative self-perceptions from childhood might I have brought into my adult life without realizing it? The second part of the approach is about coming to realize that our negative self-perceptions were in fact errors. We need to come to the clearest insight we can get that our real selves were in fact both innocent and good. After that, schema therapy involves identifying the coping strategies we developed over the years that have become self-defeating and working to change them.

Obviously, this can be a complicated process, but not necessarily. I have seen people gain tremendous insights and make lasting positive changes in their self-perceptions and behaviors virtually overnight. However, a therapist is still a good idea, partly because people are often afraid to revisit their pasts, fearing what they might find. As mentioned above, they generally seem to fear that they will only rediscover their perceived faults, defectiveness, and where they went wrong by their own inherent badness. Of course, this is never the case. What they discover is their innocence and goodness.

Fearing that this emotionally challenging work could trigger relapse, substance abuse counselors generally advise putting it off until one has become well stabilized and supported in an abstinent lifestyle. However, as I have said, for many people this deeper self-work cannot wait—

without it they will not achieve stabilization and will continue to relapse. For achieving recovery from alcohol dependence, I have organized the following three-phase process you can practice on your own. I refer to this as the practice of *self-validation*.

Phase One: Recognition of emotional overage

Learn to recognize when you are in emotional overage. As you go through your days and nights, try to be mindful of your feelings. Whenever you catch yourself with distressing emotions like fear, anxiety, depression, or jealousy, for any reason, ask yourself, "Could I be experiencing emotional overage?" Again, emotional overage (E/O) is whenever our feelings are disproportionate to the situation we are experiencing. Of course, this is not always easy to identify.

Sadly, many people seem to live their entire lives without ever realizing when they are emotionally overreacting. Sometimes when I suggest to clients that they try this self-validation exercise, they return after a week and report that they forgot or never got around to it. They say they were too busy being distressed about this or that situation. They got so totally caught up in their emotional struggles that they were unable to stop and think, "Ah! I am experiencing emotions right now," let alone, "Could I be in emotional overage?" Thus, I am asking you do something that you may be quite unfamiliar with. However, as the well known adage goes: *It is a definition of insanity to continue to do the same thing and expect different results.*

Be aware that your pattern of emotional responding has been shaped over many, many years. When I was in the 8th grade, I played a round of golf to see if I could become a member of our junior high school golf club. I had not played much golf at all before that, so I did not make the cut score. Well, I continued to play a little, but without instruction, so I grooved in a bad swing, resulting in decades of playing with what is called a *slice*. My point is that only after committing to many hours at the driving range in my 40s was I able to groove-in a better swing and successfully iron out the slice. What I am suggesting to you, in no uncertain terms, is that if you want to correct negative core beliefs and liberate yourself from the tyranny of self-defeating behavior patterns, you are going to have to literally do things differently, and you are going to need to practice.

If you practice mindfulness and tracking feelings as described in strategy number one above, you may be well on your way to developing the ability to recognize when you are in E/O. Most people report an internal debate process as this evolves, something like, "Alright, so Aunt Lucy said *that* about me. That really does upset me, but should I be *this* upset? Maybe it really *is* that bad ... or is it? Am I overreacting?" If you begin to experience this sort of internal dialogue, this is great. If you are doing this, you are on the right track. In some instances, it is quite clear when we are in E/O, but in situations where you are not sure, I recommend that you simply take a guess that you possibly are.

Assuming in your own mind that you are in E/O sets up a good experiment by giving you a chance to complete the rest of the exercise. Now, keeping in mind the power of negative emotions for positive change, welcome the E/O you have recognized by saying something like, "Ah! There you are again, my old friend emotional overage [or specify a feeling or a behavior pattern such as anger, anxiety, sorrow, or self-deprecation], reminding me to validate myself. Thank you for showing up." With the recognition that you are in emotional overage, you can move to the next phase.

Phase Two: Discover the source of your E/O

Remember, the intensity and duration of any emotional distress, on any hypothetical scale, that is beyond the pale of what is directly proportionate to the situation, is not caused by the situation. The situation has merely retriggered an emotional response pattern unfortunately learned, probably in your childhood. For the second phase of the self-validation exercise, cast your mind back to any time in your childhood that you may have had the same or similar feelings. Although the situations, people, and places may be very different, ask yourself, "When have I felt this way before?"

If nothing clearly comes to mind, do not worry. Mother Nature wants the young to survive. In childhood we have a built-in capacity to shut out, ignore, and otherwise suppress unpleasant experiences; her parents are fighting in the living room, but the little girl is quietly absorbed with activities in her room. However, what we *suppress* in childhood often becomes *repressed* in adulthood, such that we can no longer remember some things even if we want to. I have always found a correlation between the extent of emotionally challenging events in childhood and the extent to which a person can recall childhood events in general. In some cases, whole blocks of time, months and years, are apparently lost to this phenomenon. Not being able to remember much about childhood is often a red flag that some level of abuse or neglect occurred. Fortunately, I have also found that for the purposes of this self-validation exercise, one need not recall very many specific emotional experiences in childhood. In fact, any recollection generally will do. So if you do not come up with a childhood moment specific to your current emotion, that is just fine. I suggest merely recalling *any* time in childhood when you were in some way less than content. Again, all roads lead to Rome, so any memory you pick can get you there—an understanding of your childhood schema or core beliefs.

Try to focus on a single episode in childhood that reminds you, at least to some extent, of your present E/O experience. Visualize the moment as clearly as you can. Where were you? Who else was there and in some way involved? Now imagine you have taken a time machine back to that moment and place. When you step out, you approach the child that you were, wherever you imagine him or her to be, e.g., in your bedroom, on the back steps, walking home from school. The point of this is to temporarily get out of your adult rational mind, because you want to understand how you felt and what you thought back then. Now, in the safety of your imagination, tell the child that you are his or her future adult come to visit for a few minutes. Ask the child, "You look unhappy; what's wrong?" What does the child say is happening? Can she or he describe the circumstances of her or his unhappiness? You might help by saying, "Why did your [mom, dad, sibling, teacher] say [or do] that to you?" Or "Where are your parents?" However the child responds, follow up with this tough question, "Well, other children's parents don't do that. They love their little boys and girls. What's wrong with you?" Usually at this point, people will imagine their child part responding with statements such as, "I'm bad, I guess," or "I'm not good enough," or "I'm not important." Perhaps you might respond with, "You mean like fruit on a tree, you're the one that is rotten inside?" What does your child part say to this? Does he or she say, "Yeah, that's how I am"?

Phase Three: Self-revalidation

If you did not hear a self-disparaging response from your imagined child, perhaps you actually had a healthy self-perception in childhood, which would be wonderful, and this deeper emotional recovery work is not necessary for you. However, if a parent has treated a child badly, it is very unlikely that the child will respond to your tough question with, "No, I do not perceive anything inherently wrong with me. Actually, I hold myself in high regard. I'm just fine. My parents, however, have ongoing struggles with deep-seated feelings of inadequacy and unfortunately overcompensate by treating us children inappropriately." Children cannot reason like that, or speak that way. In childhood we are very egocentric, and parents are like God to us, so we assume anything wrong—parents' complaints, feelings, criticisms, unavailability—is somehow connected to, or because of, some shortcoming within ourselves.

More likely, to your tough question, you heard the origins of a negative self-perception as suggested in Phase Two. Perhaps you heard something to the effect, "I guess I'm not good enough." Or, "I'm bad inside." If so, did you, as an adult, buy in? As you listened, did you believe the child was, in fact, defective? What then would you say before you left? "Gee, that's too bad kid, you'll just have to try to deal with it"? More likely, when you imagine hearing the child saying, "I guess I am no good," you would think, "Oh no, this child is getting the wrong idea about [himself or herself]." This is the seminal insight, the realization of your own innocence and goodness, the realization that based on the way you were treated, through no fault of your own, you have belabored all of your life under *false* negative self-perceptions. Now imagine what you would say to the child before you left. I hope you would say something like, "Hey there, don't start believing that. There is no badness in you. If there is any badness, it is outside of you, not in you. You are made of all the right stuff." This, of course, would be the truth.

But, as it was, you may have gotten some negatives in your self-perception. Common ones include:

- Schema of defectiveness
- Schema of mistrust of others
- Schema of failure
- Schema of unrelenting standards

Schema therapists have identified many others (Young, Klosko & Weishaar, 2003).

Now, we have a couple of saving graces. First, the negative perceptions are errors; remember the maternity ward bassinet babies—all innocent. Also, if you had had a kindly aunt or uncle when you were a child who talked with you about your perceptions once per week, reassuring you of your actual innocence and goodness, you probably would not be experiencing E/O in your adult life. The second saving grace is that although no one was there for you then, you are now a wise adult and can, if you try, reassure and revalidate your child part.

After you recognize, even welcome, emotional overage, and when you can visualize your child-self with the insight of your innocence and goodness, then you can revalidate yourself by saying something like the following: "I was a good kid, as valid and anyone. There was no fault or badness in me. I was doing the best anyone could under adverse circumstances." Then zoom yourself back to the present, saying things like, "And I am doing the best I can now. I am even entitled to expect other people to meet some of my needs. I do not have to be responsible for everyone else's feelings, and I do not have to be perfect. I can make mistakes and still accept myself as a worthwhile human being. I can enjoy myself and my life."

I hope you can appreciate these concepts. Unless they are abundantly clear, I again recommend that you see a private psychologist for a better understanding of how the concepts may apply in your life and to ensure that you can benefit from them. Here is the three-phase self-validation exercise, in an easy-to-follow outline.

Phase 1.   Recognize, even welcome, emotional overage when it occurs.

Phase 2.   Cast your mind back and visualize your child part until you realize your own innocence and goodness.

Phase 3.   Come back to the present with revalidating self-statements.

Feel free to adapt this exercise in any way that it works better for you—most people do.

Now, remember the golf swing repair metaphor. You will likely need to practice self-validation repeatedly. Without practice, the old swing comes back. Sometimes I imagine that I invent a sort of MRI machine for the self, a device that would allow me to image what a person is made of. I could advertise this and people would come from all over. I imagine I could charge a lot of money for this unique self-imaging service. A person would come in and have a seat, and I would say, "What brings you in?" The person would say, "Well, I heard you have this imaging device, and I have always wondered what I am actually made of." I would say, "I see. What have you thought you are made of?" The person would respond, "Well, I've always thought I must be filled with dirt, or lead, or something like that." Then, quickly, I would swing out the machine and trip the shutter. The person would immediately gasp and clutch the arms of his or her chair, but then I would say, "Oh wow! Look at this. You're made of pure white light [or solid gold], the best stuff, all the way through." The client would look at the image, let out his or her breath, and exclaim, "Oh ... my ... God!" As when Sally Field's character first discovered that Mrs. Doubtfire was actually her ex-husband, the person would sputter, "You mean ... how could ... after all this time ... if I'd only known," etc.

The person would go home elated, like the prisoner proved innocent after 20 years in prison, like a poor person winning the big lottery, like being told you have no trace of a disease you were misdiagnosed with years ago. But then, like the prisoner, the lottery winner, and the patient, after years of imprisonment, poverty, and fear, it would be very hard to overcome the old habit of negative perceptions and behaviors. After a week, my clients would return, depressed again, saying that nobody treated them any differently, and they soon found themselves resuming the same old self-defeating patterns. To such a client I would then say, "Oh, I guess I forgot to give you this," and hand them a picture of their pure real selves. "Here, take this with you, and keep it close. Pull it out to remind yourself of your true goodness every time you are in emotional overage or are otherwise feeling bad or mistreated."

We do not have such an imaging device, but the three-phase self-revalidation exercise is a close approximation. Every time you go through this exercise, you can at least feel a little better than before you started. You may have the sensation of pulling yourself up on little islands of well-being amid your swims in turbulent emotional seas. If you practice enough, these islands can become continents. Then you will have arrived. This is all we want—bigger islands of well-being. A little bit of swimming in the chop is an expectable part of normal life.

This is the hope of the Transactional Analysis (T.A.) approach that came out of the therapy renaissance of the 1960s, with books like *Games People Play* (Berne, 1967), *I'm OK—You're OK* (Harris, 1969), and *Scripts People Live* (Steiner, 1974). I have suggested that we are like computers, with most of our emotional problems coming from bad programming, not hard drive flaws, and what we need is to rewrite our programs. T.A. espoused this concept before anyone had even conceived of personal computers. Their metaphor was more Shakespearean: "All the world's a stage, and all the men and women merely players ..." From the T.A. perspective, we are all handed *scripts* in childhood that we have little if any control over, and we get stuck with having to act out our parts, like it or not. Their prescription is to learn to rewrite your scripts.

In the third phase of self-revalidation, it is helpful to use an actual photograph. Find a picture of yourself in childhood—one perhaps that suggests a hopeful, if troubled, innocent child. Your challenge is to adopt this child, your real self, and promise never to let him or her down again. Keep the picture with you for several weeks and look at it several times per day, saying, "I was wrong about you in childhood, I am sorry I ever split you off. I will take care of you now." In all seriousness, who else is really going to do this? You are not to blame for negative and erroneous core self-perceptions, but only you can be responsible for overcoming them. You do not have to be a psychologist to do this. You do not have to know exactly what to say, or to get it exactly right. You only need to try.

Strategy Number Five: Changing maladaptive coping patterns

Recall now our discussion of maladaptive coping strategies in the preceding section on *Where Feelings Come From*. In Dr. Jeffrey Young's conceptualization, these are the basic emotional survival strategies we naturally develop in childhood to cope with our negative schema. It is very important to accept yourself for having adapted these strategies in the first place—they probably were an important service to you initially, such as to avoid being hit or yelled at, to avoid feeling like a failure, or simply to be able to join in with others despite feeling inadequate. They only become maladaptive across time. Understanding our own maladaptive coping strategies allows us to interrupt and change them. Why should we bother to do this? Because in the long run, they are too self-sacrificing. Thus, begin by looking for examples of maladaptive coping behaviors in your daily life. Here is a discussion of some common maladaptive coping strategies:

Avoidance

Avoidance is not all bad. If done assertively (see Chapter 13, Relationships Recovery), it is often very useful. The trick is to control it, rather than allow it to control you. If you have a very social job like mine, artfully avoiding too much socializing in your free time is probably healthy. We are all entitled to some alone time. However, do you persistently avoid, hide from, and otherwise shy away from making and maintaining social relationships? Take an inventory of different periods of your life and of the friendships, family relationships, and co-worker relationships you have had. How much of a participant have you really been? And what about your work, career, or occupation? Have you tended to drop back or step forward? What about your living place, and what about leisure and recreational pursuits? If you find that indeed you are an *avoider,* perhaps it is time to think about where this came from, consider what you have been missing, and begin working on the self-validation exercise in the preceding section. Then you can begin challenging yourself as per the life areas template. Review the template for each life area, now asking the question, "Have I been *avoiding* in this area?" Then, do the needs assessment for whichever life areas you like. Set goals and make plans for your real self that are the antithesis of avoidance—goals and plans that get you to pursue social connections, leisure activities, and/or occupational opportunities.

Surrendering and Serving

This is the "If I carry your lunch pail, can I hang out with you?" lifestyle. You are not avoiding at all, but you are feeling too responsible for others in your life and are overserving, with the erroneous assumption that you are defective, undeserving, or otherwise a second-class citizen. Yes, human societies depend on most of us having enough compassion to be interested in, and helpful to, others. Amid an array of activities, doing something for others has the highest correlation with happiness. And yet, if overdone, it can become tragically self-sacrificing, and paradoxically it actually becomes a disservice to those we think we are serving—it rewards them for not being healthily responsible for themselves.

For a week or so, notice your social interactions. How much do you offer and do for others versus how much do others offer and do for you? I suggest that you then try the following:

- Allow yourself to experiment with asking others to do some things for you
- Learn about and practice assertiveness (see Chapter 13)
- Practice setting boundaries with people (see Chapter 13)

When you avoid the impulse to please and wind up feeling that you were not nice enough to someone, experiment with appreciating that the world does not actually end as a result, and pat yourself on the back. The more strange patting yourself on the back feels, the more you must have missed it in childhood, and all the more you need to practice.

Overcompensating

People overcompensate as a defense against core feelings of defectiveness, failure, and/or other negative schema. In the extreme, this can be considered *reaction formation*. Consider a girl who in church is told that even to think of sex is a sin. She believes in God, and knows that she has already been experiencing heavy petting with her boyfriend. She is mortified and concludes she is an evil sinner, damned to purgatory for eternity. To offset this mental anguish, she strives to become the antithesis of what she thinks she is. She devotes herself to Christ and becomes a nun who is stridently intolerant of anything but the most pious behavior among all of her parishioners and students, thus escaping or mitigating her dreadful feelings of shame.

Overcompensation in general may seem less extreme than reaction formation, but it is nonetheless profound in how it can affect our lives. This is the student so driven to get straight A's that he comes apart emotionally and quits school when a teacher gives him a B. It is the star high school athlete who locks herself in her bedroom for a week, refusing to come out for meals, because she let a goal get by her in a soccer championship, or fell during her tumbling routine at the gymnastics competition. Consider how you may have overcompensated in your own life. *Some* striving in life is a good thing, but overcompensation is *mis-er-a-ble!*

Another, perhaps more desperate form of overcompensation as a maladaptive coping strategy is to get too tough in relation to other people. It is most tempting to blame and shame oneself here, but it really is not fair. If you developed a tough exterior in childhood, even to the point of becoming a bully, did you ever consider that maybe you needed to, or that that was what you were taught to do? You probably need to forgive yourself. And, certainly, we all need a tough side in this world, to not be abused or taken advantage of. The challenge in adult life is finding the right balance. It is not a good thing to be without a tough side, but we must not let it control us. I encourage people who have a tough-guy or tough-woman coping strategy to simply learn to put it farther back on their shoulders, and rest assured that it is there if they really need it. If this applies to you, practice letting others relate to your gentler, perhaps more vulnerable side. Generally, this actually endears people to us and brings greater, not less, respect. In cases where it does not, realize that no one can really hurt you now; you are all grown up and are no longer dependent on anyone. You are all grown up, and you always have your hard-earned tough side if you really need it. Just remember, anybody can stand up and fight. That is not so hard. What is more challenging and takes real courage is to share of ourselves openly and honestly, and when necessary, to walk away from a fight.

The way out of an overcompensation maladaptive coping strategy is first to recognize that you do this—that it applies to you. Consider all of your major endeavors across your life so far. Was the letter grade more important to you than the content of the class? Was winning more important than enjoyment of the sport? Now consider your present life. Again, look at the life areas template. For each area, question whether a current pursuit or future goal of yours is something you really enjoy, or is it about achievement for the sake of achievement? Is it for status or for what you imagine others think is cool or respectable, or do you simply like it for your own enjoyment? Consider the protagonist in Ayn Rand's *The Fountainhead* (1943). The architectural firm he worked for gave a big project to another employee. Our man so loved creating architecture that he asked the fellow who got the project if he could do the drafting for him without signing his name. So he did the work anonymously. Although the finished project was award winning, he didn't mind *not* getting the credit; he had had his fun and was *internally* satisfied. Could you do something like that? In any life area, what might you enjoy doing even if no one ever knew? I suggest you experiment with the idea.

Strategy Number Six: Building a positive inner voice

This strategy is an important advancement for recovering from the more deeply held erroneous negative self-perceptions that may continue to affect your mood and behaviors today. The term *inculcation* in psychology refers to the instillation of self-perception and is part of the process of how we each get our own personalities. When we are little, we do not have much of an understanding of who we are. Our parents repeatedly deliver both praising and disparaging statements, which eventually become imbedded in our own minds and become part of our own self-perceptions. In many ways, how we relate to ourselves and to others is a result of the unique mix of the personalities of each of our parents now forged into our own personalities. This is necessary for each of us to control our own behavior when we are grown up. In Schema Therapy, Dr. Young points out that, depending largely on how our parents treat us, we eventually acquire healthy and/or unhealthy internal parent voices that either help us or plague us all of our lives—unless we actively change these inner parent voices.

First, learn to identify different internal parent voices. Here are three major types adapted from the Schema Therapy approach.

The nurturing and valuing parent voice. This is necessary for parents to deliver because humans, perhaps much more than other mammals, have evolved a need for emotional nurturing in order to manage the complexities of adult human social interaction and all of the choices we will face. Building the child's self-esteem is the most important parent function. When parents frequently say prizing, positive things to their children, the children learn to prize themselves, usually for the rest of their lives. Parents are doing their part when they say things like, "You did that so well. That is so pretty. You are the best child a [mother or father] could have. I love you so much." To the child, this validates self-worth. Such children will emerge from childhood with the automatic ability to do this for themselves, with the inculcated healthy parent voices now part of their own personalities: "I look good. I did that well. I am a good person."

People who did not get consistent and believable nurturing and valuing from their parents tend to be unable to nurture and value themselves. Positive internal cognitions were not inculcated. Without this ability, people have a hard time motivating themselves and have a tendency to feel depressed.

If you feel that you did not get sufficient nurturing and valuing from your parents, take heart, you can definitely develop this ability for yourself. Try this: Make a list of things you appreciate or like about yourself. This can be difficult. For many people it is a lot easier to make a list of things they do not like about themselves. I encourage you to try. Think of little things such as perhaps merely the way morning light comes through the window, or the way your fingernails look. Include anything you do that you enjoy, certain relationships you may have, and anything you are grateful for—the color of your socks, the way you walk, or the way you listen to people. Work on your list at breakfast every morning. Change and add to the list across time. Now, importantly, read the list, in a meaningful, appreciative way, every morning. It appears that just doing this once per week significantly elevates most people's moods in just several weeks. The reason is that if you start the morning with positive thoughts, it tends to set the pattern for how you interpret everything for the rest of your day.

Also, as you go through your days, think about the concept of a healthy, valuing parent voice, and how you are entitled to this. Then simply practice doing it for yourself. At your workplace, with people, or alone just driving down the street, take a moment to say prizing things to yourself: "I deserve some happiness. I like myself. I love this weather. Life is good." Again, like my bad golf swing, practice, practice, practice is what straightens it out.

The reassuring parent voice.

> The best laid schemes o' mice an' men
> Gang aft a-gley
>
> From *To a Mouse,* by Robert Burns

This one is especially important. Here is why: In case you haven't noticed, many things in life do not work out. Indeed, the best laid plans of mice and men often do go awry. Things break, spill, or fall apart. This is normal. Spilled milk, missed appointments, rainy days, jobs gone sideways—all normal. What we need in childhood are parents who realize this and model healthy coping, with statements like, "That's okay, we all spill milk—I'll just get you another glass. It's only thunder. I'll hold you until it's over. It won't hurt you. You'll like school. The other children will like you. I know how you feel; at some point we all get a teacher we can't seem to relate to." This is healthy parental reassurance.

When I leave clients in the waiting room for more than several minutes, I feel guilty. When I bring them into my office, I apologize. To myself I say, "Alright Chris, you know you can do better than that. But, hey, nobody is perfect; I am still a good and reliable therapist overall and I will do better." I can do this because, many times, my parents offered such reassurances—when I dropped the fly ball, when the glass broke, and so forth. I was fortunate to have this reassurance ability inculcated into the healthy parent part of my own personality. Now, if I had had parents who were predominately critical in all spilt milk-type situations, things would be different. If I let a client wait too long, I might think, "Chris, you idiot. Whatever made you think you could be a psychologist? You'll never be any good at this." Of course, these *un*healthy parent voices would leave me feeling depressed.

One morning on my way to work, while stopped at a light, I noticed a car pulled over around the corner with a flat tire. I recognized the driver as a client of mine. As I pulled around, I thought I might stop and help the fellow, but he already had the jack out and was actually whistling a tune. He clearly had things under control. Not three weeks later, I saw another client, not far around the same corner, also with a flat. As I pulled around, this fellow was kicking the side of his car shouting obscenities. I cruised on by. When I later saw the first man in my office, I asked him how it was that he seemed so untroubled with his flat tire. He said, "I don't know, I guess I have always felt that I am a handy guy, so I just told myself that everybody gets flat tires and that I would be able to fix it just fine." Here was a man who, without realizing it, automatically had his father's voice in his head: "My, you hit that nail just right son. You're pretty good with your hands," or "That's alright; we all drop the ball sometimes." Now the second fellow had a different set of thoughts about his flat tire: "Why does everything bad always have to happen to me? I am such a damn loser. I'll never be able to fix this thing." When he told me of this, I could almost hear his father's voice: "Give me that damn hammer son. You're going to screw up. You'll never do anything right."

When the milk spills in your life, what sort of voices do you hear? Again, it is never too late. You can begin practicing this self-reassurance immediately because at least some things seem to go wrong in our lives every day. Here is how to begin to develop a healthy self-reassuring voice all on your own. Once again, be an anthropologist in a participant observation study of your own life. Get a small notebook and carry it with you every day, everywhere you go. Be astute, and record everything that disappoints you or goes wrong each day for a week. For each "went wrong" event, stop whatever self-berating you might catch yourself automatically doing, think of what a healthy parent might say, and jot down a set of reassuring self-statements. This exercise, like the healthy self-nurturing exercise, is likely to feel strange and uncomfortable at first. Just practice it for a while. Practice until it feels as right as rain. You deserve it!

The self-directing parent voice. Lest you think that the prizing and reassuring healthy parent voices license you to be a complete hedonist and shirk all responsibility and accountability, there is another important voice to consider. It is that inculcated parent voice of correction, discipline, sensitivity to others, and motivation. Mother Nature has evolved a healthy inclination in the young of all mammals to explore their environments and limits. Clearly, this has survival value, but also, if not monitored, can get us in serious trouble in a hurry. That is why we place stoppers in unused electrical outlets, fence off stairways, move breakables out of reach, etc., when we have toddlers in the house. When children get into things that are uncivil or potentially dangerous, we have to correct their misbehavior. They need direction and steerage. We also need to help children develop the motivation to engage in behaviors that they might not immediately want to do, like pick up their rooms, help with dishes, and do school work. There are two ways to do all of this directing and correcting. Let me give you an example: A parent briefly loses track of where her toddler is. Stepping into the laundry room she sees Kiddo playing in a pile of detergent he has managed to spill over. Now, the unhealthy parent demonstrates control by shouting, *"No!"* rushing in, hoisting the kid up by the arm and swatting on him on the behind, yelling, *"You're bad,"* and throwing him in the corner of his room, saying, *"Don't you dare move 'til I say so,"* and then going out slamming the door. Imagine what Kiddo gets inculcated into his own personality and coping style. He, or she, will become painfully self-critical. The healthy parent handles the situation a bit differently. Upon discovering Kiddo playing in the spilled laundry detergent, she realizes it was a lapse in her own responsibility. Her child is only doing some natural exploring. So she says in a concerned but soothing tone of voice, "Oh Honey! There you are. I was worried about you." She gets down on the floor. "This is soap. Yuk! You don't want to put this in your mouth. This is nice but we don't play in soap." She gently picks him up, saying, "I know. I'll show you where we can play." She then takes him into the family room, gets out a pile of blocks, and engages him in how to stack them up. Now what does Kiddo learn? That some places are not okay to play, everybody makes mistakes, and if one thing doesn't work out, another thing will. The result will be self-motivation and the ability to direct oneself in healthy ways.

If you find that you have a hard time getting motivated about life's challenges and joys, if you are hard on yourself for things that do not work out, practice positive self-direction with statements like, "I need to get up and do this now. I can delay gratification as well as anyone. I will be glad I did."

Strategy Number Seven: Defeating the Three P's

I call this strategy the Three P's. It comes out of research on cognitive characteristics or thinking habits that distinguish depressed people from nondepressed people. Depression researcher Martin Seligman describes this in his book *Learned Optimism* (1991). The first P is the tendency to take things too *personally*. There are different styles of responding, for example, when a boss rejects a project someone has been working on all week. If your learned response is, "Damn, I'm no good at this. I am such a failure," you will feel more unhappy than the situation calls for. You are taking it too personally. If, on the other hand, your response is, "Oh well, the boss's judgment is lapsing," or, "Oh well nobody gets all their projects accepted," you will not feel as bad.

To overcome the habit of taking things too personally, realize that you were probably taught to do so from an early age through no fault of your own. So, from the start, don't take your habit of taking things too personally, too personally. Then, see if you can groove in another new swing. Learn to be mindful of any situations where you begin feeling that something that is not working out, especially with someone else, is due to some inherent flaw in you—situations where you catch yourself rushing to apologize, or automatically start demeaning yourself as a failure or loser. Then bring in the healthier, reassuring parent voice you have been working on. "I know it's not my fault. So-and-so is making a poor judgment. Well, it's a good thing I don't have to be responsible for his [or her] feelings. And hey, if it is my fault, I'll just apologize and be done with it; everybody makes mistakes."

The second P is the learned tendency to interpret most potentially aversive situations as *permanent*. When the boss rejects your project, or a co-worker bad-mouths you, or you lose on the tennis court, your tendency is to imagine this is how it will always be. "I'll never get it right. Things will never work the way I want," and, "This proves I will always fail." These are the mantras of people who assume something they are unhappy about is going to be permanent.

Gratefully, things change. My recommendation is that you become mindful of any tendency you may have to interpret potentially bad situations as permanent. Then learn to consider in each instance that things actually do change, through our own efforts or, as often, through the passage of time alone. The company person with the rejected project who says, "I'll never get my projects accepted, and the boss will never respect me," is going to feel depressed as a result. The person who says, "Well that's fine, not continuing with this project will allow me to get going next week on that winner of a project I've had on the back burner," is going to feel a lot better.

Even in situations that may actually be permanent, at least our attitudes about them can change, and surprisingly, often times things we think are bad actually prove to be a benefit in our lives in some way later on. I have always found a solace in what I learned long ago as the *Ancient Japanese Farmer's Tale*. Where the story comes from, I do not know. There may be many versions. This is only what I can recall.

Long ago, near a village in ancient Japan, there lived a very old farmer with his only son. One day the farmer's horse ran away. Villagers stopped by offering condolences: "Poor old man, we are sorry for you. Without your horse you will not be able to get your crops in and you will go hungry this winter." The old man thanked them for stopping by but told them to try not to worry: "We really do not know if this is such a bad thing. All we know is that my horse has run away." The villagers leave, saying goodbye and "That's good, keep your spirits up." The next day the horse returns with 20 wild horses following it. The old man's son manages to corral all of them. The villagers learn of this and return saying, "You were right old man. It was not a bad thing that your horse ran away, it was a good thing. Now you are rich with horses." The old man chuckles and says, "Okay, but again, we do not know whether this is a good thing. All we know is that I have 21 horses."

"Yes, well, we think you are pretty lucky," say the villagers, and they return to the village.

The next week, the farmer's only son breaks his leg trying to break-in all those horses. The villagers come out again, saying, "Old man, that is amazing. You were right again. It was a bad thing that you got all those horses. Now your son has a broken leg. You won't be able to get your crops in and you will go hungry after all." The old man, by this point a little annoyed with the villagers' attitudes, responds, "Look, you are doing it again. We do not know whether this is a bad thing or a good thing. All we know is that my son has a broken leg." The villagers say, "Okay, we think you're daft, but good luck anyway," and they return to the village.

The next week the military sweeps through the area, taking all able-bodied young men off to a distant war. After a while, the villagers return to visit the old farmer.

"Old man, you were right again. Because of his broken leg, your son was not taken. Now all of our sons are off to a war, while you still have yours." The old man looks off into the distance for a moment and then turns to the villagers.

"When will you ever learn to stop judging things before you can possibly know what will eventually transpire? What will be a good thing or bad thing is in the hands of divinity, time, happenstance, and myriad forces beyond our control."

This story is probably told in different settings and with additional vignettes on the theme. Clearly, it illustrates that not only do things change, but at least some things we think at first are bad can often turn out to be good. Learn to avoid taking things so permanently. Remember the *Japanese Farmer's Tale*, and teach yourself in all potentially aversive situations to ask this question early-on: What possible positives could eventually come out of this?

The third P is for *pervasively*. In this case, the person whose project is rejected does not leave his or her upset at the office. After taking it too personally and too permanently, he or she tends to drag through the weekend, continuing to ruminate about the perceived failure, unable to enjoy any other activities. The emotionally healthy person says, "Oh well, too bad for them." And that is the end of thinking about work again until Monday. He or she gets home for the weekend with, "Hi Honey. What do you want to do for dinner? I can't wait to get on that bike ride tomorrow."

We need to appreciate, in the first place, the reality that all mammals experience times of distress. Should we really expect not to? The difference between humans and other animals is that other animals are better able to compartmentalize and separate times of distress from times of peace. I see the deer blissfully resting in the afternoon sunshine in our backyard. They do not seem to be worried about anything. Then a dog barks and they are up and running. When humans got self-consciousness, we also got the woeful capacity to endlessly ruminate about all sorts of potentially negative events—even when they are not presently occurring. You know you are a human being when you have to wait for test results. Animals do not do this.

> I think I could turn and live with animals, they're so placid and self contain'd,
>
> I stand and look at them long and long.
>
> They do not sweat and whine about their condition,
>
> They do not lie awake in the dark and weep for their sins,
>
> They do not make me sick discussing their duty to God,
>
> Not one is dissatisfied, not one is demented with the mania of owning things,
>
> Not one kneels to another, nor to his kind that lived thousands of years ago,
>
> Not one is respectable or unhappy over the earth
>
> —Walt Whitman

Okay, so Walt was not entirely accurate in his observations, but his romanticized point is not missed. Our human ability to anticipate futures has had great survival value, but at the price of way too much unnecessary worry.

As with taking things too personally and permanently, if you tend to let emotional distress from one area of your life pervade into another, you were probably taught to do so. There may also be a learned gender difference in this tendency. Many different types of research studies over several decades find that women are more depressed than men. One reason may be that, unlike boys, girls are not taught to expect that they will have much control over the externals of their lives. When I was in elementary school in the 1950s, we boys were told to get ready to become the doctors, lawyers, business owners, and leaders of everything—get ready to run the world. Little girls were steered to home economics, in and of itself a very valuable endeavor, but that was it. This iniquitous situation was not much better in junior high school in the early 1960s. Boys were not allowed to take home economics, and I never saw a girl in a shop class or mechanical drawing class. Thus, as adults, in broad averages, women may have a greater tendency to have perceptions of powerlessness, hopelessness, and helplessness than men, and feel more depressed as a result. For the last three-plus decades, we have been trying to change this. Nevertheless, it remains a leading theory as to why women tend to be more depressed than men.

Also, women tend to *ruminate* more than men about negative situations. This rumination has a role in letting negative thoughts and their attendant negative moods pervade into areas of our lives in which they really have no business. On the golf course, I occasionally hear a fellow complain about something.

"They changed the project schedule at work again—man that really bummed me out." Another player says, "Hey, that's too bad, but you should work for our CEO, what an idiot." That is it—finished. The next words are something like, "great putt!" and it's on to the next hole. That was all that was needed or wanted—no ruminating, no more letting a negative situation in one area of life pervade into another. I think the Oprah Winfrey phenomenon is fantastic. It has been a great new consciousness raising venue for all of us. However, sometimes I wonder if there isn't a subtle reinforcement of rumination going on. At times, at least, I think the program demonstrates this, but, your call.

Of course the ability to reason has had huge survival value for human beings. But then our tendency to ruminate and let negative situations pervade into our ability to enjoy the positive situations of our lives is one of the leading causes of depression and anxiety. Many of my older clients recall a book called *Zorba the Greek* by Nikos Kazantzakis (1952), later made into a movie starring Antony Quinn. It is the story of an old guy on the Greek island of Crete who had lived through a lot of troubles. The locals loved him because of his unflagging optimism—he always got them dancing. On board a ship returning to Crete he meets a somewhat troubled young British writer who is going to Crete to reopen his father's abandoned mine—but really to find himself. They strike a deal for Zorba to help him reopen the mine, and at one point the young man turns to Zorba and says "Incidentally, you never told me, are you married?" Zorba replies "Am I not a man? And is a man not stupid? I'm a man, so I married. Wife, children, house, everything. The full catastrophe." He persistently encourages the young man to stop over-thinking—that we all have things we could ruminate about, but that we must nevertheless release ourselves to live life to the fullest without dwelling on the past or worrying about what will or will not work out. At the end of Anthony Quinn's career circa 2002, he was teaching acting in Hollywood. A reporter doing a story on him was pointing out how all the young actors adored him because he was so grandfatherly and wise. But then the reporter changed gears and said something like "By the way Mr. Quinn, I've done my homework on you. You've had many lovers, three failed marriages, and at least a dozen children not all of whom survived." Anthony, whom one might have thought would have been a bit thrown, didn't miss a beat. After 50 years he recalled his line. With a distant smile he said "Oh yes. I've had the full catastrophe of all of it." Subsequently, a psychologist got on to this and published a book called *Full Catastrophe Living* (Kabat-Zinn, 2009), the gist of which is, regarding life, what did you expect?

To me, the Zorba message is that beyond any reasonable modicum of personal and social responsibility, it is important to accept and let go of, rather than to endlessly ruminate about, all of the past, present and potential future negatives that are just natural parts of each of our lives. Consider the coyote crossing the vast prairie of its life. It walks up a canyon for three day only to discover it dead ends. Another day it is encounters a den of rattle snakes...another day it's stuck on an ice flow in a river. But then the next day it enjoys a grassy field in the sunshine, free of worries about the harsher realities of crossing the often rugged terrain of its life. Should we really expect human life to be magically different?

In order to offset your tendency to let negative emotions in one area of your life pervade into other areas of your life, try the following. I call this the *two column technique*. I sometimes imagine that each of our lives is like a sheet of paper with a line drawn down the center creating two columns. In your left column are all of your regrets, losses, perceived failings, and negative emotions. The truth is that the older we get the more items we each have listed on that side of the page. Such is life. In the right column, however, can be listed all of the good, or at least potentially good, things about your life—anything you have succeeded at or anything potentially enjoyable. We humans tend to believe that if we have anything at all in the left column, we therefore cannot possibly enjoy anything in the right column. Thus our emotions from the left column bleed across the line, pervading into the right column. This, of course, is utterly irrational and unnecessary. Remember my story about the three-legged dog romping blissful on the beach. In his left column was the fact that he was indeed missing a leg. He didn't care one bit. He was 100 percent happy in his right column, which, that day, was the sunny beach. In your own life try to clearly delineate what is in the left column versus what is in the right column. Then work at adding items to the right column and maintaining a very thick and impenetrable line down the center of the page effectively walling off the left column.

Remember the three P's. Try to develop internal radar that vigilantly scans for episodes of taking things too personally, permanently, and pervasively in your daily living. Then experiment with interrupting the habit. Apply a healthy parent voice of reassurance, and refocus on possibly positive outcomes. Then give yourself permission to compartmentalize your worries and enjoy what you are doing in the present.

Co-occurring Mental Health Problems—Dual Diagnosis

Avoid a classic error. Recall that alcohol dependence directly causes what would otherwise appear to be freestanding mental health problems. Just as habituation to pain medication lowers one's physical pain threshold, making every little pain unbearable, alcohol dependence lowers one's ability to cope emotionally. Emotional dysregulation (uncontrollable ups and downs) is an expected product of alcohol dependence. Therefore, it really is not fair to assume that just because the active alcoholic is clearly struggling with mood, anxiety, attentional, and behavioral problems, that he or she has an independent mental health problem. Often a colleague will phone to discuss a case with me. I will say "yes, indeed, it sounds like your client has an alcohol dependency." Then the caller will say, "Yes, that's what I thought." I then politely offer to see the client/patient, but the colleague will say, "Okay, thank you, I will make the referral, but first I've got to work him through his depression." This, unfortunately, is a mistake. It is a fundamental truism for treating co-occurring disorders that the addiction must be treated first. Otherwise, we are just spitting into a strong counterproductive wind. Myriad professionals have repeatedly learned the hard way that depression, anxiety, and other mental health problems will not respond to treatment while the client is actively substance dependent. So, while I am sure you have many very real symptoms of a mental health problem such as mood or anxiety problems, do not be too quick to assume that what you are experiencing is independent of alcohol dependence.

Research shows that large numbers of alcohol-dependent individuals meet psychiatric criteria for additional problems, from 47 percent of alcoholics in the population (Helzer and Pryzbeck, 1988) to as much as 77 percent of alcoholics in treatment (Hesselbrok et al., 1985). However, in most cases these other diagnoses are artifactual features associated with addiction. For example, research by Brown and Shucket (1988) found that while 42 percent of alcoholics studied met criteria for clinically significant depression, after only 3 weeks of abstinence fewer than 6 percent still did. It was also found that anxiety measure scores among alcoholics become significantly lower with abstinence, steadily declining across 3 months.

Dealing with the Real McCoy

When it comes to the possibility of an independent mental health problem, however, I really must encourage you to see a professional. Alcohol-dependent people with true co-occurring mental health problems have lower odds of alcohol dependence recovery. This is the field of *dual diagnosis*, also referred to as co-occurring disorders. It requires a clinician experienced in both mental health and chemical dependency to conduct the necessary differential diagnosis assessment accurately.

Assumed mental health problems tend to evaporate with sobriety for most people. However, for some, preexisting mental health problems are the driving force behind alcohol use in the first place. When these people quit drinking, their mental health problems may not resolve spontaneously. In some cases, they will actually worsen. That is, if a person had an anxiety, mood, or other mental health problem prior to finding a solace in alcohol, the symptoms may reemerge or increase with sobriety. This is called *decompensation*. This is why professional assessment is so important. If someone has a true co-occurring mental health problem, it will need attention and treatment, or at least careful monitoring, early in abstinence. Otherwise, the individual will be at elevated risk of relapse in the already daunting challenge of recovery. Below is a list of mental health disorders that commonly co-occur with alcohol use problems.

Mood disorders:

- Major depression (the down-and-out depression where normal life functioning becomes impossible)
- Bipolar (depression that may alternate with times of feeling absurdly up)
- Dysthymia (a low-grade but pervasive depression in which the person can function but is unhappy)
- Cyclothymia (mood swings but capable of basic functioning in most life areas)

Anxiety disorders:

- Panic (brief episodes of feeling terrified that one is going to die due to racing heart or losing control over breathing)
- Agoraphobia (becoming so afraid of panic that one isolates at home)
- Simple phobias (intense anxiety toward one or several things like heights, snakes, spiders, water)

- Generalized anxiety disorder (being overly worried about more than one thing most of the time)
- Acute or posttraumatic stress disorder (intense anxiety following traumatic experience)
- Obsessive/compulsive disorder (obsessions are any form of unwanted and troubling thoughts that a person has difficulty stopping. Compulsions are any irrational behaviors that one loses control over in the belief that they will keep something bad from happening)

Personality disorders:

- Antisocial (lacking compassion, often lawbreaking)
- Borderline (takes things too personally and rages at others or becomes depressed)
- Histrionic (drama queens and kings)
- Narcissistic (self-centered and grandiose)

Psychosis:

- Schizophrenia (a brain illness resulting is distorted reality)

This list is not at all exhaustive. Many other psychiatric disorders can be seen to co-occur with alcohol use problems.

How Dual-Diagnosis Assessment Is Done

Of the dozens of mental health disorders that may co-occur with alcohol dependence, mood and anxiety disorders are most commonly caused by the alcohol dependence itself, rather than the other way around, whereas schizophrenia, a serious brain disease, is usually primary when seen to co-occur with alcohol dependence. I have never seen a case of an alcohol use problem causing schizophrenia. To be proficient at dual-diagnosis assessment, one needs to be as much a Sherlock Holmes or a Colombo as a psychologist. Differential diagnosis involves several important considerations:

Primacy. This is the chicken-and-egg part of the assessment—as in, which came first. The specialist asks questions to determine if a person had any symptoms of mental health disorders in childhood or at any time *prior* to beginning alcohol use. These questions need to explore anxiety, mood, relationship, learning, and behavioral problems at earlier times in the person's life. In many cases, not merely inherited metabolic hardwiring compels a person to become alcohol dependent. The other big driver is mental health problems. The person, consciously or not, discovers a self-medication in alcohol for his or her anxiety, mood, or other mental problems. If symptoms of one or more mental health problems are found to precede onset of drinking in a person's life, then the mental health problem is said to be *primary* and the alcohol problem *secondary*. Of course, in some people both problems can stand alone. This would be a very pure case of dual diagnosis. However, some dual-diagnosis cases are primarily mental health problems, and others are primarily alcohol problems. An analysis of data from the huge Mental Health Epidemiological Catchment Areas Study found that in 78 percent of the men with an alcohol use problem, alcohol dependence preceded the onset of depression. This was true of 66 percent of the women (Helzer & Pryzbeck, 1988). This is consistent with thousands of assessments I have done. In most cases involving depression and alcohol dependence, it is the alcohol dependence that is primary.

What becomes of mental health symptoms in times of abstinence? This is a very important part of dual-diagnosis assessment. In some cases, even without symptoms of a mental health problem prior to alcohol use, such problems can emerge at least somewhat independent of a person's drinking. Many people with drinking problems report times (weeks and months or even years) of abstinence. Most people with an alcohol use problem are not in *constant* denial. Although they may underestimate the challenge, at times they recognize the problem and make attempts to quit. If the alcohol dependence is primary, during these times of abstinence, a person's symptoms of mental health problems should subside across several weeks. Of course, a good clinician will take into account other variables that could account for mental health symptoms that continue. For example, it is not fair to diagnose depression in a newly sober person whose spouse has recently died. That would more likely be normal bereavement. Also, there is naturally quite a bit of emotional dysregulation during acute and post-acute withdrawal. The person's life situations in any times of abstinence must be considered. For example, if someone says he or she was depressed about not having a job, or was anxious about a health problem or unstable relationship, that distress may have been syntonic with (proportionate to) their actual situation and not indicative of a mental health disorder at the time. Therefore, diagnosis of mental health problems because of symptoms noticed shortly after quitting drinking can be premature.

The longer any episodes of abstinence may have lasted and the more episodes we can inquire about, the easier the diagnosis of a mental health disorder is. Mary tells us there have been 3 times in her adult life that she managed to stay completely sober for from 3 to 6 months. Although she never had anxiety problems in childhood or during years of alcohol use, with each episode of sobriety, she experiences unrelenting panic attacks. In her case, we need to recognize her bona fide anxiety disorder and provide appropriate treatment.

Severity. Regardless of primacy based on when symptoms first appear in a person's life, severity of symptoms must often influence diagnoses. Just imagine an emergency room doctor fresh out of medical school facing a patient in the waiting room. The patient is in tennis clothes clutching his ankle with one hand and clutching his chest with the other. The doctor inquires of the man when he first noticed the symptoms. The patient tells him the ankle pain started about an hour ago when he fell on the tennis court, and the chest pain began shortly after arriving at the ER. So based on rules of primacy, the doc takes the patient into the exam room and starts treatment of his sprained ankle.

Thus, for some individuals, all other factors notwithstanding, severe symptoms of a mental health disorder need to be addressed or the person is unlikely to stay sober. The question of whether the mental health issue was caused by the drinking or vice versa does not much matter to the panicking patient, or to the suicidally depressed patient.

A comprehensive discussion of co-occurring mental health disorders and their role in alcohol use problems and recovery is far beyond the scope of this book. So, if you are concerned about a mood, anxiety, or other mental health problem that may be causally related to your drinking problem and compromising your recovery, I recommend that you see a professional trained in dual diagnosis. If you and/or a dual-diagnosis professional find no convincing evidence that you had a preexisting mental health disorder, or that one did not *independently* emerge in your drinking years, then you only need to focus on your recovery from alcohol dependence, as suggested, using the forward-going life areas template. Your anxiety/mood issues will likely abate within a few weeks of abstinence. If, on the other hand, there is evidence of an independent mental health problem, then it is doubly important that you focus on the emotional recovery strategies presented in this chapter and work with a private therapist. My experience is that although quitting drinking can confront a person with his or her other mental health problem, this is actually a very good thing. It provides the opportunity to discover something very important about one's self. If this applies to you, remember that mental health problems are *all* treatable. Quitting drinking and facing your fears can truly be the beginning of your personal liberation. It will become another gift in recovery.

In closing this chapter on emotional recovery, let me offer one more point. It seems like everyone I know has or has had some sort of emotional problems: mood problems, attentional difficulties, obsessive/compulsive problems, and/or emotional wounds from all sorts of experiences. So a variation of the axiom for a long life that I cited in Chapter 8 comes to mind: *The secret to a happy life cannot realistically be to have no emotional problems or scars, but rather to accept the problems and scars that you have and manage them well.*

Recommended Reading for Chapter 11

A Guide to Rational Living, by Albert Ellis & Robert Harper.

Breaking the Patterns of Depressio, by Michael Yapko.

Feel the Fear and do it Anyway, by Susan Jeffers.

Learned Optimism, by Martin Seligman.

Reinventing Your Life: The Breakthrough Program to End Negative Behavior ... and Feel Great Again, by JeffreyYoung, Janet Klosko & Aaron Beck.

The Feeling Good Handbook, by David Burns.

The Four Agreements: A Practical Guide to Personal Freedom, A Toltec Wisdom Book, by Miguel Ruiz.

When AA Doesn't Work for You: Rational Steps to Quitting Alcohol, by Albert Ellis & Emmett Velten.

Chapter 12

Leisure/Recreational Recovery

Problem:	*All work and no play jeopardizes Jack's and Jill's recoveries.*
Solution:	*Learn to play.*

I have witnessed a direct correlation between the quantity and frequency of people's drinking and proportionate declines in their participation in healthy leisure and recreational activities. This has been most obvious among inpatient treatment populations. At the beginning of my treatment center talks on leisure and recreational recovery, after distributing pencils and paper, I would say, "See if you can each make a list of 20 things you love to do." Well, by the time a person is in an inpatient treatment program, this turns out to be quite a challenge. As with the feelings list, most of the pages remained blank. When someone did manage to list a couple of activities, I would say, "Okay, John, what's on your list?"

"Boating and snowmobiling," he might respond. I would then say, "Okay, when's the last time you went boating?" Typically, I would get back something like, "I guess we sold the boat in '82, and come to think of it, I gave my brother the snowmobile somewhere around that same time." Leisure and recreational pursuits are often seriously compromised as alcohol dependence advances. Why go off doing something on a weekend when you can drink beer in your back yard, or wine in the kitchen?

The goal of recovery is to create a better-balanced lifestyle, and the leisure side of life is far more important than most people ever realize, or realize too late. The chairperson of the Sociology Department at

Northern Michigan University circa 1969 had a sign on his office door that I have never forgotten. It read: "Work hard now so you can afford a good stomach pump when you're old." Then there is the terse adage, "What do you want on your tombstone? 'Glad I spent all that time at the office?'" The person who wins in the end is neither the one with the most money nor the one with the most toys, but rather the one who has done more of what he or she wanted to do.

The paleontologist Richard Leakey (1979) notes that the ancient band-level hunter/gatherers probably worked about only 30 hours per week. This was not because they belonged to a strong union. This was because humans evolved to survive hard work (originally hunting and gathering) by intermittent and regular mentally and physically recuperative rest and relaxation. What changed this happened only very recently in our evolution. As discussed in the section on finding a model to live by, the change occurred with the agricultural revolution and ahead of our ability to cope with the profound social changes that came with it. Also, as the human population grew in Africa, and people began migrating north, they had to become more and more industrious to meet the challenges of new environments with colder winters. They needed more durable dwellings, more advanced tools, clothing, weapons, and the capacity to store food for long winters. People worked harder. The industrial revolution sprang very quickly from the challenges of living in the northern climate. Certainly, we have proved to be a very adaptable species, but I do not believe we have had sufficient evolutionary time to psychologically adapt to this workload increase. Witness the high rates of hypertension and myriad other stress-related diseases and social problems in modern cultures. We are not getting the necessary breaks in our daily, weekly, and annual workloads. I read in our local newspaper that European nations average something like 35 vacation days per year. Italians have the most with over 40 days off per year. Even the industrious Japanese have 29. We Americans have 12. What happened to our right to pursue happiness?

When I was just a young boy, I happened to meet our mail carrier at the front door. As he handed me our mail, a large flock of crows was squawking-up a loud cacophony in our elm tree. I said, "Gee those crows are making a lot of noise." He then responded with a small lecture on the scientific name and nature of crows. I said, "Man, you sure know a lot about crows." To this he responded, "Well I ought to. I happen to be president of our local Audubon Society. Bird-watching is my *avocation.*" After he left, I went inside and asked my mother what the word "avocation" meant. She explained that it was something a person did apart from his or her regular occupation, out of sheer interest and pleasure—something that people often had more expertise in than in their regular profession. A mill worker was an avid weekend trout fisher. A physician entered his model airplanes in competitions. A professor taught cross-country skiing at a local resort in her spare time. Somehow, perhaps somewhere between Sputnik and the cold war, my generation seems to have lost touch with the purpose and importance of developing avocations—leisure and recreational passions.

Not participating in leisure and recreation pursuits can breed serious emotional problems and increase relapse risk as well as increase vulnerability to stress-related physical diseases. Devotion to leisure and recreational endeavors provides a powerful hedge against emotional despair across our lifetimes, and especially through midlife transition. At least one of our defense shields needs to be an avocational passion. Remember, the kids grow up, the job ends, health issues emerge, and sometimes marriages end. What then will we have to identify with and contain our fears? A leisure/recreational passion can sustain us by providing at least one point of identity, one shield that can contain our fears regardless of other changes. This is not to say it needs to be or should be just one thing. You can have as many passions as you can manage, and you can change them across time. I used to like downhill skiing. Now I prefer skate skiing. I used to like rock climbing and river rafting. Now I like mountain biking, golf, and building projects. I am also planning new hobbies such as painting and sculpting.

Many times I have seen men and women fall to despair at retirement, divorce, health crisis, or other midlife challenges, and as a result drinking problems begin or increase. Clearly, for those who have developed the leisure habit and have one or two leisure passions, the onset or advancement of drinking problems is far less likely in transitional times. Picture the newly retired executive who throws himself into his passion for trout fishing and tying flies. He voluntarily becomes the "CEO" of the local trout fishing club. He is not going to hang around the old corporate watering hole, or worry about his adult children living in other parts of the country. He is going to be emotionally healthy and hearty.

The trouble is, for lack of healthy role modeling, or due to an overcompensational sense of responsibility, many of us do not develop the leisure habit. As it turns out, to be healthily involved in leisure pursuits often takes just as much time, money, and practice as we put into our occupations. Ideally, such activities are great fun from the start. I think skiing is this way. The riveting thrill of one's first run down the bunny slope is hard to recapture when one is an expert. Learning to play a musical instrument, on the other hand, takes a real ability to delay gratification and practice long hours on the mere hope that someday it will sound good. Generally, if you do not start the leisure habit when you are young, it may seem surprisingly difficult to initiate when you are older. Golf, for example, is difficult to become proficient at when you begin at 60.

What to Do

Using your Life Areas Template, highlight the Leisure/Recreation area. As with each of the areas, focus first on "Needs" identification. Then begin by completing the "Love List" exercise below. The instructions are as follows:

List as many interests/activities as you can think of that you have ever enjoyed or that you have ever thought you might enjoy. Take your time. For a few days or a week, notice what other people are doing among your friends and in your community, look in magazines and on television. Ask people involved in certain activities how they got started and what it took. Do not hold back or automatically exclude yourself from any possibility. Fill out the rest of the form as indicated by the column headings: How much does that activity cost; does it require other people; does it require training and practice; does it require advance planning or can you do it spontaneously? I like to have a mix of activities. A trip to go surfing or cross-country skiing takes considerable advance planning and expense. Getting on my mountain bike or lifting weights in my home gym can be done almost instantly on a whim and at this point costs nothing. Some things I like to do solo. Some activities, such as tennis, require at least one other person. Other activities, such as golf, can be done alone, but are preferably engaged in with other people.

The Love List

ACTIVITIES/ INTERESTS	Cost	Other people or alone?	Training required ?	Advance planning required?	Altered state of consciousness sought	Substances used in past
1						
2						
3						
4						
5						
6						
7						
8						
9						
10						
11						
12						
13						
14						
15						
16						
17						
18						
19						
20						

Remember that the primary reason people drink alcohol or use other drugs—whether consciously aware of this or not—is to alter their state of consciousness from a less pleasant place to a more pleasant place, for example, to relax, to energize, to escape, or for excitement. In the last column write down alcohol (and each other drug you may have been involved with). In the second to the last column write down the altered state of consciousness you think you were seeking when drinking or using any other drug. Finally, next to each altered state sought, write down the number of any activity or activities that could produce that state. Whenever you feel like drinking or using, try to bring to conscious awareness what altered state you are seeking and substitute a healthier, and ultimately more enjoyable, activity.

Once you have completed the Love List, take an educated guess at an activity that might work for you. If all else fails, put it on the wall and throw a dart at it, or use any more sophisticated method of making a random choice. Then, as per the Life Areas Template, set a goal. Determine the means to achieving the goal, get it scheduled on your calendar, and get started. Mary Sue decides she might like to paint with watercolors as a new hobby. She sets a goal of having a studio space, easels, pallets, and paints all set up and underway in three months. She realizes that the last time she painted anything was in kindergarten, and that was with her fingers. So she needs some training. It will also require some capital outlay. Therefore, as the means by which to achieve her goal, she reallocates some of her money and starts the "Introduction to Watercolors" class at the community college or signs on with an artist who offers lessons. You can think of myriad examples for all sorts of leisure activities that other people do, but the point is to make yourself an example.

Further Considerations

Do not hold back because you are not absolutely sure an activity is right for you. Remember, you are not making a signed-in-blood oath to participate in any activity in perpetuity. You can stop anything at any point you want. Just look at anything you start as only an experiment. Put a time limit on it if you want. For example, John is going to play tennis for 6 months. If he is not really enjoying it after 6 months, he will drop it and try something else.

Also, don't fall victim to the perfectionist's script for self defeat described in Chapter 9. If this has been roadblock for you remember to simply strive to be average at new activities, rather than perfect, and you may be able to at least begin.

Try as many activities as you like, but at a minimum try at least one new leisure endeavor each year. Consistently use your alcohol abstinence date, your bellybutton birthday, an equinox or solstice, or New Year's Eve as an annual starting point.

Get the right stuff. Whatever leisure activities you pursue, try to get the best equipment, gear, and/or clothing that you can possibly afford for the activity. This makes it more fun, and more likely that you will stick with it.

Do not give up on an activity too soon. Most things take some practice. Stick with a thing until it pays off.

Chapter 13

Relationships Recovery

Problems:

- *Your partner relationship has been compromised due to your drinking.*

- *You are considering a new relationship early in your recovery.*

- *Your family relationships have been damaged due to your drinking.*

- *You have become a social isolate due to your drinking.*

- *Your co-worker relationships have been compromised.*

Solutions:

Learn how to

- *Repair your existing relationship.*

- *Decide whether or not to start a new relationship.*

- *Identify and repair family relationship problems.*

- *Build friendships.*

- *Manage co-worker relationships.*

Working in the addictions treatment field, one of the first things you learn is that there are no truly voluntary clients. Approximately 90 percent of people in treatment programs are there by court mandate—predominately for driving under the influence (DUI) offenses. The remaining would-be voluntary clients usually have some other issue fueling their motivation to be in treatment. Classic examples are things like seeking treatment as a condition of reemployment, or because of a health crisis, or due to a spouse's threat to leave. Therefore, a more realistic moniker is "nonmandated" rather than "voluntary" when it comes to reasons folks are in treatment.

In my experience with thousands of individuals with alcohol use problems, the most urgent life area cost is to relationships. Apart from the legal consequence of driving under the influence of alcohol, the most common reason adults identify that got them to seek treatment or otherwise quit drinking is because of the concerns of a wife, husband, boyfriend, girlfriend, other family member, friend, or employer. Health problems or psychological concerns are also common but are less often listed as the stimulus for seeking help among the nonmandated treatment population. I have only rarely heard clients say that their chief reason for coming to treatment was that they felt their leisure pursuits were compromised by their alcohol use. Thus, relationship recovery is the area of recovery that people most frequently feel urgent about and identify as the first area of recovery they want to work on.

Within the area of relationship recovery, there are several different types of relationships that may have been affected. I loosely divide these into four categories:

- Primary partner relationships
- Friendships
- Family member relationships
- Co-worker relationships

Certainly, there are other categories of relationships you may wish to consider, such as with one's greater community of people (service providers, doctors, teachers, lawyers, etc.), with one's Higher Power, and/or with one's self.

About Primary Partner Relationships

There are several considerations about *primary partner* relationships important to discuss. To begin with, there are two different types of primary partner relationship dilemmas that people early in recovery often have to contend with. For people with an existing relationship, the question is, "How can I keep, or must I let go of my *current* partner ?" For single people, the question often is, "Shall I start a *new* relationship?" Of course, some people have both dilemmas. The AA/treatment program complex has a very specific position on these questions, and that is, don't make any relationship changes in your first year of recovery. But again, as with so many other aspects of recovery, there are significant individual differences. No set rule can apply to all people at all times. I constantly remind myself not to play God, Jesus, Buddha, Mohammed, or Laozi. The question of whether you should or should not make an important change in your relationship status is up to you.

No Happy Hermits

Sometimes clients tell me they are happy being single, as if they were born to be hermits. In a sense, they are happier, but they are often mistaking the avoidance of their overblown relationship anxiety and mistrust of others for being happy. They are merely feeling relief from anxiety, not optimally happy.

As with all animals, humans have a need to connect with a mate—a need that has evolved over thousands of generations for survival of the species. Quite simply, where in history a man and women tended to stay together, their children better survived, thus genetically passing on that "tendency to stay." Any tendency in a person to not seek and stay in relationships fell out of the gene pool for lack of successful reproduction. As I have contended, due to the agricultural and industrial revolutions, humans lost their natural ability for effective parenting and family relating. This has left myriad humans with interpersonal mistrust and self-doubt, rendering them too inhibited to relax and enjoy their genetic potential to find gratification in having a mate. Research consistently finds that happiness does not correlate with IQ, income, geography, occupations, etc. The only consistent correlate of happiness is the extent to which any of us feel positively, safely, emotionally connected to anyone else.

Love and Reciprocity

So what makes relationships work or fall apart? Back in the 1970s, we thought it had to do with the extent to which people reciprocally exchanged positive reinforcements with each other. This was the "I'll scratch your back if you scratch mine" model. We had people complete lists of reinforcers—things they would like or wanted from their partners—and matched-off elaborate mutual exchange deals: I'll cook, if you do the dishes. I'll clean the bathrooms if you engage in conversation. You schlep the kids around and I'll manage the bills, etc. Nice idea, but this turned out to be too much work for most people, and real improvements in relationship satisfaction were few. By and large, having some satisfactory exchange agreements is a good thing. I encourage you to establish some exchange deals if this makes sense to you in your particular relationship situation.

However, I have learned that something almost antithetical to the mutual exchange hypothesis is even better. That is, marriages are really only good to the extent that rewards are exchanged *without regard* for reciprocation. For example, my wife and I have tended to trade off preparing dinner for doing the dishes. However, if after finishing a meal that I prepared, I see that she is exhausted from a long workday and is sacked out on the couch, I quietly do the dishes, without keeping score, just because I enjoy making her happy.

The Areas of Compatibility Fallacy

What really makes one person right or wrong for another person? If you ask a young couple about to get married whether they think they will meet each other's needs, you usually get a puzzled or indignant look and a response something like, "What do you mean? *Of course!* We love each other ... *duh!*" Unfortunately, the chance that they will discover otherwise is about 50 percent.

In many non-Western societies, marriages are arranged and couples are compelled to tough it out and make it work due to very strong cultural norms and pressure to do so. In Western society, we pick our own mates practically at random, largely by happenstance, whenever we "fall in love." Mother Nature wants only one thing: *procreation.* Young couples are blind to any differences they may have as they are driven to get together. Of course, once they have cohabitated for a few weeks and the procreative urge is satisfied, they begin to discover differences. She leaves the cap off the toothpaste and does not close drawers. He expects to play golf and drink beer with his friends as usual on Saturdays. Her family opens presents Christmas Eve; his, on Christmas morning. Each begins to realize this is not what he or she expected, not what they bargained for. Doubt and fear grow. Blame leads to counterblame and one or both rush to individuate.

"He didn't tell me that ... ."

"I never knew she ... ."

At this point, about half of couples just keep going. They stay separated, and if married, get divorced. Nevertheless, about half manage to work it out. How do they do this?

In the old days (the ancient 1970s), we assumed that alignment of areas of compatibility was the most important thing for a relationship to be successful. We gave young couples what are called compatibility scales. We had everybody rate their partner in comparison to their ideal partner on several different dimensions. These include such areas as political and religious beliefs, financial status, sex, leisure interests, social interest, etc. (see the *Desirable Mate Features Profile* in the next section). It was thought that the more areas of compatibility a couple shared, the better the union. Of course, it is easy to think this way because conflicts over such areas are exactly what couples present to counselors. When asked what brings them in, they say they are fighting over money, time, child raising, sex, or some other area of incompatibility. In truth, this is another example of something seeming so obvious but not really being the problem. Research on older couples, content with their marriages, shows they too had and have plenty of differences.

Mother Nature blindsides us to differences to ensure procreation. And as it turns out, just as mixed-breed mutts tend to be healthier than purebreds, some differences between the parents make for stronger or better-adapted offspring in humans. So if we tell a young couple that the differences they have in areas of compatibility are too great for the marriage to work, we are monkeying with natural selection and human evolution.

In fact, many perceived differences between two people are actually benefits, and not just for the offspring. If one is a spendthrift and the other a tightwad, they probably bring each other to a healthier center. If one is fanatical about outdoor leisure pursuits and the other a workaholic, they will likely have a beneficial influence on each other. And the Sunday supplement was wrong; parents should not use the exact same parenting strategy. They are two different people with different personalities and ways of relating. The children need to experience this or they will not be able to accommodate different personalities in the world outside the family.

Of course, not all areas are advantageous or reconcilable. If one desperately wants children and the other abjectly refuses to even consider the idea, this may not work. If one believes in open sex and the other needs a reliably faithful partner, this may not work either. However, the point is that the success or failure of marriages is not predictable by, or predicated on, these commonly listed areas of compatibility. Eighty-year-old Herald says he and Mary have been happily married for over 50 years. I say, "But Herald, you told me you disagree with liberal politics."

"Oh, that!" he chuckles. "Well she goes to her committee meeting once a week and we have learned to just not talk about it."

You do not even have to actually reconcile all of your differences in order to have a successful marriage. Some things are apparently okay just to put aside. You are two different people. Some differences are healthy for you. Did you really want to marry yourself?

The Two Areas of Compatibility That Really Do Matter

Having said that good relationships do not actually depend on compatibility in all areas, there are probably two line items of compatibility that really do need to match up. The first one has been identified through decades of research on marital discord, especially that by John Gottman at the University of Washington. The finding is that conflict in marriage is normal (Gottman, 1999). I am worried, especially where alcohol is involved, when someone tells me, "Oh, we never argue or fight." I get the picture of one person overly dominating the other, or of a shy couple suffering dissatisfactions silently for years due to fearing or not knowing how to conflict. You are two different people, with different moods, wants, and expectations at any moment. You cannot read each other's minds; you are going to step on each other's toes.

So conflict itself is not the problem. The problem is *how* to conflict. Gottman's research involved having couples come and stay in apartments for a few days where everything they did and said was recorded. The researchers would then follow up years later to see who was still married. What was found has been most instructive. Couples who had conflicts in certain identifiable ways were divorced, and those who managed their conflicts in other identifiable ways were still together. As it turns out, how couples manage conflict is the strongest predictor of who will or will not stay together. Far less predictive is whether couples agree or disagree about managing money, child raising, leisure time, or any other area of compatibility. I highly recommend Gottman's book *The Seven Principles for Making Marriage Work* (1999) to learn about the "four horsemen of the apocalypse of marriage." What I have gleaned from this, and from my experience with countless couples, is that there are destructive ways to argue and there are constructive ways. To make marriages work, we must first learn what *not* to do in arguments, and then how to argue more productively.

The second necessary area of compatibility I feel is the ultimate one. It is the only one that really matters, for without it the union may be worse than pointless. If not compatible on this one line item, two lives are tragically sacrificed. It is the area of what Gottman has called *emotional connection.* This is not just any emotional connection, because there are couples connected by fear, demand, threat, and other negative inner personal emotions. The type of emotional connection that makes a marriage valuable is a positive, safe, and enduring connection: It is the quality of really liking and having compassion, if not hot passion, for your partner. It is that you understand a lot about each other's emotional needs and can go an appreciable distance in meeting them. It is having an emotional confidant and best friend.

I think that each of us deserves and can find a partner in whom we find or build these qualities. In fact, this is the real reason people come to couples' counseling—not because of the money conflict, or the child-rearing disagreement, or any of these superficial stated reasons for seeking help. What really brings them in is that they are experiencing a painful breach in the emotional connection they once had or thought they had. This, of course, is much more difficult for them to talk about, so they divert to other more obvious external issues. Many couples with an alcohol use problem experience this emotional disconnection, and it is the one compatibility line item that needs to be restored. Please know that if you feel you and your partner have indeed lost that connection, it does not mean you cannot get it back. Really, this is the goal of almost all couples' counseling. How to get it back involves starting with hope, a reasonable modicum of remaining love, or just blind faith, and a willingness to try new strategies.

Recovery of Your Existing, Though Damaged, Primary Partner Relationship

Who knows how to make love stay?
Answer me that and I will tell you whether or not to kill yourself. Answer me that and I will ease your mind about the beginning and the end of time. Answer me that and I will reveal to you the purpose of the moon.

—Tom Robbins
From Still Life with Woodpecker, Chapter 2

When I say primary relationship, I am talking about your romantic, or would-be romantic, partner, whether boyfriend or girlfriend, husband or wife. If this relationship has been compromised in any way related to your drinking, there is much to do. We will look at several important questions about relationships, including whether they are really worth it, what makes them fail, and what makes them work. Philosophers and poets, of course, have weighed in heavily on these questions for many millennia. Also, as in so many areas of science since WWII, research over the last 50 years has produced significant gains in knowledge about what makes relationships succeed or fail, and very useful strategies for rebuilding damaged relationships.

Something many people in early recovery need to do is take a serious look at their motives for wanting to stay in their primary relationship. If, after serious reflection, staying in it is what you want to do, we can then explore strategies to rebuild and improve your primary relationship. First, should you stay?

Should You Remain in the Relationship in the First Place—Is the Struggle to Rebuild It Really Worth It?

You may not actually be right for each other. Lots of couples have based their relationship and understanding of each other on drinking. Did, perhaps, you and your partner first meet while drinking at a party or a bar? This is common, of course, in our culture. Sometimes alcohol use has thinly held together a couple who would otherwise be incompatible. Early in sobriety, many couples look at each other as if meeting for the first time, practically as strangers, and ask the question, Who are we now? One can become flooded with fear that the relationship has been a farce and may have to end. If you have questioned the fundamental compatibility between you and your partner, you are well advised to not act on impulse and break up too early in your recovery. The first few months of recovery can bring many emotions and confusing questions. Take your time just to stabilize everything for a while. Then consider the following.

I am sometimes compelled to confront a person with the following two-part question: "Are you sure you want to stay with your partner ... and if so, why?" This usually perplexes and frustrates clients as they suddenly realize that they actually do not know and struggle to iterate what is so important about the relationship. Some people will simply say, "I just love [him or her]," but are totally unable to define what this means or why. Others will stammer out, "Well, we've been together for X number of years," as if that alone was a powerful injunction to stay together at all cost. Never mind that for the past seven of those years he or she has done nothing but question the relationship, accuse, belittle, intimidate, withhold or demand sex, and otherwise keep the you thoroughly miserable. "So, Susan, you tell me you've been desperately unhappy in your abusive marriage without getting any of your needs meet for the past 10 years. What is it again you will be missing if you leave?" Sometimes in these situations with a man or a woman, I think, "My God, by now wouldn't it be a great relief just to have that person out of your life?"

If your relationship seems to have gone sideways, charging into salvaging it is not a good idea without first answering these simple questions. Get together with a trusted friend and go over them carefully. They are:

- What have you *really* gotten from the relationship that you need so desperately to keep? Make a costs/benefits analysis. Honestly list what you think has been valuable to you and, as honestly, what has not. The next section will help you figure this out. Feel free at this point to jump ahead. Keep in mind that no one meets 100 percent of another person's needs. It really is best that way. With all of one person's needs met by the other person, that person would become overly responsible for the other, and the other could become overly dependent. It is really a question of percentage. There is no set figure; it is an individual, subjective thing. If the benefits exceed the costs, you possibly have a relationship worth keeping. If not, well, some things may need to change. Again, see the next section to help clarify this.

- Are you blindly rushing to save the relationship simply because you would view separating as a personal failure? This is when people respond to my what's-so-good-about-your-marriage question with, "Well, I've been divorced twice before and I promised myself I never would again—I would just feel like such a failure." Some people would rather crawl across hot coals for 20 years of personal sacrifice than to admit defeat or failure. More power to you if this is your priority. However, you might want to explore how you ever got so hung up about failure. When nothing else matches up, staying together merely to avoid labeling yourself a failure will result in the sacrifice of two lives, paradoxically constituting a failure.

- Are you mistaking the need to avoid feelings of abandonment or to escape loneliness for being in love? This is a very common self-sacrificing perceptual error. I think that although most of us can function solo, in general, most of us are better off bonded. We have evolved affiliation and romantic needs. This is more profound for some people than for others, to the point where no matter how tragically mismatched, they work desperately at staying with their partner because of secret or out-in-the-open abandonment fears. An old adage comes to mind—do you really want to remain standing on a burning cliff just because you can't see where you will land if you jump?

- Are you mistaking love for what is really entanglement in a competition? Some couples are fiercely competitive. They remind me of high school relationships, with all the jealous plotting and scheming for dominance and control. Power-testing in relationships really needs to go away after high school. If power is what your partner needs, is he or she really the right person for you? Would you ever feel safe emotionally? Feeling emotionally safe with your partner is probably the most important element in a relationship.

Setting the Stage for Primary Relationship Recovery

If you feel that your partner is the right mate for you and rebuilding your relationship is an important area of recovery to you, there are a number of things you can do to succeed at the task.

1. First and foremost, do a *mea culpa*. Confess. Confess it all, and apologize genuinely. This will be easier if you realize that although you are the only one who can be responsible for the drinking and its costs, at least you yourself know you are not to blame. It is a disease of the mind that struck you. But do not expect your partner to understand that at this point. The years of trying to get your partner to think that everything was his or her fault need to end. You need to ask yourself, Do I really want it to work out? Because if you do, this means deployment of a "busing" strategy—bending over backward to right a prior wrong. Tell your partner that you are deeply and profoundly sorry for all the ways your drinking affected her or him. This can include but is not limited to alcohol-related lying, infidelity, financial losses, your insensitive treatment of him or her, and most importantly, your emotional unavailability. Emotional unavailability is the number one complaint from partners of alcoholics.

2. Do not expect immediate forgiveness. In most cases, it simply will not be possible. Spouses have generally suffered more than their alcohol-dependent partners are able to realize because it is a painful realization. The time will come when you will deserve and can expect forgiveness, but not in the first year or so of your recovery, assuming everything else goes okay.

> We must sit on the edge of the well of darkness
>
> And fish for the fallen light with patience.
>
> —Pablo Neruda

If they have not become actively alcohol dependent themselves, spouses typically have developed *codependent* traits in order to cope with the confusion and fear that come with trying to figure out their alcoholic spouse and struggling to keep the union together. This includes emotional pain with fear and anger, self-sacrificing, and covering up, or covering for, your drinking problems. Suggest that your spouse see a counselor; offer to pay for it, and promise to attend any sessions if requested. Read about co-dependency (your spouse may already have). Start with the classic *Co-dependent No More* by Melanie Beattie (1992) and go from there. And for heaven's sake, if he or she thinks you should be in counseling too, swallow your pride, stuff your fear, and go for it.

3. Offer an abstinence guarantee. This may sound crazy, and it is certainly antithetical to what you would hear in a treatment program or AA. In the system, it is always one day at a time, and no one can promise that abstinence will last—it is not humanly possible. However, it is only natural for spouses to want it to be over for good. It takes a lot of gentle explaining to help spouses understand that when their alcoholic partner gets out of treatment or otherwise quits, he or she is not "done." I estimate that among people who try treatment programs, it takes an average of two to three programs for most to get lasting recovery. Remember, it is medically defined as one of a number of diseases of relapse. Initially quitting is just the beginning of a long process of recovery, and although they are difficult for spouses to accept, some slips are a natural type of learning in early recovery. You can see that it can be very helpful to have a counselor involved in processing this with you and your spouse. You must try to validate, rather than refute, your partner's fears and complaints. You will need to allow his or her expressions of pain and anger. Spouses deserve support for this. If you do not allow it, just imagine the eventual consequences of their pent-up pain. An experienced counselor's office is a good venue for processing your partner's pain and anger.

Spouses cannot automatically know what to do—what they should or should not do to support your recovery effort. Many times, given co-dependency dynamics, they try to do too much. It is generally advisable that only the recovering person be responsible for his or her recovery, and the spouse should not feel responsible or attempt to control it. You must forgive him or her for trying, but a most marvelous dynamic then invariably occurs. You may find yourself feeling resentful of your spouse's concerns and questions such as, "Are you doing this [or not doing that] about your recovery." Feeling ashamed enough already, your spouse's inquiries and directives at the very least steal your thunder, and at the most make you feel belittled, resentful, unmotivated, and angry. You may feel infantilized and eventually find yourself protesting loudly or not communicating at all about your recovery progress or setbacks. At this point, the relationship you wanted so badly to repair becomes conflicted again.

So here is what to do. Tell your loved one that she or he is working too hard on your recovery and it makes you feel guilty and sad—she or he has already had to give so much. Say that you love him or her very much and want to offer every protection you can. Offer a "limited" guarantee, and volunteer to put it in writing. State that if you drink again, you will:

- Report this within 24 hours
- Move out, at least temporarily, to a friend's or relative's home or to a motel, voluntarily and without argument
- See your counselor or go to a treatment program without question

If you both think this is too extreme, leave out the "move out" clause or otherwise adjust it to better suit both of you. Assuming this goes okay, do the following:

4. *Authorize* your partner to inquire about your recovery status once per day. If it is at your request that they do this, it is a lot easier to take and not feel resentful about. And seriously, do you really want your partner to be walking around on eggshells, anxiously wondering how you are doing? I don't think so. If someone is worrying about how I am doing about anything, I sure as heck want him or her to ask.

Then, when under your advance authorization your spouse asks about how you are feeling or about where you are with your recovery, you need to respond with, "Thank you for asking, as I have encouraged you to do," and then answer the question honestly and sincerely. In exchange, your spouse needs to not ask too many questions too frequently and to say "Thank you for telling me" regardless of what good or bad news you share. You deserve support too. This is no different from people asking their diabetic spouses if they have checked their blood sugar. Face it, as applies to the management of any health issues, your spouse has a legitimate stake in your recovery. You need to pay sincere attention to his or her concerns.

Healthy Relationship Conflict Management

Remember, all couples have at least some conflicts. Learning to do this well is critical to whether you do or do not survive as a couple. Here are some important guidelines.

Put a total moratorium on hostile physical contact, threats, or posturing

Physical assaults or threats always makes things worse. Couples involved in this either break up or live unhappy lives together. It is not worth it either way. Hostile behaviors include:

- Any threatening or intimidating words or acts
- Pushing
- Hitting
- Slapping
- Pointing
- Shouting
- Raised hands
- Picked-up objects
- Throwing things
- Mean scowling or intimidating expressions

No criticizing (compared to fair complaining)

In *criticizing*, we are telling other people what they did wrong or where they screwed up and otherwise point out their faults. This is destructive. And saying, "I was just giving constructive criticism" is a cop-out—unless the person has asked for constructive criticism. Alternatively, in *complaining*, we are talking about our *own* feelings and our *own* needs. This is a necessary and constructive relationship skill. As an example, I had gotten home from work ahead of my wife one evening. When she came in, as is our custom, we had a hug and a kiss, and I asked, "So how was your day, Honey?" She responded with, "Well, Chris, to tell you the truth, it started out awful. I realized I was going to be a little late this morning. I spilled the coffee, rushed around the kitchen, grabbed my coat, ran out, started the car, and there was your pickup blocking the driveway. I thought we agreed you would keep the truck beside the garage. I had to run back in, hunt for your keys, and move the truck. I was pretty upset by the time I left. Will you please remember to park the truck on the side?"

Now, I may have felt like a scolded boy, but I had to filter out, did she criticize me? No. Not one bit. She merely *complained*. I swallowed my pride and said, "Of course. You are right. I should have moved the truck. I am really sorry. Here, let me fix you something to eat."

Now, if instead, she had come in saying, "Chris, you insensitive idiot. You never do anything you say you will. You are thoughtless and greedy. If you leave the truck in the driveway one more time, I am going to sell it," I would not have to respond at all. Notice also that in her credible complaint, she also added a request. In the example of criticizing, she threw in a demand.

Work on understanding the difference between *criticizing and demanding* versus *complaining and requesting*. The former are unfair and destructive in arguments; the latter are fair and constructive. Discuss this with your partner, and authorize each other to use fair complaining and requesting. I submit to you that even a small improvement here will make a significant improvement in your relationship.

No endless defending

Gottman's research found a high correlation between being too defensive in arguments and marital failure. When we are defending in an argument, we are not listening any further than to merely figure out what we are going to say in rebuttal. Excessive rebuttal really stops progress. This is kind of a hard one to catch. It becomes so automatic as a dodge to avoid blame that we do not realize when we are doing it. In therapy, I spend a lot of time just pointing out defending. And most of the times I do this, people automatically reply with more defending, "No, I am only saying that she got that wrong, what I really did was this … ." Defending, though simple to comprehend, turns out to be surprisingly difficult to identify when it is happening and difficult to give up. Defending sounds like this:

"That's not how it was; here's how it was … ."

"I only did that because … ."

"I couldn't do that because … ."

Make an agreement with your partner to point out defending when either of you hear it. Stopping excessive defensiveness is a good way to become more mutually supportive.

No shows of contempt

Contempt is worse than simply criticizing. Its intent is to intimidate, hurt, punish, and/or control the other person—very destructive. You know you have crossed that line when you engage in any of the following:

Ridiculing, condescension, shaming, blaming, sarcasm, sneering, facetiousness, vindictiveness, spitefulness, put-downs, name calling, swearing, or accusations such as:

"You never … ."

"You're so … ."

"You're the one who … ."

"You always have to … ."

No stonewalling

Stonewalling is identified in Gottman's research as the single most destructive tactic a person can deploy in the mismanagement of relationship conflicts. This is when one person folds arms, walks away, and refuses to speak to the other. It is passive aggressive. In effect, the act is saying, "You are so [wrong, bad, insignificant] that I am not even going to speak to you." It can last for days. It is a mean-spirited attempt to punish and control the other person, who is then left hanging, desperately wanting to process and with no recourse other than to seek an emotional confidant outside the marriage. Is this what you would really want to have happen? It is my belief that being each other's emotional confidant is the most important feature of a worthwhile relationship.

Stay on one topic at a time

Couples who tend to switch topics in arguments likely will not make it. The argument may start with the burnt toast but somehow morphs into why one failed to fix the toaster. Then it becomes an issue of who is too cheap to buy a new toaster. This then leads to why one is not employed, and who does all the work around here anyway, and if one had not insisted on buying the SUV, maybe there would be enough money, and who screwed up in that other (probably unrelated) incident back in 2002?

You see what I mean. I have often interrupted couples arguing away in my office and asked, "Now what was this argument about?" What I get back are blank expressions suggesting that the question is stupid, but then troubled expressions with the realization that they no longer know what started it, followed by searching their memory banks for the answer. They have to run the reel of the argument backward quite a ways to reach it. "Oh yes! It was the channel changer incident."

It is out of fear of rejection, ego face-saving, and just plain bad habits that couples move off the target of the argument with forms of defensive counterblaming, tactics of derailment to a new set of accusations, or dredging the past. We usually have learned these combat-focused strategies vicariously from our families of origin, and innocently enough—after all, who really teaches us anything about how to manage relationship conflicts?

Healthy couples are able to stay on one topic per argument. After some brief arguing, they work cooperatively toward resolution. They quickly become solution-focused rather than combat-focused. Derailing to a different topic, flipping it back, or dredging the past are considered unproductive and obtusely unfair. Try instead saying things like, "Wait a minute, it seems we have gotten off track and have started a different argument than the one we started with. Let's go back and see if we can come to an agreement on the first argument."

Make sure you both have the same understanding of what you are arguing about

Couples frequently start talking about different aspects of the same problem at the same time, often without realizing it. He is yelling at her about leaving the keys in the car, while she is focused on how insensitive he treated the desk clerk. One is talking about an event while the other wants to process an emotion and an interpersonal dynamic, but nobody clarifies this.

Successful couples tend to make sure they are talking about the same issue. If cross-topic arguing is happening to you, learn to stop and question, "Wait a minute, I don't think we are talking about the same thing. What issue are you concerned with? I will agree to talk about that issue, if we can talk about the one I am concerned about when we are finished. Okay?"

Speak assertively rather than aggressively

Dr. Joseph Wolpe was the father of behavior therapy. He invented systematic desensitization treatments for anxiety disorders that are used to treat all sorts of fears and phobias. He was a brilliant British, South African research psychiatrist who came to teach in the USA in the 1950s and '60s. While here, he noticed that many men he saw in therapy suffered the same problem. At work or at home they would tend to let a lot of distressing interpersonal situations, communications, and behaviors of others go by without knowing how to express themselves, thus getting their own feelings ridden roughshod over. Perhaps these men were too shy to confront iniquitous behaviors in others, or feared their own anger. In any case, something would eventually come along that would be the last straw, and they would go off on someone—a co-worker or family member. Then they would be referred to therapy. Wolpe noticed that this dynamic did not seem to happen to a lot of other men he knew. He realized that most guys in contentious situations with others spent a lot more time in a broader middle ground he called being *assertive*. The other extremes he called being *sub-assertive* or being *aggressive*.

Sub-assertive   Assertive   Aggressive

```
---------------------|--------------------------------|----------------------
```

Wolpe developed what he called assertion training for men. The first important understanding is that when we are being *aggressive,* we are attempting to control a situation and get our needs met by threatening or intimidating the other person through criticizing, yelling, posturing, scowling, and/or demanding behaviors. This generally fails, however. Being aggressive tends to provoke the other person, who then becomes entrenched in his or her defenses and retaliates. And if we do get compliance through being aggressive, it will only be at a perfunctory level and will create disrespect and resentment. When we are being *assertive*, on the other hand, are not going at the other person, we are only talking about *our own* feelings and needs. When being assertive, we are keeping the other person's defenses down, earning respect, and by requesting instead of demanding, we are more likely to get cooperation.

When I was a young man, I had a job writing reviews of self-help books for a college library. In my personal life and as a psychologist, I have read countless self-help books. Many have been very beautiful and thought provoking. However, if I had only been allowed to read one genre, I would have selected books on assertiveness. Although comparatively didactic and dry stuff, it has been the most useful throughout my life for all sorts of relationship situations.

The perfect assertive statement might have three components. First, a statement of how you feel, then a brief description of the situation, and lastly, a statement of what you would like to have happen. Say I go into a restaurant to meet a colleague for lunch. We sit down and wait, and wait, for some service. Then some people sit down at table next to us and right away get menus. Now, some years back I might have been nonassertive and done nothing—wouldn't want to have made an embarrassing fuss. We would eventually be served, and I would go back to my office late, displacing my frustration on some poor underling. Or, I might have abruptly stood up, shouted aggressive disparaging remarks at the restaurant staff, and stormed out, thus landing my colleague and me out on the sidewalk, too late to find another place for lunch. Alternatively, I could be assertive. I could hail the waitperson, maybe even get up and tap him or her on the shoulder. "Excuse me, I can see you are pretty busy today, but we are feeling neglected [feeling statement] over here. You may not have seen, but we were here before those people, and I'm afraid we are on sort of a tight schedule [situation statement]; could we get some menus [what I want to have happen], or shall we go someplace else?" Without the aggressivity, I am more likely to get cooperation. I am likely to hear something like, "Oh, you're right, I am so sorry, I'll bring menus right away."

There are many more strategies in assertiveness. In the late great 1960s, the women's movement caught on to it and there are now more books about assertiveness for women than for men. I highly recommend that you study it up. A couple of good books are *Your Perfect Right*, now in its ninth addition (Alberti & Emmons, 2008), and *How to Be an Assertive (Not Aggressive) Woman* (Bear, 1976). There are many more on the topic. Clearly, assertiveness is extremely helpful in managing disagreements in couple relationships.

Complete each argument by the end of the day

Couples unlikely to make it never complete an argument, go to bed upset, and the next day a new argument emerges. It is an endless cycle of rolling arguments. Grandmother had sound advice: "Never go to bed mad." It is really very unpleasant and sad to try to go to sleep when upset, and so unnecessary when the two people involved are lying right next to each other. It is an over-the-top example of a relationship problem directly affecting physical health. In this way, it is cruel to both partners. Quote Grandmother: "At the end of the day, kiss and make up," even if you cannot get complete closure on an argument. You each deserve a restful sleep, and actually have it within your power to offer this to each other. So swallow your pride, take a deep breath, reach over and squeeze his or her hand, and say "I still love you." And for heaven's sake, if you are on the receiving end of this, reciprocate. You both, at least, will sleep better.

Use time-outs

Driving in an unfamiliar city, racing to get to the airport, I am yelling at my wife about the lack of appropriate signage on the freeway. She says, "There's the exit." I yell, "No damn it, it is the next one." Five miles later the next exit proves she was right. Well, with my blood still boiling I just cannot get myself to apologize—not just then. I need a few minutes, quite a few actually, time to physiologically calm down, before I can say, "You were right, Dear, I should have listened to you, I am sorry I yelled … ."

Most of us get upset and lose our tempers with our spouses somewhere along the line. It is only human—or more accurately, it is only mammalian, because anger happens to all animals. It is part of the flight-or-fight response. This is a naturally evolved survival response involving the autonomic division of the central nervous system, specifically the sympathetic division. It is not really sympathetic as we generally use the term. It is sympathetic in the sense that it wants us to successfully offset a threat by fighting hard or by getting away. We perceive a threat, adrenaline is released, pulse rate and blood pressure jump, blood is pumped to the big muscles and the brain, eyes dilate, and respiration is increased. In this state, it is very difficult, maybe impossible, to sensitively hear what one's partner is saying, let alone respond compassionately. We need time to calm down. Research by Dr. Neil Jacobson involving hardwiring couples to measure physiological responses while arguing found that it takes men about half an hour to calm down, but it takes women only about five minutes. Why the difference? Across the span of human evolution, it was the man who could stay physically energized the longest who survived, therefore passing along this trait to his sons. This was the guy who could chase a gazelle for ten miles, hit it with a spear, track it another five miles, haul it over his shoulder, and carry it all the way back to camp. This was the man who, because of a strongly beating heart, defeated the other fellow in a fight. On the other hand, women seem to have evolved the "tend-

and-mend" response. This was the woman who could calm people down. This was the woman who could keep the babies quiet under the bushes until emergencies passed.

In any case, taking time-outs is something healthy couples do when they realize they are too upset to be cooperative. On the surface, it may appear to an observer that stonewalling is occurring. The critical difference is that time-outs are by mutual agreement, whether spoken or unspoken.

I suggest that you talk about this strategy with your partner. To help make it work, again, remember that time-outs need to be mutually agreed upon. Also, they are better if time-limited. That is, agree that after taking a time-out, you will discuss the issue again at a specific time, preferably before the end of the day. It is advisable to not discuss hot issues within an hour or two of going to bed, because you need to be relaxed by then to get a good night's sleep.

Use problem-solving guidelines

As I have said, healthy couples tend to get solution-focused in their arguments. Here is a method to do this using a problem-solving system. The strategies are similar to those used in industries to stay in business for many decades, even for centuries. Corporations like Ford Motor or Boeing have conflicts too—big ones, usually pitting labor against management. Over the years, they have developed problem-solving systems. When a conflict emerges, they call in the arbiter. This person then follows guidelines usually involving a number of steps. The first step, in anybody's system, is to determine what exactly is the problem to be solved. So the arbiter gets together with the laborers and on a flip chart identifies a list of all the problems they can brainstorm: "They don't give us enough break time, not enough health benefits, our pay is too low," etc. Then the arbiter gets together with management and gets a similar list: "They want too much money, their breaks are abused, health benefits are too expensive," etc. Then the arbiter does a magical thing. He or she has each side elect several individuals to be placed on a single committee tasked to come up with possible resolutions to the problems. There is something special about being on a small committee that makes people want to be more sensible, helpful, and cooperative. The arbiter sets a cooperative atmosphere and then focuses the committee on one problem at a time, discussing the issues and then brainstorming possible solutions. The best ideas are taken back to the larger groups to be voted on and acted on.

Couples should not have to rely on an arbiter to negotiate each conflict. What they need is a method of solving their own problems. This problem-solving system for couples has only three steps. Within the three steps are most of the communication tools you need for effectively managing any problem you may encounter. When couples practice these steps, they slowly get what they have been missing: a sense of safety and trust that they can solve problems, and the return of the most important thing in a relationship—the experience of a positive, genuine, and safe emotional connection. I suggest that you review the model together and try it out on any issue that the two of you have been unable to resolve. If you cannot get through it in good faith, I strongly encourage you to see a couples' counselor. Below is the model I recommend:

Assertive Problem-Solving for Couples

1. *Identify the problem.* This is often the hardest part. We all too often miss and obscure the issue of contention because we are so busy defending our feelings, playing the blame-counterblame game, or rushing ahead to what we each think should happen.

If you are wondering about some issue or potential issue involving your partner, ask for his or her help. Do not say, "Hey ... I've got a beef with you," or anything aggressive sounding. Instead, try to engage his or her cooperation assertively by saying something like, "I think we have a problem here. Let's try to solve it, together," or "I want you to help me. I'm worried about ... ." Or if a conflict is underway, one of you needs to say, "Okay, what is *the actual problem* we need to resolve?" Then actively support each other in taking turns making statements of the problem—*technically. Do not talk about your feelings at this point, or your speculations as to the causes, or your idea of a solution.* Avoid all of that at this stage. Fight the impulse to defend yourself. Force yourself to respectfully elicit your partner's perception of what *the problem* is.

When you can agree on what the problem is, write it down as a statement. Make it neutral, not blaming or condemning one another, e.g.,

"*We* have a time management problem," not, "You are too greedy with your time." The whole exercise will not work if the problem statement explicitly or implicitly places fault on one or the other.

2. *Share feelings and needs.* The goal of this step is to become emotional confidants by suspending aggressiveness, relaxing defensiveness, learning more accurately how you each feel about the problem, facilitating useful discussion, and generating empathy for each other.

After you have written down a neutral statement of the problem to solve, take turns describing what the issue has been like for each of you emotionally. Focus only on getting in touch with and sharing your *feelings* in words. Whoever is speaking must use assertive, not aggressive, language. This step is not about dumping on your partner; it is about coming to understand your own feelings, expressing them so that your partner can understand, and coming to understand his or her feelings as well. Use "I" statements, not "You" statements. For example, "When thus-and-such happens between us, I feel discounted," not, "You are too insensitive." Do not share your thoughts on the content of the problem, its history, or who is right or wrong. Focus in on yourself to identify your feelings. Work at using words that describe *feelings* rather than reiterating the situation, blaming your partner, or pontificating about what is fair and unfair. Use feelings words from the list in Chapter 11 if it helps.

It is essential that the one whose turn it is to be listening does not interrupt, interpret, defend, judge, scowl, grimace, wince, or laugh inappropriately. Be attentive, respectful, and sincere and show that you can suspend judgment. This is your chance to prove that you really can be a good listener. Use supportive listening skills. Being nonjudgmental and empathic creates the sense of trust and safety necessary for the other to identify and divulge important emotions. While listening, use the tools counselors are taught. Start with "minimal encouragers" like eye contact (not glaring), head nodding, and saying "uh-huh" or "I see." Use occasional open-ended questions that encourage feeling identification: "What has this problem been like for you; ... how has it made you feel?" This kind of listening really helps people feel that we are supportively listening. It helps them relax and peel back the defense layers that inhibit emotional knowing and sharing.

Beyond minimal encouragers and open-ended questions, what really helps us to understand, and our partners to feel heard, is to occasionally reflect the content of what we hear them saying. For example: "So Mom said what she said to you, and then just walked out of the room." With this, the speaker knows we are paying close attention, and it will feel good to them—it feels supportive. More powerful than this is to occasionally reflect the speaker's emotion. This is a reflection of affect: "It sounds like when Mom walked out, it left you feeling humiliated."

You must work at accepting your partner's feelings whether you feel accused, disagree, or think he or she should not feel that way. It is generally counterproductive to tell someone, "You shouldn't feel that way because … ." It tends to confuse and hurt people when others do not accept what they are in fact really feeling. *Feelings are always real.* It is essential that feelings receive validation even when we think they have no rational basis. Feelings and rationality are two different things but equally real.

The broader benefit in this approach is that beyond possibly resolving a specific problem, it also promotes emotional closeness—to become again each other's emotional confidant, the only compatibility line item that really counts in a relationship. Think about this. If you are not your partner's emotional confidant, to whom will he or she turn? You do not have to go through life paying counselors for this. So even during this exercise, you must work at getting your partner to trust that you are listening and that you care about his or her feelings. Neither of you will be able to relax or get in touch with and risk sharing core feelings if you cannot even trust your partner to listen supportively.

When the speaker, encouraged by supportive listening, can think of nothing else to say to describe how he or she feels, the listener needs to paraphrase everything he or she heard, with a precise focus on repeating the actual feelings words that the speaker used. Avoid saying things like, "I hear that you think I really screwed up and you hate me." Rather say, "I hear that you feel discounted, hurt, and angry about [the problem]." Just stick to the actual words the speaker used to describe his or her feelings.

Now, using the same assertive speaking/supportive listening techniques, take turns stating what each of your *needs* are regarding the problem. For example, "I need to have the children stop fighting," or, "I need to go to my class on Tuesday nights," or, "I need to feel important to you."

A great strategy to ensure that this sharing of feelings and needs works is to use the ticket-to-talk technique. Once you have agreed on who will share feelings and needs first, he or she can hold the ticket to talk (any piece of paper or small object will do). The other cannot get the ticket to talk until he or she has, to the ticket holder's satisfaction, successfully paraphrased and accepted what the ticket holder has said, *especially the feeling words shared.* If the ticket holder does not feel completely heard, he or she should restate any parts the listener did not get and continue holding the ticket until the listener paraphrases accurately. Then the ticket is given to the other and the process is reversed until both agree they have been heard.

3. *Brainstorming and resolution.* Now, with a caring appreciation of each other's feelings and needs, brainstorm possible solutions. Take turns and encourage each other to come up with and write down a list of as many resolutions to the problem as possible.

Resolutions generally come in two types: new ideas that meet the needs of both parties or compromise solutions. Taking turns is very important, back and forth until no one can think of any other possibilities. It is critical that you not miss the following rule of brainstorming: In order to begin to feel like you are on the same team, and to generate the most free and creative thinking, never comment on or judge the appropriateness of an idea no matter how ridiculous it may sound to you. To do so greatly discourages the person offering the idea, and inhibits further creativity. No judging until the list is complete. For each idea suggested, try to think of as many variations as possible and list these as well.

When it is agreed that no more ideas can be thought of, then review each item for compatibility with each of your already stated needs. Then select the idea(s) that seem to have the best balance. Agree to implement the chosen idea(s) *experimentally.* Review the tested plans after one week, or at any mutually agreed upon interval, and adjust as needed or repeat the process. If an idea cannot be agreed upon, take a break, anywhere from a few minutes to a week, and then review the above steps to see if the problem statement was appropriately stated or should be restated. Then see if needs and feelings were accurately stated and understood. And then work again at brainstorming.

Remember: You are trying to become each other's emotional confidant. To do this you have to stop defending and blaming. You need to speak and listen differently. You need to show that you can understand your partner and that he or she can trust you to accept and support, or at least accommodate, his or her very real feelings. Ultimately, don't look for blame or find fault, *solve problems*.

Sexual Recovery

For many couples, the loss of healthy sexual relating is one of the most emotionally painful costs of excessive drinking. Under the influence of alcohol, people sometimes seem to perform sex more easily. This, of course, can be a happy result, especially for those otherwise struggling with sexual inhibition. However, this same disinhibiting effect also leads to bad choices and negative effects such as wrong partners and sexually transmitted diseases. Countless times I have heard the lamentable, sometimes tragic, stories, of individuals awakening in the morning flooded with guilt and fear about a sexual experience that would never have been initiated or completed if the person had been sober. An excellent book on this topic is *Smashed*, by Koren Zailckas. It is the author's personal story of being actively alcoholic through her college years (Zailckas, 2005).

If an affair, on either side or both, was in some way related to your drinking, then special attention will need to be given to this issue. Experts figure that nine out of ten affairs don't work out. If active alcohol dependence was involved the figure is probably closer to ten out of ten. In any case. If you love your original partner, don't beat yourself up for too long—get busy trying to help him or her begin to heal, and be prepared for this to take a long time. Here, I cannot more strongly recommend that you actually see a counselor. I also recommend a book called *After the Affair* by Janis Spring (1996). It is a good starting place for healing to begin if an affair was in the mix.

The other major sexual cost for thousands of drinkers is loss of sexual functioning from the numbing of the nervous system heavy alcohol consumption causes. This is generally experienced as embarrassing and humiliating, to the extent that the problem often recurrences even when sober. We Americans, inspired by Hollywood's spectacular performances where everything works, place grand expectations on ourselves. The stars look great. Zippers and buttons fly away, and amazing mutual organisms occur whether in a bedroom, an elevator, a backseat, or on a kitchen table. In the animal kingdom things are actually a lot more hit or miss. The Bull Moose wanders the forest for 11 months before he even finds a female. Then he is rebuffed many times before a successful joining occurs. The Galapagos tortoise actually falls off the female he tries to mount 50 times or more for every one successful mating. We humans, for whatever reasons, become emotionally unraveled at the slightest thing that doesn't go perfectly when it comes to sex. Identifying the many different types of male and female sexual problems is too far a'field for inclusion in this book. However, If you are having problems in the area of sexual interest and performance I recommend that you have a discussion with a qualified psychologist. The good news is that after several decades of excellent research there are very effective therapeutic strategies and, of course, new medications available. Also, there are many self help books on the topic. I recommend *Seven Weeks to Better Sex* by Domeena Renshaw, MD (2004), because it is well backed by research.

Beyond Conflict Management—How to Build a More Satisfying Primary Relationship

Historically, pain and suffering have driven medical and psychological research. In psychology, it is exciting to see a strong new research movement with a focus on wellness as opposed to pathology. This body of work has been looking at the parameters of happiness. There has, however, been surprisingly little research into what makes for happy couples. Although there are plenty of private opinion books, the preponderance of scientific inquiry has been on how marriages fail. But what if a couple manages conflicts in productive, healthy ways? Beyond that, what can they do to enhance their relationship satisfaction?

Here again, research by John Gottman (2002) helps us out. If we want to increase relationship happiness we need to enhance the sense of a positive "emotional connection." Here is how it works: There are two parts—two things you can easily do to increase contentment in your primary relationship.

The first is to increase your overtures and requests for positive interaction with your partner. These are called "bids for emotional connection." These seem to occur naturally in healthy relationships. They are mostly simple conversational gambits such as, "Honey, did you see how the Wilson's redid their deck?" or, "Did you read about the president's new position on the environment?" Why do we say things like this? It is not merely to hear the melodious sound of our own voices. No, such statements are really requests, consciously or subconsciously, for a brief emotional connection through sharing thoughts and feelings in a gratifying sort of mind-melding. Beyond initiating small talk, bids for emotional connection include suggesting any sort of shared activities, such as to prepare a meal together, go for a bike ride, do a weekend trip, share sex, or indulge in big-ticket items such as a cruise ship adventure. The list is endless. The point is to make a conscious effort to increase your bids for emotional connection with your partner.

Secondly, if not already obvious to you, it is critical that any bids for emotional connection are favorably responded to. It is essential that the person to whom a bid is offered "turn toward" it, rather than away from it. When my wife says, "How about the Wilson's deck," I might turn away from her bid by ignoring it, saying something rude, or otherwise being dismissive of her interest in the topic. Not a good choice really, not if I want a happy marriage. A better choice is to turn toward her bid with something like, "How about that? What do think of that cable railing?"

Many couples have told me that just practicing this simple exercise—making a conscious effort to increase bids for emotional connection and to turn toward them—made an appreciable improvement in their relationship contentment. One reason it works so easily is that it is so quickly rewarding. The inherent reinforcement of positive interaction makes the exercise readily become a self-perpetuating habit.

Many times people experience an increasing absence of romance in their relationships as years go by. Unfortunately it seems to seldom occur to anyone that this can change. But like everything else, you can't continue the same pattern and expect different results. Consider working at being romantic with your partner: Bring flowers, dress seductively, go on a date, smooch, and tell your partner that he or she looks marvelous. Of course millions of poems, books and movies are about this topic. I often recommend a movie titled *Don Juan DeMarco*, starring Marlon Brando and Johnny Depp. This is a delightful story of a young man with the delusion that he is the world's greatest lover. Especially for guys, make sure you watch until the very end when the point of the movie is so beautifully revealed (p.s., John Gottman also recommends this movie).

Starting a New Primary Relationship in Recovery

It is well to note that under the 12-step system of AA, and as ardently recommended by most treatment programs, one is advised not to make any relationship changes in early recovery. This makes sense when you consider how interwoven relationship and drinking problems can be, and how emotionally confusing and fragile early recovery is. Changes and challenges in relationships are inherently distressing. People in early recovery need time just to learn about what happened to them and to restabilize their lives. Time and again, we see people relapse when they make desperate relationship changes or when relationship challenges flair up too early in their recovery. The standard guideline is to gain one full year of recovery before making any significant relationship changes (or for that matter, any other big changes, such as in living place or career).

And yet, I have found that this rule is not only unnecessary for some people, but adhering to it can, in some cases, actually precipitate relapse. What, for example, is recommendable to a newly sober woman whose husband loves her but two months ago had finally made her move out because of her drinking? Does not making any relationship changes mean that she must stay apart from her husband for the next one year? Or does it mean she should stay with him for the next one year, even if she would rather continue apart? What if early in his recovery a potentially healthy relationship becomes available to a lonely middle-aged man? Shall he pass it up at the urging of his AA sponsor or treatment program counselor? There may be serious risk to his recovery either way. Personally, in that situation I tend to think we all need healthy relationships, they are hard to find, and we cannot afford to be too risk averse. *We need to live our lives as if things will work!* The alternative, living as if things will not work, will certainly lead to loss. The former, at the very least, may not.

> To cheat oneself out of love
> is the most terrible deception;
> it is an eternal loss
> for which there is no reparation,
> either in time or in eternity.
> —Soren Kierkegaard

On the other hand, a newly sober woman who has a painful history of going from one shallow alcoholic relationship to another may be very well advised to live independently until she learns who she is, becomes independent in other areas of her life, discovers what she really wants in a relationship, and has a well established recovery going before she enters any new relationship.

In any case, after your first year of recovery or sooner, if you want to consider a new relationship, here are my suggestions.

- *Prioritize* your recovery—your hard-earned sobriety—in any and all of your relationship choices. In any relationship choice you need to ask yourself honestly, what will more likely destabilize your recovery? To stay or to go? To hold off or to commit?
- Talk over any anticipated relationship changes with a trusted friend, relative, or counselor.
- If you are considering entering into a new relationship, identify your motives.

The big question regarding your motives for entering into a new relationship is, are you just wanting to escape yourself and the daunting challenge of independence, or does the person you are falling for really have the qualities that are right for you? If you are so riddled with self-doubt that you tend to approach any potential relationship focused on fear of rejection, you will run into the problem of perpetually mistaking someone's acceptance of you for being in love with him or her. The subconscious error is, "He/she didn't reject me. Therefore I must love him/her." After you have given your heart away, you eventually discover the significant differences between you and your new partner. Relationships thus predicated seldom work out. To avoid this faulty selection process, try the following: Take some time to make a list of desirable features you want in an ideal mate. Add whatever you want to the list, and jot down your wishes for each.

Desirable Mate Features Profile

The Areas of Recovery

Area	What I want
Politics	
Religious beliefs/practices	
Financial strength/practices	
Age parameters	
Appearance	
Health and fitness	
Personal hygiene	
Child-raising beliefs/wishes	
Social interests	
Leisure interests/pursuits	
Sexuality	
Division of labor beliefs	
Disagreement management style	
Emotional connection	
Other features important to me	

Now rate the features in their order of importance to you. For example, for some people child-raising beliefs are more important than politics. For others, leisure interests are the most important thing. All that matters here is what is important to *you*.

Then, keep your list in your hip pocket (at least mentally), and when you encounter a possible mate, on a date or any other situation, *do not let your heartstrings go until you learn whether the person truly measures up*. This ought to take several dates or encounters with any one person—it takes a while to really learn about a person's politics, religious beliefs, leisure and social interests, etc. But remember, the two most important items to learn about are, (a) how does the person manage arguments, and (b) can the person make a positive, safe, and genuine emotional connection with you? I urge you to take these two items most seriously, above all others. To review, research shows that how people argue, fight, or otherwise manage disagreements is the strongest predictor of who will or will not end up staying together (Gottman, 1999). And, a marriage without a satisfying emotional connection is merely a business arrangement at best, but more likely the sacrifice of two people's lives.

Making an advance list of desirable features reverses the whole dynamic of how you approach dates and potential partners. You are now thinking, "Is he or she right for me?" rather than, "Am I good enough for him or her?"

Family Relationships

The negative effects of alcohol use problems on family relationships are legendary. Perhaps the best commonly known system for understanding the dynamics of the alcoholic family is that espoused by Sharon Wegscheider-Cruse (1989). She likens the family unit to a decorative mobile that hangs from a ceiling. If you blow on one part, all the other parts must move to counterbalance and restabilize the unit. When an alcohol use problem occurs in one or more members of a family, the changes in his or her behavior will affect all the other members—they will need to adjust the way they relate to each other and ultimately to all other people in their lives. The adaptive roles that family members tend to assume are identified as follows:

The Dependent

This, of course, is the family member with the alcohol dependence problem. Typical of the disorder, dependent persons tend to realize at some level that they are emotionally and possibly physically dependent on alcohol. They have a fear that they cannot do without the alcohol, resist believing that they have the problem, and fear discovery. So they cover this fear with a "wall of defenses" designed to keep the others from realizing the problem. This wall of defenses may include congeniality, hyperproductivity, or anger and hostility. The other family members will be confused by this, and not know how to relate to the Dependent person, subsequently developing their own defenses.

The Chief Enabler

This person, usually the spouse, has the task of holding the family together. If the alcoholic is not making enough money, spending too much, or blowing jobs, the Chief Enabler will get a job, or learn to make do with less. If the Dependent is unable to make it to work, the Chief Enabler will cover up—phoning the boss to say that the spouse is ill. All of these well-intentioned behaviors, of course, actually facilitate continuance of the problem by staving off the much-needed confrontations that could break the Dependent's denial and help him or her initiate recovery. The Chief Enabler is, of course, at risk of developing his or her own drinking problem out of hopelessness and helplessness and the depression this causes.

The Hero

This is one of the children, most often the firstborn but not necessarily. This kid is keen to the parental problems, stuffs his or her own fear and self-doubt, and becomes really good at something as a defense. The goals are to show the outside world what a good family this really is, and to take some heat off the parents. Typically, the hero becomes either a great academic overperformer or a great athletic overperformer.

The Scapegoat

If one child is the known family hero, well then that role is taken, and the next child, feeling totally useless, needs to rebel and become the troublemaker. These kids may run with the negative-influence peers, screw up at school, use alcohol and other drugs, and get in trouble with the police. Family therapists consider this the role of noble sacrifice. The Scapegoat's secret mission is to provide a distraction that the community can obviously see, in order to take the focus off troubled Mom and Dad. The modus operandi of the Scapegoat is to act out with anger and high-risk behaviors what the family is unable to confront in more healthy ways.

The Lost Child

This one fears trouble and yearns for peace and tranquility. Family discord is emotionally anguishing for the Lost Child, who feels powerless to do anything about it. So these kids take a "don't rock the boat" approach. They avoid relationships and try to blend into the background at home and at school. With a reserved exterior, no one realizes how troubled the Lost Child really is. No one inquires or tries to help.

The Family Mascot

Here is the little charming personality—the little Miss or Mister Sunshine, the family entertainer, and the class clown. The Mascot simultaneously seeks validation that is not reliably available at home, and attempts to bring comic relief to an otherwise tragic scene. Ultimately, this is the employee at the watercooler cracking jokes, but then knocking back martinis at home to ease the stress of being on stage.

If you identify with any of these roles, take heart. They occur in all families to greater and lesser extents, whether alcohol is involved or not. I think I have inadvertently tried all of these roles and more. The main thing is that if you can recognize any of these characteristics in yourself or in any of your family members, you can do something about it. You can stop enabling. You can prize the heroes for just being who they really are, especially when they do not make that four-point GPA or drop the pass in the end zone. You can get help for the scapegoat. You can notice the lost child and help the mascot relax. And of course, you, despite whatever roles you have taken in your family, can stop drinking and start being good to yourself.

Recovering family relationships that have been damaged in some way related to your drinking can take a long time. Here the AA practice of making amends has real serviceability. Remember, like the diabetic or the paraplegic, you don't have to apologize for what happened to you as if what happened to you was by your own malevolent intent. But to tell a family member that you are indeed sorry for how your condition effected them, can go a long way in beginning to heal the relationship. Unfortunately, you may not be able to salvage relationships with all family members. Once you make your apology the ball is in the other person's court. Be prepared that some people may not be able to respond favorably. If this happens, I suggest that you not respond angrily or dismissively, but rather graciously. Give the person space, and let go. You've done the best you can. Accept the loss with compassion for each of you.

This is especially painful if the person who will not forgive you is a son or daughter. In these situations, while they may have slammed the door, you must respect their space, let go as best you can, but always keep *your* door open. Be patient. Gratefully, things usually change across time.

Friendship Recovery

Friendships is the third area of relationship recovery as I classify them, but often the most important. This is especially true when one's primary relationship, family relationships, and co-worker relations are not very solid or not there at all. Friendships can actually be more enduring than the other types of relationships. Think of people who have been divorced a couple of times and never speak to their ex-spouses, but who have always maintained several close friendships from childhood. Whereas ex-partners, family members, and co-workers go away, old friendships never die. More than this, recent research from the Australian Longitudinal Study of Aging found that old people with good friendship connections significantly outlive those with no friendships or those with close family relationships only (Giles et al., 2005). It seems that close relationships with spouses, siblings, adult children, and grandchildren in one's old age are nice, but will not boost longevity as much as having good friends.

Several factors conspire against newly sober folks in the area of friendship recovery:

Lack of Social Self-Confidence

No particular personality type predicts active alcoholism. However, after years of drinking, alcohol becomes not only one's emotional manager, but also one's *social* manager. This creates an actual deficit in social relating skills when one is not using alcohol. Thus, alcoholics in early recovery tend to have in common a lack of social self-confidence.

This lack of social confidence is not really a personality deficit or "character defect" but rather a social skills deficit. Simply put, it was a lot easier to relate to people behind the fog of alcohol, but now what do I do with my bare face hanging out?

Continuing or Ending Drinking-Based Friendships

In early recovery a person is typically faced with the daunting challenge of developing new friends, or having no friends at all. Over a number of years, people with drinking problems increasingly gravitate to the company of other heavy drinkers, or begin to isolate, losing a social life altogether. After quitting drinking, people naturally want to be able to continue to associate with their drinking friends, but this seldom works out. The old AA adage seems to be true for most people: "You have to change your playgrounds and playmates." As you may discover, this is often the biggest single challenge in recovery. Just when you could use the most social support, the people you would normally turn to are suddenly bad influences. And, of course, the old friends want you to continue to get together with them as well. They invariably offer to support your abstinence. Countless times, I have heard clients say, "Oh, don't worry, my friends all say it is fine with them if I don't drink—they support my abstinence. They even said they would make sure I don't drink."

Although well intended, this is unfortunately a notorious script for relapse. The first couple of times out with drinking friends will work because you will have your vigilance up and friends will be outwardly showing that they can support your abstinence. After the first experience, you will think, "Well, I did it. Wow! That wasn't so bad. See? I can be with drinking friends and not drink." Because this at first seems easy, you will naturally be less uptight about it on subsequent occasions and will naturally lose your vigilance across time. Then, on a bad, unwary evening with your friends, you will suddenly find yourself drinking again. Perhaps you will have been experiencing some stress in your life, and with your mood turning south, in the company of drinking friends, you will either ask for or accept a drink, and you will be surprised to find how quickly your friends support your drinking again.

Societal Stigma

In early recovery, people become aware of a societal stigmatization of alcoholism and struggle with how to present or avoid the issue with friends or potential friends. Part of this dynamic is often an increasing sense of embarrassment and shame from episodes of overdrinking with friends in the past. Shame and embarrassment frequently become so acute that they are in fact a major source of relapse. Most, but not all, people who quit drinking are surprised to discover how difficult it is to consistently turn down drinks socially offered.

I highly recommend that you avoid social situations where drinking can occur in the first place—perhaps for a year or so. Eventually, however, or when unavoidable, I advocate an honest no excuse approach whenever others are drinking or when the topic of alcohol use otherwise comes up. It is important to fight feeling ashamed; you did not ask for the alcohol problem any more than a person asks for arthritis. You are doing your best to be well. You do not need to make excuses or apologize for not drinking with friends or in social situations where alcohol is being consumed. Being assertive here is not merely an option, it is essential.

In the short run, however, if you are not ready for this frankness about your abstinence, there is nothing wrong with skirting the issue or just saying, for example, that you are on a health kick and counting calories. Information about your history with alcohol or why you are not drinking is your private business. You can dispense such information on a need to know basis at your discretion.

Preexisting Social Anxiety

Often, social self-doubt is a major driver of one's drinking problem in the first place. In this case, when initially sober a person can find it doubly difficult simply to avoid becoming totally isolated. This also becomes a prescription for relapse. With these considerations, it becomes seriously challenging to reinvent one's social life and establish healthy friendships in recovery. Understandably reluctant at first, many people find that AA provides a fast track for this task. Whether you do or do not try that route, here are my suggestions:

If you lack social self-confidence, try to view this as a temporary condition, not a dyed-in-the-wool character defect. It is most likely that you have merely become unfamiliar with presenting yourself straight and have compromised your prior sociability. You are just a bit rusty because alcohol has done the job for years, and it will only take a little practice to regain your social confidence. Just get busy practicing and your confidence will return.

If you feel that you are more chronically inhibited and suffer a bona fide social anxiety problem for which excessive drinking was a self-medication, this area of recovery is all the more crucial to work on. Try to look at it this way; if you quit drinking, you will finally have the opportunity to overcome your problem. Again, you must avoid the temptation to think that yours is an immutable problem. I'll bet you a dime to a dollar, that due to your particular childhood circumstances, you merely did not *learn* to be socially confident. You can learn to be significantly more confident now. However, I guarantee you will not be able to do this if you only practice socializing while under the influence of alcohol. As discussed in Chapter 6, imagined social skill gained while inebriated is state-dependent. It will not convey when sober. Social confidence has to be learned sober.

Millions of us have suffered social anxiety, from simple shyness to crippling social phobia with outright panic when around other people. Wherever you consider yourself to be on this continuum, you need to accept yourself and accept that you really do have this condition. You cannot wait to be magically freed of your social anxiety before doing something about it. *Accept* that you are prone to this irrational anxiety, but also *commit* to working on making it better. Again, *Acceptance and Commitment Therapy* captures what I am talking about (Hayes et al., 1999). And now is the time to take the attitude wisely expressed by Susan Jeffers in the title of her book: *Feel the Fear and Do It Anyway* (1987).

Begin before your social fear subsides. Looking at your recovery template, highlight the area of friendships and think about your needs and entitlement. If you really do not believe you are entitled to have friends, I urge you to see a psychologist to overcome this undoubtedly irrational perception. Now set a goal. I suggest something like having two friends with whom you do things regularly by four months from now. Then forge your strategy considering the following ideas.

Make a list of all the friends within reach that you have or have had. From this pool can you identify those without any alcohol use problems, or better still, which are non-drinkers? Of this group, assuming you could generate a list (and not everyone can), twice per week invite a different person to lunch or coffee. After you have seen everyone on the list, pick the ones you feel you enjoy the most and make additional invitations, for example, to go to a movie together or shopping, etc. Perhaps after a couple of months you will have achieved your goal.

If you cannot generate a list of acquaintances to begin with, you will need to start from scratch. Use shared interests to make new friends. A shared interest is the grain of sand around which the pearl of friendship forms. For example, if you join a book club, theater group, bike club, or underwater basket weaving class, such groups are inherently social and invariably have other get-togethers, such as potlucks, to increase social connecting. Again, AA is ideal for this. In addition to meetings, AA groups offer sober social outings at various times.

Desensitize your social anxiety. The socially anxious person has learned to be excessively self-conscious when in social situations. This is a learned autonomic overreactivity, and you can unlearn it. What you need are some simple tools of conversation. Really, it is not very complicated. First, realize that just about everyone is at least a little self-conscious, and if you are among the ranks, it is nothing to be ashamed of or to apologize for. Next, I suggest that you start a little experiment to become more comfortable at interacting with people. It is about the simple art of conversation. First, you must seek out rather than avoid opportunities for social interaction. When the opportunity is at hand, begin the experiment by asking someone a not too personal question:

- So, Art, did you do anything interesting this summer?
- Mary, what did you think of that assignment?
- I see you drive a Honda. How do you like it?

Then, follow up whatever response you get with ... wait for it ... *another question*. Something like, "So at the lake last summer, how big was that fish you caught?" It is amazingly simple. If you only practice this one little strategy, you will reduce your self-consciousness significantly and get along anywhere with just about anyone. Why? Because people love to talk about themselves. Use the listening skills I identified in the section on Assertive Problem-Solving for Couples. Just listen attentively by looking at the person (not glaring), nodding your head, and occasionally saying, "uh-huh." In counseling practice, these attentive listening behaviors are known as "minimal encouragers" because they let the person know you are paying attention, with interest, and without judgment.

Now, add to this conversation experiment with actually responding to any questions that may be directed back to you. If, for example, someone says, "So how was *your* summer?" Do not respond with your usual, "Okay … I guess." That is not sufficient. You need to take the opportunity to desensitize your anxiety by trying to elaborate, even embellish, your response with as many words as you can possibly muster.

To have some fun, in a group of people try playing what I call the "start the conversation game." Without announcing what you are doing, throw out a general question about anything and see where the group conversation winds up a half-hour later. If you start with something like, "Did you read about that earthquake in Chile?", after a half-hour you may be surprised that the group, through a series of loose connections, winds up in a rousing conversation about Fidel Castro. At that point, you may begin to feel a growing sense of confidence that you can actually participate in social situations quite well.

If all of this seems too challenging to you, just start smaller. Practice on people you may already be comfortable with, family members or close friends. You can even practice on people you do not know and whose opinions will not matter in your life: store clerks, people in line with you, anybody with whom you are not actually going to have a relationship. These are going to be brief, time-limited conversations about the weather, or the cost of movies, or what have you. The more you practice this, the greater your confidence will grow. In time, you will feel safe and in control in most social situations. Confronting irrational fears is the best way to overcome them.

The asking questions and responding strategy provides a good beginning, but to really gain appreciable friendships, you will need to do two more things. First, you will need to occasionally take the risk of sharing on a more personal level. Tell someone you are beginning to trust something about what makes you happy, or what makes you sad, or what worries you, or what makes you feel inept or vulnerable. See what sort of response you get. If the person responds with compassion, and perhaps shares something personal back, this should feel quite good to you, and you may have found a worthy friend. If instead the person is judgmental, clams up, or seems dismissive, then this may not be a worthy friend and you can feel free to go the other way. Second, see if you can be somewhat emotionally supportive to the other person. Inquire about how some particular thing may have made him or her feel. Respond with empathy, show that you care, without judgment, and can relate to or otherwise accept their feelings without assuming responsibility for them. This is what friends do and why friendships are so important.

Like most behavior change attempts, your efforts will be more effective, enduring, and rewarding if you set goals, monitor your progress, and set yourself up some rewards for intermediate goals achieved. Moving to a new home several years ago, my wife and I wanted to expand our network of friends. We decided to invite interesting couples to dinner once per month for the first year at our new house. We noted our progress on a calendar. It was inherently rewarding, and after a year, in addition to having had a lot of fun, we established a set of couples with whom we now do things regularly.

Public speaking anxiety is a special type of social anxiety. Many people tell me that they have friends and no problem feeling relaxed in one-to-one relationships, but the thought of getting up in front of a group terrifies them. Fear of public speaking is very common and very beatable. As with other irrational fears, it just requires direct confrontation to desensitize. I highly recommend that you try joining Toastmasters (sorry about the name; this worldwide public speaking club has nothing to do with drinking). Toastmasters clubs are available in every town with a population over about two people—every community of any size has at least one. Google "Toastmasters International" to find a club near you. It provides a safe forum for overcoming public speaking anxiety. There you will get a chance to talk repeatedly in front of a group where every member can appreciate your anxiety. If you do this on a weekly basis, you will significantly reduce your anxiety. Alternatively, enroll in a speech class at a college near you, or write out a plan of your own to systematically practice speaking in front of larger and larger groups of people in as many forums as you can find. If this is too difficult, see a counselor who knows how to treat public speaking anxiety.

Co-Worker Relationship Recovery

This little corner of recovery is seldom written about but often experienced. If, in the course of your drinking, your behavior toward others with whom you work, or your work performance, was compromised, this will be an important area of recovery for you. Here are some things to consider:

As mentioned in the discussion on recovery of family relationships, within the 12 steps of AA there is a directive to "make amends" to others who may have in some way been harmed by your drinking behavior. I do not think this is any more necessary for alcoholics than for people whose behavior for *any* reason has unintentionally harmed someone else. If an epileptic has a seizure that results in failing to fulfill work responsibilities, tipping over someone's shopping cart, missing an appointment, or frightening someone, they might well want to say that they are sorry it happened. Many things are like this in life. So, yes, if at all possible, make apologies to people affected by your drinking, e.g., the co-worker who had to cover your shift, the one you told off, etc. If you do this, however, I suggest that you follow these guidelines:

- Be sincere. It may not be a laughing matter to the person you are apologizing to.
- Don't overdo it. Keep it brief and succinct. Few things are more obnoxious than over apologizing. Imagine you are a person who missed a lot of work because you were hit by a car walking to work. Sure, you would say you are sorry, and thanks, to your co-workers who had to fill in for you, but you would not overdo it and you would not go around like the proverbial dog with its tail between its legs for days on end.
- Do not make unrealistic promises. Just say you are dedicated to staying sober and continuing to be the good, but fallible, human being you really are.
- If someone does not accept your apology, do not get mad, just let it go.

Remember that your workplace and co-workers are not your home or your family. There seems to be a direct correlation between the extent to which a person does not have other fulfilling relationships and the extent to which he or she takes workplace relationships too seriously. Without significant private-life relationships, coworker relationships can fill the void, becoming unreasonably important on an emotional level. This makes for lots of interpersonal conflicts at work. Even when co-worker relationships happen to become family-like in a positive way, this often keeps a person from developing private-life friendships. Try to work from the point of view that co-worker relationships need only be as good as necessary to get jobs done in a reasonably enjoyable way. *Aspire to get your major relationship needs met outside your workplace.*

In closing this chapter, I imagine most of us can agree that relationships are both the most rewarding and the most challenging aspect of our lives. About all we can say was once summed up by Woody Allen. Relationships reminded him of his uncle who thought he was a chicken—they are crazy, but, well, we all need the eggs. I say, keep alcohol out of the mix and you might make some pretty good omelets.

Recommended Reading for Chapter 13

After the Affair: Healing the Pain and Rebuilding Trust When a Partner Has Been Unfaithful, by Janis Spring.

Boundaries in Marriage, by Henry Cloud & John Townsend.

Codependent No More: How to Stop Controlling Others and Start Caring for Yourself, by Melody Beattie.

How to be an Assertive (Not Aggressive) Woman in Life, in Love, and on the Job: The Total Guide to Self-Assertiveness, by Jean Baer.

Passionate Marriage: Sex, Love, and Intimacy in Emotionally Committed Relationships, by David Scharch.

Seven Weeks to Better Sex, by Domeena Renshaw, M.D.

Smashed: Story of a Drunken Childhood, by Koren Zailckas.

The Relationship Cure: A 5 Step Guide to Strengthening Your Marriage, Family, and Friendships, by John Gottman.

The Seven Principles for Making Marriage Work, by John Gottman.

What Makes Love Last? How to Build Trust and Avoid Betrayal, by John Gottman.

Your Perfect Right: Assertiveness and Equality in Your Life and Relationships (9th edition), by Robert Alberti & Michael Emmons.

Chapter 14

Career/Occupation Recovery

Problem:	*With the added challenge of recovery from alcohol dependence, the already baffling challenge of occupational choices can seem hopelessly overwhelming. Going without satisfaction in the productivity life area leads to feelings of despair, and to relapse.*
Solution:	*Overcome your inhibitions and self-doubt, do your homework, and experience the liberation that comes with taking control of your career pathway.*

Costs to work life are not incurred by all people with alcohol use problems. Many times, it is the last area of life affected. In AA they say it is because for the active alcoholic, no matter what else goes wrong, they have got to keep the bartender paid. I think this is often true, but not the only reason. Compared to leisure pursuits, health, and in many cases even marriages, many people most strongly identify with their occupations. Sometimes it is the only place we get any sense of a stable identity, and at least some semblance of self-esteem.

When occupational costs occur, they range in severity from as mild as a onetime experience of going to work with a hangover, to calling in sick, to interpersonal conflicts, to compromised performance, to being fired, and finally to becoming so debilitated that one cannot work at all. Sometimes the costs are not so obvious, but are nonetheless profound. There are people who stay in miserable jobs for years because drinking a bottle of wine or a six-pack of beer (or both) every night keeps them from feeling acutely distressed enough to seek a new job.

If you need some help in the area of career/occupational recovery, here are my thoughts and suggestions.

Let the Past Go

"Last night as I was sleeping,

I dreamt – marvelous error! –

that I had a beehive here inside my heart.

and the golden bees

were making white combs

…and sweet honey

from my old failures….." – Antonio Machado

Whatever you may have blown is blown. Forgive yourself and get prepared to move on. You are not a bad person because you had a drinking problem. You may need to start afresh, but this can be a wonderful thing. In my parents' generation, a person tended to prepare for or drift into one profession and that was it for life. This has completely changed over the past 50 years. Now most people make several career changes during their lives. It is even encouraged.

You get to reinvent yourself. To do this you may need to liberate yourself as much as possible from the way you presently perceive yourself in relation to everyone else in the world. We often self-sabotage our own best interests because we so strongly identify with our set roles and relationships. We are husbands, wives, sons, daughters, brothers, sisters, plumbers, lawyers, and any other relationship that defines us. But *sometimes the roles that define us also confine us*. In the service of self-liberation, in therapy we help people imagine life without their current defining roles. There are many strategies. Here is one I like called "Planet X." It is referred to as a "role stripping" exercise. It is designed to help people imagine how they might live if free of externally imposed definitions of themselves and free of the self-defeating expectations that follow. It goes like this:

Imagine that a huge asteroid is about to strike Earth. Somehow, you manage to get on a rocket ship that blasts off just in time. From a hundred thousand miles out you look back in horror to see the world totally blown apart. Every person, place, and thing, you have every known is gone forever. In despair, you look around and discover that you are the only one on the ship. You get into a capsule within the ship that puts you in a state of suspended animation, and the ship hurls through space at hyper-light speed for 10 million years. Then it crash-lands on a planet at the other end of the universe. You manage to get out before the ship burns up. You find yourself on a planet that is laid out exactly as Earth was, with all the same countries and cities, but, of course, you do not know anyone. You have several thousand dollars in your pocket.

Five years pass. You wake up one morning. What kind of living place are you in? What does it look like? What do you have for breakfast? Is anybody else there? Where do you go that day? What do you do for a living? What do you do for fun?

Imagine Planet X once in a while, and imagine how you might live there. It may help you let go of unnecessary self-recrimination, unfulfilling roles, and disingenuous expectations. It may help you discover who you really are or want to be. It may help you begin to turn what you thought were pipedreams into reality. I wish you well.

Develop a Sense of Entitlement

Like every being on earth, you have a genetic imperative and entitlement to survive and thrive. You owe it to yourself to try again. As mentioned in Chapter 9, in comparing big lottery winners to initially successful business owners who went bankrupt, after five years 80 percent of the lottery winners were back at their old jobs and lifestyles after pretty much squandering the money, whereas 80 percent of the failed business owners were back on top and wealthy again. What is the difference? The lottery winners lacked the sense of entitlement that the business owners had. For the successful, failures are attributed to outside causes, such as unforeseen vagaries of the market, rather than to any personal faults. They simply learn from the experience, chalk it off to experience, and move on with a continuing assumption of entitlement to succeed.

Do Not Be Too Risk Averse

If you can imagine enjoying a certain type of occupation but hold back because you see some obstacles and fear failure, you may be what is called too risk averse. The problem is that just settling for what is safely in reach may not really make you happy.

> Ships in harbors are safe.
>
> But that is not what ships
>
> are built for.
>
> —Anonymous

Risk-taking at times is necessary in building careers. Ask anyone successful and happy in his or her career. I cannot think of anyone I know who did not take risks. In my own life, every job, school, or career move I have ever made required considerable risk. Did things always work out? Of course not. That is why it is called *risk*-taking. Isn't everything we try really just another experiment? To wait for certainty that a plan will work out is unrealistic. We need to grant ourselves permission to try things without waiting for guarantees that will never come.

Building Your Courage

When it comes to careers, *do not expect to know exactly what you should commit to.* If all you have is a hunch, that will have to do.

Scholars used to theorize that we must go through several stages of career choice. Children are thought to be in only a fanciful period of career choice, and teenagers in a tentative period of choice at best. Indeed, many ideas teens have are not very realistic, but based rather on fleeting romantic notions of what a great identity they will have if they become a Learjet pilot, or a special agent for the CIA, or a marine biologist playing with dolphins all day. The choice process can only get more realistic as we age and our life experiences broaden. Because of this, in the late 1960s people supported the idea that one should not try to decide too young. We were encouraged to go to college and take general studies for a while, and to not pick a major for as long as possible. This made sense. Too often in my practice I meet people—dentists, lawyers, factory workers, what have you—who are terribly unhappy in their careers, and wondering who allowed that 15- to 20-year-old to make such a momentous career choice without having experienced enough of the world and possibilities and before having any idea who he or she was. I feel that we were well advised in my generation to take it slowly. Since then, something seems to have gone wrong. Somewhere in the 1990s, I began to see *middle school* children who were feeling like failures because they had not decided what they should study in college and had not put together a portfolio to be prepared to get accepted by the right college when the time came. They were being pushed by anxious, competitive parents and teachers to define interests and choices while still only in a fanciful period of career choice. Their young minds and inexperience make any choices at that point ludicrous.

If your career took a hit because of your alcohol use problem, or if you have never been sure what career you are best suited for and are dissatisfied with what you got, you are not alone. Amid thousands and thousands of career possibilities, most people are never really exposed to more than a handful from which to choose. Yet, in reality, most people could be successful at and enjoy a huge variety of occupations. My point is, stop assuming that you should know, or that something is wrong with you if you do not know, what occupation will guarantee your happiness. I submit to you that if you can generate a short list of occupations that you can imagine you might like, it does not matter which one you choose. It only matters that you choose. Your happiness will depend far less on the job than on your attitude about work and life in general.

Strategize Using the Life Areas Template

Reread the section on how to use the Life Areas Template. Specify the world of work, assess needs, set goals, make plans, and get started. Here are some ideas that may help.

Capitalize on Happenstance

Do our occupations come to us by drift, choice, or chance? In the first half of the last century, theorists assumed that people moved into careers through rational decision-making processes. Under this model, one systematically begins to identify specific interests and abilities in his or her teen years and then selects a career based upon its match with those interests and abilities. Like so many assumptions of yore, the theory has proved unrealistic. In reality, for most people, what drives career choice is everything but a rational decision-making process. Apart from the possibility of divine directives, unplanned and unforeseen influences in the real world play the most powerful role in career choice. Research, for example, on nurses and teachers finds that most people tend to drift into their careers as other options fall by the wayside. The class you wanted was full, so you took another one. The instructor got you involved in a project that led to meeting someone else who got you interested in moving to Tucson, where you got a job with organization B because organization A was not hiring. Drift and happenstance play a huge role in our lives.

This, I hope, will not sound as if I am suddenly giving you license to just take life one day at a time and see what happens. Not at all, for plan we must. Otherwise, you are merely drifting. In drifting, we are hoping that the fates will someday smile on us and we will discover our inner calling, with the attendant bags of money that come with such wishful dreaming. In my youth, Eastern ways of thought became popular. Chanting certain nonsense syllables was supposed to bring the chanter anything he or she desired. Perhaps if I had stuck with it just a bit longer I might have gotten that Mercedes-Benz and the $12 million. Oh well. The current resurrection of this practice has us all wishing for wonderful things to come to us through magically thinking, "My thoughts will pull what I want to me." Okay, there is some hope there. However, if you want a Mercedes, it is not going to drop gently out of a wonderful caring universe onto your driveway because you willed it to do so. No. You are going to have to work for it. You are going to have to make some plans and take some steps.

Merely drifting is not what is meant by capitalizing on happenstance. What this means is that as you plan, ardently plan, and pursue an occupation, be open to exploring the unplanned, tangential events, interests, people, and opportunities that emerge as you go. To do otherwise could be like a treasure hunter passing right by the hull of a treasure-laden ancient Spanish galleon because his nose is stuck in his map.

Use Job-Getting Strategies

If it is just a job you want right now, any old job, try the following:

- Dust off or create a resume. Again, all the resume templates you could possibly want are available online. Do not bother sending it out unsolicited; that just does not work.

- Download a standard job application form. There are dozens of them free on the Internet. Fill one out as completely as you can. Having this done and in your pocket makes it a lot easier to walk in cold to different businesses to ask for work.

- If a college campus is situated in your area, go there. They all have career resource centers that are usually publicly funded and therefore open to the public. They usually have postings of all sorts of jobs—part-time, temporary, and permanent—from area employers.

- Walk into possible job sites cold. With your resume and your model job application in hand, you can walk in anywhere and easily fill out their job application. Calling in advance is going to prove a waste of time. It is too easy for employers to steer away someone they are not looking at face to face. Sure, check the newspaper, but that is not where the jobs are to be found. Walk into bookstores, restaurants, car lots, flower shops, and art galleries—wherever you want. Ask if there are any jobs available.

Simple sounding, isn't it? But for some, very difficult to do. We are inhibited because we fear rejection. Of course, it is an irrational fear. We imagine that if we ask about work at some establishment, the person there might loudly say, "Oh my God! Look everyone, this pathetic excuse for a human being is asking for a job." Then everyone there looks angry, or laughs, points to the door, and yells, "Get out you idiot, and don't come back."

This in not going to happen! In fact, people will treat you with interest and respect. After all, haven't we all been in that position?

People actually want to be helpful. If they do not have any work available, just ask them if they know of anyone who may be hiring. To help overcome your inhibition, practice what you might say with a friend or family member. Richard Bolles (2010), the author of the classic job-finding book *What Color Is Your Parachute*, recommends heading out on a job-hunting morning with the goal of seeing how many "No" responses you can get, because the truth is, the more "No's" you collect, the closer you are to a "Yes."

If what you want is an occupation or career, not merely a temporary job, consider the following:

- Start by reading a career-finding book like Bolles' *What Color Is Your Parachute* (2010). It is always current because he updates it every year. When you identify what it is that you are willing to pursue, set a goal. Then create a time line that tracks backward from the date you hope to reach your goal. This process is described in more detail in Chapter 9, on using the Life Areas Template. From the date farthest out, identify what will need to be accomplished at various points in time right back to the present.

- Visit a college career resource center and request career counseling. Sometimes there is a nominal fee for such services, but often they are free because, again, most colleges are publicly funded. They usually have career interest inventories, career information, and personal career counseling. For example, look at a book called *The Occupational Outlook Handbook* (2009). It is published every other year by the U.S. Department of Labor. Not only are hundreds of occupations identified within the pages of this tome, but for each there is information on what the work is really like, what training or degrees are necessary, where the jobs are, what kind of money can be expected, and what the future outlook is.

- Deploy guerrilla tactics. Bolles outlines a strategy that beats all others. It is a sort of backdoor strategy that can be adapted myriad ways to fit any individual's particular needs and situation. In a nutshell, it goes something like this: Do not bother blindly firing out your resume for position openings in your targeted field. Millions of people do this every day. This will get you nowhere. I remember in the middle 1970s trying this woeful strategy in hopes of getting a job in a college counseling center. I was well qualified with a master's degree and had completed a counseling internship at a college. I got zero positive responses for several months. After actually phoning some schools directly, I learned that for each opening they were getting hundreds of qualified applicants. One west coast community college counseling center director told me, "Don't feel too bad. We had over 2,000 resumes with cover letters sent for one open position." The jobs usually went to inside candidates. So instead of the shotgun approach, do some research on a specific company or entity you wish to work for. See if you can identify any challenges ahead for that company, or problems they may be having. Learn what some other companies in the same or a related field have done to face such challenges. Then identify and ask to meet a person of influence within the company or entity you have researched. Tell the person that you have an interest in the field and would like simply to talk with him or her about how the company operates. Offer to buy the person lunch. Completely avoid any semblance of a suggestion that you are looking for a job. Forget about getting a job; at this point you are legitimately trying to learn about an interesting field. When you meet the person, show great interest in what the person knows about the field. Inquire about the challenges or problems you already know they have. Then ask if they have considered some of the possible solutions you have already thought about. If you have done your homework, do not be surprised if they offer you a job. Now, if you think about it, you can tailor this concept to meet your particular interests and needs. How do you suppose I got into a couple of very competitive graduate programs? I studied up several professors' research and strolled into their offices to casually talk about their work as related to my interests. And what do you know? In the course of conversation, they got interested in me, asked what my plans were, invited me to take classes with them and to apply for admission, offering all the help they could. All it takes is a little creativity. No need to be deceiving. You can say that you are interested in working in that field/business/industry, and this is exactly why you want to learn more about it from an expert on the inside.

Create a Healthy Work Life

Once you get a job, or if you have a job, then you will want to make your work as enjoyable as possible. In recovery, *a balanced life is the goal*. This means do not take your work life too seriously. As mentioned in Chapter 12 on leisure and recreational recovery, European countries average 30-plus vacation days per years; Americans, 12. American economists argue that we have a higher gross national product. European economists say they have a higher quality of life—they actually use quality of life as a factor in their economic formulas.

Do not let your work define you entirely. I hope that you enjoy your work. I hope that you feel creative and positive about your occupation. However, strive for other definitions of yourself, with your family, friends, leisure interests, health maintenance, and living place. When I was directing treatment programs, many challenges would arise. For example, faced with funding cuts requiring program changes, staff would say, "Chris, thank heavens you can manage this. How do you stay so calm?" I would respond (admittedly for my own benefit as well as theirs), "Well, if I made a list of priorities in my life, I get the top 10 met outside of here, and so whatever happens here can't upset me very much." It is emotionally healthy to more broadly define yourself outside of work, to the extent that your work challenges never have to seem overwhelming.

Avoid viewing your workplace and co-workers as your home and family. As a rule, work settings must operate on a different basis than friendships or families. There have to be *impersonal* rules, specific goals and tasks, strict hierarchies of authority, performance evaluations, etc. that would drive families and friendships apart. Seeing the work group as your family is going to lead to too much emotionality over what are just business interactions. The extent to which people do this is proportionate to a lack of healthy, supportive family and friendship relationships outside work. If you find yourself experiencing this phenomenon, the thing to do is identify what you are missing elsewhere in your life. Use the template to set new goals and plans in other life areas, and hopefully develop the feeling of family with people outside of your work place.

Avoid burnout. To do this, realize that the mind needs a reliable sense of "break." Set work limits as tightly as you can. Strive to make clear boundaries between work and not work. Set consistent hours and do not take work home with you. Not doing these things is a script for burnout. This is especially important if you are your own boss. People I know who are their own boss complain that they have the toughest boss they have ever had. When your income is solely dependent on your own productivity, overworking becomes extremely compelling. It calls to you like the sirens called to Homer's delirious sailors. But like with the doomed sailors, it will destroy you. When I went from directing treatment programs to full-time private practice about 15 years ago, I still had kids at home and a mortgage to pay, so I was ready to work hard. Yet I had seen enough burned-out private practitioners to set some advance limits on my work. I agreed with myself that I would only work five days per week, never see clients in the evening or on weekends, and never bring work home. If you can, it is better to stay late at work to finish something you were thinking of bringing home to do. Bringing it home does not teach your mind a reliable sense of break. You may find yourself debating this at the end of an otherwise normal workday. You might think you can finish it at home after dinner, or come to work a little early tomorrow to finish it. Try this: Stop and consider the poor person to whom you are leaving the work. That person, of course, is you. You would never do a thing like that to a co-worker, why do it to yourself? Now imagine how good that person (you) will feel tonight and in the morning because you already finished the work before leaving the office. Not doing this leads to burning out because it fails to teach your mind to relax with the trust that clear breaks will reliably come.

Many people tell me they fear that if they take this strategy, they will become less productive. Quite clearly, however, because your mind stays significantly more relaxed with the knowledge of well-defined breaks, you become more productive. There is an old adage, "Work fills its allotted space." With work limits reliably in place, one has more cognitive energy to focus, enjoys work more, and works more efficiently. Therefore, in all these years, I have often worked 10- or even 12-hour days, but I have held to my initial plan. Thus, I have not burned out. I always look forward to coming to the office, and I am well focused each day. My mind has learned to comfortably know exactly when the breaks from work are coming. I make a clear demarcation between work and not work, and this has been very satisfying. I am more relaxed at home and more efficient at work. Most importantly, I have had a life with family, friends, fitness, regular recreation activities, and vacations.

All of these concepts and strategies become doubly important if you want to avoid relapse on alcohol. Fortunately, managing your career/occupation and working for a balanced life, is not only essential for sobriety, it is also very fulfilling.

Recommended Reading for Chapter 14

Occupational Outlook Handbook, 2010 – 11th Edition, by Bureau of Labor Statistics, U.S. Department of Labor. Edition, Bulletin 2800. Superintendent of Documents, U.S. Government Printing Office. Web site: [http://www.bls.gov/oco/]

What Color is Your Parachute: A Practical Manual for Job-Hunters and Career-Changers, by Richard Bolles.

Chapter 15

Living-Place Recovery

Problem:	Not living where you want to live in a home the way you like it is depressing. Depression is a major relapse trigger.
How to win:	Discover where you want to live and find a way to get there, or learn to accept where you are.

My life would be pretty good by now if not

for two things that have followed me all my life:

Bad luck and poor choices.

—Lines spoken by Owen Wilson in the character of Jack Ryan in the film *The Big Bounce* (2004), from the book by Elmore Leonard

I see the recovery area of living place as involving several levels. First, there is the geography of where one lives on the planet. This is the big picture—the country, the state, the region, city, or rural area. The second level is the exact location within that bigger area, right down to the neighborhood and lot. Last is the actual dwelling type, inside and out, be it a house, apartment, condominium, or yurt.

Like many other important things about happiness in life, we are just not taught about living place selection in school. We are not encouraged to factor living place preferences into life planning at all. It is almost as if it is taboo to think of where on the planet we would like to live.

Advisers see where one lives as only incidental to career pursuits—we are expected to focus on preparing for an occupation, period. Indeed, for some people, where they live is apparently not important. Witness college seniors lining up at the corporate booths on career day, willing to go anywhere for the right job. On the other hand, I have known people of all ages who have moved to some place on the globe, willing to do any sort of work, hell-bent just to be there. Either way, I think our ancient ancestors did care a lot about where they lived and had considerable freedom to be where they wanted to be. I think you as well have the right to consider seriously where you want to live your life. Believing that you are where you want to be and having your place the way you want it can be a very gratifying area of your life, emotionally important, and important for your recovery.

Compared with the range of problems anybody can have regarding where he or she lives or wishes to live, those with histories of alcohol dependence can have some special issues:

- Staying where they really do not want to live because drinking keeps them from feeling the raw edge of unhappiness that would otherwise stimulate a move. They are overmedicated and unable to take advantage of negative emotions that would provide adequate motivation to make needed changes.
- Committing the classic "geographic cure." People are often surprised at how difficult it is to stay sober. They begin to think they cannot achieve any lasting abstinence without getting away. They come to feel that getting out of Dodge is the only way to avoid all the local friends, places, other drink-inducing stimuli and nefarious behavior patterns. So, naturally, they think that if they move to such-and-such a place, they will surely have a better chance at sobriety. I know of no research that shows how often this fails. In my experience with countless people who have tried it, however, it clearly fails much more often than it succeeds. In the treatment field, the geographic cure is frowned upon; it is seen as just another manifestation of denial that delays recovery in earnest. If you cannot get recovery in your current location, you are not likely to achieve it anywhere else.

- As a sort of amotivational syndrome slowly takes over with advancing alcohol dependence, one's actual home or apartment can become something of a mess. Alcohol dependence tends to lead to disorganization in a person's life, and it becomes increasingly difficult to keep up with making the household clean and nice, let alone keep up with basic maintenance and repairs. Things can literally fall apart. This becomes increasingly depressing to the drinker and can even lead to the point where one simply believes he or she must move. The cleanup task can seem so overwhelming. Of course, there are always the drinkers who work diligently at keeping their home as neat as a pin to convince themselves and others that they couldn't possibly have an alcohol problem. Hyperattention to neatness can be a cover-up for many things.

There is no right or wrong place to live, or any type of dwelling that is superior to any other. No matter what anyone tells you, it is an entirely individual preference. Such preferences are generally highly subjective. If you want to stay in your hometown or move back to it forever, there is nothing inherently wrong with this. If you have wanderlust, moves to distant places may be right for you. In any case, here are my suggestions:

Apply the template strategy for the area of Living Place. If you are not satisfied with where you are, spend some time brainstorming your needs/wants. Where else, all obstacles aside, do you see yourself? If you are unsure, make a list of location factors that may be important to you. Consider any of the following factors:

- Weather
- Population characteristics
- Recreational opportunities
- Schools, entertainment, restaurants, arts
- Job opportunities
- Cost of living
- Coastal versus inland
- Mountains versus plains
- Urban versus rural

Now make a list of possible places to live. Stimulate your imagination by looking in magazines and on television, and research places on the Internet. Check out websites of different places, and use Google Earth to get a closer look at possible locales. Contact the Chamber of Commerce of any town of interest to request information about the community.

For any move considered, do costs/benefits analysis by contrasting the pros and cons on the grid below:

	Gains/Positives	Losses/Negatives
Social		
Occupational/ Financial/ Cost of living		
Climate		
Other factors important to me - - -		

If you are considering a move, avoid the geographic cure mistake. Consult counselors, friends, and family for honest feedback. Visit any place or places you are considering moving to before making any decisions or other changes. Remember the adage, "Wherever you go, there *you* are," and do not expect your personality to change along with your new locale. Be prepared; you will have all the same challenges in finding work, making friends, and overcoming depression, anxiety, or whatever you think you will be leaving behind, plus a host of new, unforeseen challenges.

If you decide to move somewhere, locate and make contact with recovery support systems there before you go. This could be AA, Smart Recovery, Women for Sobriety, or Life Ring. Try to communicate with a live abstinence support person to meet when you arrive.

Use "stress inoculation." This is a strategy invented by Don Meichenbaum for coping with situations that do not work out as planned. When we get a vaccination, we are getting an inert dose of a virus that stimulates our immune systems to produce antibodies that will respond favorability if we are subsequently exposed to the live virus. Similarly, if you imagine all the things that could go wrong on your move, the more likely it is you will be able to cope emotionally and adapt, rather than flee prematurely, in the face of unexpected realities at the new location. Thus, instead of, "Oh no! I had no idea it would be like this," you will think, "Ah! I knew some things would not be as planned, and this is one of them." Remember the Marines' motto: Arrive, assess, and adapt.

Despite all of your planning, remember that mere happenstance will play a huge role in how your life turns out at any new location. Things unknown in the physical realities of a place, people you will meet, and unforeseen events will play a powerful role. More than merely accepting this, I suggest that you look forward to the unknowns and embrace them for the positive opportunities they may bring. Your initial hopes and plans can only take you so far; the rest is in the hands of happenstance, or if you prefer, God. If you believe in God, take some solace in this one-liner: If you want to hear God laugh, tell him you've got a plan.

If you like where you live or cannot live quite where you would prefer, work on fixing it up to your liking. It is great to have a place you enjoy coming home to. Fresh paint, trimmed trees, a new deck, or new stereo can go a long way in helping you feel right about where you live.

Chapter 16

Philosophical/Spiritual/Religious Recovery

Problem:	*Humans are very cerebral beings, with daunting powers of perception. Naiveté, doubt, and confusion about one's place in the universe can lead to a less fulfilling and more troubled life.*
Solution:	*Prosper emotionally by allowing yourself to explore and develop a philosophical, spiritual, and/or religious understanding of where you fit in the universe.*

This chapter is very short but by no means unimportant. Like some of the other areas of recovery, full discussion of philosophical/spiritual recovery is beyond the scope of this book—or in this case, beyond the scope of my knowledge. Just as I am not an exercise physiologist or a career development specialist, I am not a theologian, and I am but an armchair philosopher at best. That said, here are some observations about the area of philosophical/spiritual recovery that I have gleaned from working in the addiction field for many years. More than with the other areas of recovery, here it is important to trust yourself and make your own definitions.

There is something about alcohol dependence that makes things go away—relationships, health, money, careers, and happiness. Not to be left out of this litany, unfortunately, is one's view of existence or sense of connectedness with the unknown. During active alcohol dependence, people tend to suspend their relationship with God, if they had one to begin with. The nonreligious likewise seem to abandon whatever philosophy of life they had, or worse, develop a very dour worldview.

Philosophy, Spirituality, and Religiosity

Although there are many exceptions and no clear boundaries, it may be helpful to conceptualize a difference between what is philosophical, what is spiritual, and what is religious. An appreciable difference is that a philosophy is arguably a somewhat more scientific set of beliefs about human existence that is not necessarily based on a belief in a God or gods, whereas spirituality and religiosity tend to imply a more emotional experience of the vast unknown, usually with the faith that God or a higher power exists. Furthermore, although not mutually exclusive, there seems to be vague but appreciable difference between being religious versus being spiritual. Each person seems to have his or her own sense of what is meant by these terms. Spirituality generally alludes to a relatively imprecise and ethereal but positive sense of personal connectedness with an unknowable universe. With a religion, as opposed to the broader sense of spirituality, there is a specific set of beliefs, usually written down in a sacred book or manuscript. Of course, within any organized religion, followers will usually range from those who strictly adhere to the literal letter of the law to those who follow more figurative and liberal interpretations.

The 12-Step View

In the 12-step movement, of course, there is an enormous emphasis on belief in a higher power. In the Big Book, people who cannot accept this are referred to as "those poor unfortunates." I have indeed seen scores of people in the program who attribute their long-lasting recovery to their sense of contact with a higher power. They profess that the best recoveries, if not all recoveries, are spiritually based. Again, there is a bias here because it is those who found a home in AA who so profess. What about all those (silent majority?) who never took to or did not stay with AA and yet are sober? It is like claiming that four out of five dentists prefer Mega-Bright toothpaste based on a survey of dentists attending a free conference in the Bahamas sponsored by the Mega-Bright Corporation.

The architects of AA clearly understood the "power greater than ourselves" to be the Christian God. Whether this does or does not appeal to you, I encourage you to read the Big Book. Another book I recommend that has been very popular among people who have interest in a Christian perspective on recovery is Gerald May's book *Addiction and Grace* (1988). The author is a true scholar and I feel the book is a good read for anyone.

Why Believe in Anything?

Psychologists do not conduct any research into the question of whether God exists. Like everybody else, some are believers and some are not, but psychologists have long been interested in the question of why people believe, and what benefits, if any, a belief in God may provide. Humans have apparently evolved a propensity to believe in a power greater than themselves for good reasons.

Language and reasoning evolved because of the tremendous survival advantages that came with such cognitive advances; we became better hunters, better planners and organizers. Along with this, however, came self-awareness and the daunting knowledge of potential harms and eventual death. Perhaps because of this, people who could imagine (or accept) that there was an all-powerful entity that would make the right things happen may have had an emotional edge in surviving hard challenges—droughts, floods, famine, etc. They would have been slightly more likely to have surviving off-spring. Thus passing on in the gene pool a tendency to find solace in a spiritual belief. Also, many people clearly enjoy an emotional lift, even in the absence of challenging times, that also likely increases longevity and successful child raising.

This suggests that most of us could benefit in our lives from some sort of satisfying beliefs about our lives and place in the universe. Thus, why not capitalize on this nicely evolved, or God-given, human propensity, and culture within yourself a philosophy, or faith, with which you can enjoy a sense of wonder, as well as resource to draw on for encouragement when facing life's inevitable challenges—such as overcoming an alcohol dependence problem? For many of you this comes naturally, and I merely encourage you to pursue and fully participate in what you believe in. For others, who perhaps want nothing to do with society's chief religions or systems of belief, I recommend rounding out this recovery area by developing a well thought out philosophy of life.

Building Your Own Philosophical/Spiritual/Religious Recovery

Clearly, your philosophy or faith is your business. To find the balanced living that this book is all about I only encourage you to pursue, embrace, and gain from your own faith or philosophy to live by. Here are some points for consideration.

- People who perceive their recovery as spiritually based seem to do really well at staying sober. I know of no research studies that identify what percentage of successfully recovering people would make this claim compared to those who would attribute their recovery to other factors. That spiritually based recovery is highly correlated with lasting sobriety is based solely on my observations of thousands of people in recovery. On the other hand, I know many people who are apparently in solid and enduring recoveries who profess that they are entirely atheistic.
- Consider connecting or reconnecting with an established religion, make an effort to start anew. If you are unsure about which religion you might like, I recommend reading material that compares different religions. There are numerous books and material on the Internet. If you want the greatest objectivity, you might go to your local college or university bookstore and find a textbook on comparative religion. I am not going to even begin to list major religions here—not because I don't find them interesting but because I would likely overlook some that are important to someone somewhere.
- If you consider yourself a Christian and want to advance your recovery in this regard, try a church-based 12-step recovery support group. Those who do tell me that what they appreciate is that at least there no question about who the

Higher Power is—not a seagull, not the fourth moon of Saturn.

- Also, if Christian, consider May's recommendation that rather than hoping or expecting God to run your recovery for you, work on simply accepting the grace of God—that God loves you absolutely—and assume some personal responsibility for your life and abstinence.
- Whether you wish to be very spiritual and religious or not, consider studying, developing, and appreciating your own philosophy of life. Of course, you could just make one up, but I recommend at least a casual study of philosophy. Again, there are countless resources available to do this. There are books that briefly compare different philosophies and there are comprehensive tomes on the history of philosophy and on specific philosophers and their theories. Of course, there are nice summaries on the web. It is also exciting to look beyond Western philosophy and study systems of knowledge from Eastern and other cultures.
- If you just want to experience a sense of spirituality without restriction, find ways to enhance this. For example, routinely engage yourself in activities such as hiking in forests, biking in the country, cruising art galleries, or serving at the local soup kitchen in order to open yourself to the rich sense of spirituality that is inherent in such activities.

Suggested Reading for Chapter 16

History of Western Philosophy (second edition), by Bertrand Russell.

World Philosophies, by Ninean Smart; edited by Oliver Leaman.

Classics of Western Philosophy (seventh edition), edited by Steven M. Cahn.

Philosophy for Dummies, by Tom Morris.

On the Web

Internet Encyclopedia of Philosophy, www.iep.utm.edu.

Religious Facts: Just the facts on religion, www.religionfacts.com.

Enlightened Spirituality, www.enlightened-spirituality.org.

Part 5

The Art of Staying Sober

Chapter 17

Understanding Relapse

Problem:	*Failure to thoroughly understand the dynamics of relapse will leave you vulnerable to relapse.*
How to win:	*The more you know about what drives relapse, the greater your protection—once again, forearmed is forewarned.*

We have all heard cigarette smokers joke, "Quitting is easy! I've done it many times." Indeed, practically any desired behavior change is at first not very difficult. This is true of starting a fitness regimen or teeth flossing campaign, cutting out white flour or sugar from your diet, and practically any behavior change we can imagine. Of course, with any behavior change, the hard part is maintaining that change.

I strongly recommend that you actively study relapse prevention strategies, both here and from any other sources (some of which you can find in the Reference section of this book). In the Introduction, I likened recovery to my experience in constructing a lawn shed. The point was that to do a good job of it, I had to study books on how lawn sheds are built and draw up a plan. With recovery, it is the same. Why try to reinvent the wheel? Even in taking up far simpler activities such as tennis, golf, or skiing, one's proficiency is vastly accelerated by studying what others know. Learning what has already been discovered by others will save you a world of hurt. Nowhere is this more true than with the challenge of relapse prevention.

We now understand that recovery and quitting are two different things. Merely quitting is only a tiny step. *Recovery is a vast world far beyond the mere act of initially quitting drinking.* In scientific language, stopping the use of alcohol would be considered a "necessary but not sufficient condition" for recovery. Without an understanding of this, relapses abound.

A relapse in one's battle against something like pneumonia is the return of the disease and its nefarious symptoms after a period of being symptom-free. In recovery from an alcohol use problem, the same meaning applies, but much more broadly. In AA, it is said that a person is often "in relapse" well ahead of actually imbibing any alcohol. What this refers to is the return of a person's toxic pattern of thinking, feeling, socializing, or otherwise behaving in ways that used to be associated with, or will likely lead to, drinking.

The Paradox of Relapse

In treatment programs and in private practices, counselors stress the need for *total* abstinence as the only measure of success and tend to catastrophize slips as utter failure. In reality, it is rare to find a person who never drinks again after his or her very first quit attempt. The truth is that some slips are a normal part of recovery. For all the volumes written about relapse prevention, the best strategies for most people are learned the hard way—through real experience. However, we substance abuse counselors are reluctant to tell people this because we do not want the message to be misinterpreted as a license to have slips. I do not want you to relapse, but I want you to realize, if it happens, that it is a natural part of early recovery, and I do not want you to feel too bad about it—so bad about it that you just continue to drink.

Relapse verses Lapse

The relapse researcher who coined the phrase "relapse prevention," Dr. Allen Marlatt (1985), makes a useful distinction between a "relapse" and a "lapse." Planned or unplanned, the hallmark of a relapse is that it continues for weeks, months, or years. The person who gives up on recovery is said to have fallen off the wagon and is back at his or her prior pattern of drinking, with all attendant costs to life areas accruing. A lapse, on the other hand, is rarely planned and usually entails a single drinking episode or only lasts a few days at the most. The person quickly realizes the mistake, feels bad, stops drinking, and brings it to the attention of his or her counselor or other support people within a day or two. This then becomes a learning opportunity—and a normal part of recovery. Albeit troubling to the person, from the counselor's perspective it can actually be a positive thing.

The Harm Reduction Model

The harm reduction model comes directly from research, and unfortunately, there it stays. Twelve-step-modeled treatment programs seldom appreciate looking at this perspective. We Americans are great attempters of behavior change. We make plans to lose weight, quit smoking, start flossing, stop watching television, or embark on any number of self-improvement campaigns. We initiate these changes at any serviceable benchmark in time: on our birthdays, at a solstice, upon a child's birth, or in the form of resolutions at the beginning of the New Year. Whatever it may be, there is a huge failure rate across the board within about five weeks.

Drinkers are not the only ones who experience difficulties staying with their plans for behavior change. Dieters, exercisers, smoking quitters, teeth flossers, etc., all have notoriously poor adherence rates. With all other behavior change attempts, however, we are happy to accept and call successful *any* level of positive change. The guy who vowed to go to the gym six days per week and ended up averaging about three or four days per week is quite pleased with himself. He lost 10 pounds and reduced his cholesterol and blood pressure. His doctor congratulates him and says to keep up the good work. Similarly, the dentist congratulates her patient for having no cavities even though he only flossed four days per week when he had promised a daily flossing regimen. Unlike dieters, exercisers, and flossers, when it comes to alcohol use behavior change, the only measure of success has been total abstinence. Again, research on this topic finds that alcoholism is a disease of relapse, just like diabetes or hypertension. Facing reality in this way, we need not demand 100 percent adherence to count a change as successful. If at the end of a year the recovering person has had several drinks on several occasions but his health, work, energy, mood, and relationships all show improvements, his behavior change effort has not failed. It has been predominately successful. This is the *harm reduction* model. The problem is that whereas dentists, doctors, friends, and family prize those who have made quality of life improvements in their imperfect attempts, most people shame the alcoholic for a single lapse. I have had many discussions with treatment program counselors, doctors, and family members who insist that a person must be run through another cycle of inpatient treatment when the person has merely had a lapse rather than a relapse.

Again, do not let this discussion of the harm reduction model confuse you. It must not be taken as an excuse to drink. Rather strive for total abstinence. But if you have some slips early in your recovery, don't give up, just learn from this and redouble your effort.

Relapse Dynamics Demystified

To drinkers and nondrinkers alike, the causes of relapse seem to be very vague and mysterious. It is not that myriad external triggers of relapse cannot be identified; it's that they are not the same for everyone. Indeed, the lists are long and include things like low bank account balances, lost employment, relationship conflicts, continuing to associate with drinkers and in venues that promote drinking, bad hair days, and more. Also, the unseen internal physical states that can trigger slips are not too hard to appreciate, things like being hungry, too hot or too cold, or just tired. What is harder, and yet vitally important, to understand are the internal mental behaviors that drive most relapses.

As mentioned in Chapter 3, after studying relapse triggers among thousands of people in recovery, Dr. Marlatt identified three broad categories of relapse-triggering situations: negative emotional states, interpersonal conflict, and social pressure. And think about the latter two groupings: What do interpersonal conflict and peer pressure cause? Right you are—negative emotional states. In my observations of thousands of alcoholics, I find that *at least 90 percent of relapses are caused by negative emotional states*, regardless of the external triggers. This is why I continue to emphasize that alcohol dependence is a disease of the mind. This means that the most important relapse prevention strategies involve emotional management.

So what about the other 10 percent? Although much less often than bad moods, but often triggering slips, are positive emotional states (It's time to celebrate!). Beyond this, I've identified another insidious source of relapse which appears to be independent of any particular emotional state, positive or negative. I put this type of slip under the category of *fixed action patterns*, a term I am borrowing from the field of ethology, the study of animal behavior in the natural environment. Consider the mother bird that sees the baby bird's open mouth. This stimulus directly triggers a hardwired instinctual response for the mother to open her mouth and drop the worm in the baby's mouth. The bird is not actively pondering which of her offspring should get the worm or when she should feed them. This is the essence of a fixed action pattern—no cognitions or moods are involved. It is simply a stimulus followed by a response.

With human substance dependence problems, clients in recovery often report finding themselves parking in front of a bar or liquor store wondering how they got there. Deep in other thoughts while driving home from work, the person's old (now subconscious) conditioned response emerges, making it seem as if the car must have steered itself down familiar streets. Unlike the fixed action patterns of animal behavior, however, the human addict's experience is learned behavior rather than instinctual, and can be unlearned with practice.

The causes of relapse become even clearer when we understand the reason for drinking in the first place. It is not complicated. The drinker imbibes alcohol to *alter his or her state of consciousness from a less pleasant place to a more pleasant place*. It is that simple. No amount of orange juice or soda water is going to do that. Over time, the drinker's mind, consciously and subconsciously, learns to prefer and need this method. As the mind's ability to identify and manage mood on its own diminishes, a profound change occurs without the drinker realizing it. *The ability to insert rational thought between urges to drink and the behavior of drinking is lost.* Dr. Marlatt's research has indicated that the alcoholic's predrinking thoughts get reduced to of only one or two: "I'm not doing so well," and, "A drink will help," or close variants of these thoughts.

Here is how this happens. I call it the trained dolphin effect. When training a dolphin to do a double backflip, a trainer uses what is called *behavioral shaping*. This involves using a reward (a small fish snack) to reinforce and strengthen successive approximations of the target behavior (the double backflip). When the trainer enters the pool area, she rings a bell. This gets Flipper's attention. As Flipper swims around in the pool, he begins to notice that he is tossed a fish whenever he gets near the center. Soon, whenever the trainer rings the bell, Flipper jets to the center of the pool. With this learned, the trainer ups the ante. She only tosses him a fish when he gets his head out of the water in the center of the pool. Later, she withholds reward until he gets his whole body out of the water in the center of the pool. This process continues in incremental advances until eventually, when the bell is rung, the dolphin streaks to the center of the pool and does a double backflip. The behavior of performing a backflip is said to have been "shaped in" by the use of successive rewards.

In animal life, including our own, behavior is naturally shaped by what follows it. The coyote chases a rabbit under a bush and gets thorns in her nose. That is a punishment, and she learns to not charge into that type of bush. She may chase a rabbit under a different type of bush and get the rabbit without the thorns. That is a reward, and her new behavior of freely chasing rabbits under that variety of bush is reinforced. When I was a toddler, I wandered into the kitchen one day and saw a burner on the electric stove glowing cherry red. Naturally, I reached up and put my hand right on it. That is what is called one trial learning. The punishment was so swift and severe on the heels of the behavior that I never did it again. That sort of punishment has considerable control over any behavior that precedes it and is said to extinguish it—the behavior, not my hand.

Excessive alcohol use brings punishment, but only eventually. Over time, there is eventually hell to pay, in the form of lost money, shot health, wrecked relationships, destroyed careers, depressed mood, etc. Unfortunately, these punishers are too far off. They are called "long-term aversive consequences" (LACs). With drinking, there is at first a quick reward.

Tension → Urge to drink → Drink→**Reward**--------------→LACs

---

The alcohol effect is what is called a negative reinforcer because the benefit experienced by the drinker is more in what it takes away rather than what it gives. It relieves mental and physical tension, and this is a powerful reinforcer. Imagine that children who put their hands on stovetops got a wonderful physical feeling and sense of euphoria for a half hour before the burn. If this were true, hospital emergency rooms would be filled with children—and adults, too, I suppose—burning their hands over and over again. Or imagine whacking your dog with a rolled-up newspaper on Thursday because you remembered he had chased a car last Saturday. He is not going to get it.

Now back to the dolphin story. Through systematic reward, a complex sequence of dolphin behavior is shaped. At the bell the dolphin moves directly, post-haste, to the center of the pool and executes a perfect, well practiced double backflip. Similarly, the drinker, without conscious awareness, gets a complex sequence of behaviors rewarded and shaped in. This includes both external behaviors and internal thought behaviors. He or she must consider the type of alcohol beverage they want and by what method to acquire it, transport it, open it, pour it, etc. Now here is something very important to realize. It is not only what gets shaped in that is so insidious, but also what gets shaped out of the dolphin's—and our own—behavioral repertoire. The dolphin, upon hearing the bell, does not dive deep, does not swim around the periphery of the pool, and does not jump over to the next pool. The thoughts and behaviors that lead to drinking get shaped in, and all competing thoughts or alternative behaviors get shaped out.

I think of how my brother and I meet for golf on Sunday mornings in the summer. We meet for an early tee time at a course midway between the cities we each live in. Suppose, as sometime happens, I wake up at 6:00 AM excited to go but stare out the window at a cold, relentless rain (we live in the Pacific Northwest, after all). I eat breakfast hoping for some sign of an early break in the weather. Reluctantly, I phone my brother, who reports the same weather at his place. So we agree to call it off and to try again next week. I am quickly aware of feeling disappointed and a little depressed. This awareness was never shaped out by any reward for not being able to play golf. The next thoughts are coping thoughts. I think about why I should feel so down. It then comes to mind that when I was a little kid I hated school, to the point where I would feel depressed on Sunday because of having to go back to school on Monday. I then start some coping thoughts. It dawns on me that what I need on Sundays is some sense of freedom, some sort of escape. Next, it occurs to me that there is no reason this escape should be restricted to golf. It could be anything. By this point my wife is up and we are reading the paper. I say, "Honey, look, there is a new art gallery opening in La Connor. Let's drive down there today. We can check out the galleries and have chowder at a seaside café." And where does my mood go? Decidedly up.

Now, if I were an active alcoholic, this scenario would have looked a little different. Seeing the rain in the morning, assuming I got out of bed, I would think, "Well, it looks like golf is out. That sucks. Oh well, the pregame show starts at 11. I guess I'll just have to start the beers." My point is, there is no clear recognition of feelings here, let alone coping behaviors. More healthy alternative thoughts and behaviors have been shaped out of the drinker's repertoire. When I ask a client, "When you had that drink last night, did you think of anything else you could have done?", I get back a dumbfounded expression and, "What? No. There wasn't anything else I could do."

"Well, what about fixing a nice meal, going for a walk, watching TV, calling a friend, visiting a bookstore?"

"No, I didn't think of those things."

Not merely are healthy alternative *behaviors* shaped out, but so too are rational thoughts. This process, more than anything else, is what the drinker becomes the victim of. When I ask, "Did you realize that urges happen to just about everyone who quits drinking—that urges will get less intense, shorter, fewer, and farther between, the longer you stay in recovery?" The response is, "No. I thought I was failing because I kept thinking about drinking." When I inquire, "Did you realize the urge would pass?", the response is, "No. It seemed interminable." When I question, "Did you stop and think of the long-term consequences?", I get back, "Uh … not really." In their innocence, unsuspecting of the subtle but powerful reward loop, drinkers slowly lose the ability to insert rational thought and initiate alternative behaviors between urges to drink and the act of drinking. Alternative behaviors simply get shaped out. "Why did I do that again last night?" is the oft-heard lament of the anguished alcoholic. At least the dolphin gets a fish.

On a broader level, as I have pointed-out, *any* type of behavior change is difficult to maintain. Psychologists are currently studying the newly identified phenomenon of "willpower depletion." This factor may underlie the failure of many types of behavior change attempts, from exercise regimens to college programs, wherever self-control is necessary. Contrary to what we might expect, the finding is that willpower seems to decay following acts of self-control. For example, if someone determined to diet passes-up the donut tray at the office in the morning, that person is then *more likely* to cave-in, having a donut or some other high calorie treat later that day. It doesn't take much to realize what this means if you are attempting to quit drinking. The good news is that willpower and self-control have been shown to strengthen with practice.

Chapter 18

Relapse Prevention Strategies

Problem:	*The door to relapse is open when one does not practice individually crafted prevention strategies.*
How to win:	*Dedicate yourself to relapse prevention strategies designed specifically by and for yourself.*

In my experience the most helpful approach to relapse prevention starts with changing one's focus to the rewarding, forward-looking possibilities in recovery. Using the new template model reverses the contingencies of reinforcement so that not drinking becomes much more rewarding than drinking. It is about shaping in everything that was shaped out and more. In terms of a specific strategy, I recommend the following:

1. Track Your Feelings

In response to the finding that about 90 percent of relapses are triggered by negative emotional states, it is critically important to overcome alexithymia. Remember that because of regular self-medication with alcohol, the drinker loses the ability to accurately identify and cope with emotions. Take this to heart and work the understandings and ideas offered in Chapter 11. Start with becoming more mindful and accepting of your feelings. Learn to notice your feelings without judgment, and for a few weeks write them down on 3×5 cards that you can keep with you. Use the feelings list from Chapter 11.

And never forget to look for the positive intention of negative feelings. As discussed in Chapter 11, negative emotions are essential signaling systems. Get in the habit of looking for the deeper meaning of any persistent sadness, anger, or anxiety that you experience, and asking yourself what needs aren't getting met and what changes can you make.

2. Track and Reward Your Progress

Research and experience show that simply monitoring one's progress is a powerful tool for making positive behavior changes that last and become self-perpetuating. To help reinforce your sobriety, track your progress on a calendar for the first few weeks or months. Check off the days you are sober.

As noted in the discussion of stages of readiness to change (covered in Chapter 3), rewards strengthen adherence to behavior changes. For example, after each week that you stay sober, give yourself a reward that you've identified in advance. The rewards can be spaced to your liking. They can include things like buying a new article of clothing, going out for a nice dinner, or going to a movie. You do deserve rewards, so be creative and treat yourself to something you like. Remember the lyrics to the Curtis Mayfield song; *It's Alright to Have a Good Time.*

3. Develop Healthy Ways to Celebrate

As I have pointed out, perhaps about ten percent of slips come from positive emotional states—*let's celebrate.* It's only natural whenever we win the contract, make a job change, finish a project, or we or a loved one succeed at something, to want to celebrate. And it is generally healthy to do so. However, the subconscious mind is ever looking for any excuse to drink. Being aware that this is a major relapse trigger can be a big help—forewarned is forearmed. But go beyond this. Make an advance list of healthy ways you have historically, or might in the future, celebrate when the occasions arise. Examples are; treat yourself to a special dinner (sans alcohol), a weekend trip, a new article of clothing or sports equipment, or going to a movie. Try to incorporate healthy celebrating into your overall recovery plan.

4   Do Not Fall Victim to the AVE

AVE stands for the abstinence violation effect. This phenomenon was identified by Dr. Allen Marlatt at the University of Washington Addictive Behaviors Research Center. It is vitally important to understand AVE in order to protect yourself from relapse. AVE keeps millions of people from being able to maintain important behavior changes. It is involved in countless relapses among people intending to stay sober. Imagine the following scenario:

A young college woman living in a dormitory decides in January that she has gained too much weight to fit into her bathing suit by the following summer. She reasons that the problem has been her habit of stopping by the student union for an ice cream cone every night. So, as her main diet strategy, she decides to cut out all ice cream. By the end of the second semester, her plan is successful and she has lost the extra weight. Then one Friday night before final exams she is studying in her room, worried about upcoming tests. Her roommates tell her she needs a break and urge her to come to a movie with them. She does. However, it turns out to be a rather depressing film and our student is not feeling very well as they exit the theater. Before she realizes what is happening, her friends whisk her around the corner and she finds herself in an ice cream parlor. She reasons, "Well, I've stayed away from ice cream for a long time, I guess I deserve a little." So she orders a double scoop of triple chocolate chip. The next morning she feels bad about this—like a failure. At first she resolves to get back on her diet immediately. However, with a host of bad feelings and the taste of ice cream fresh in her memory, that evening she succumbs to an urge with the thought, "Oh well, I already blew it last night, so what the hell." Then it's back to eating ice cream as before.

The abstinence violation effect is a ubiquitous phenomenon. It happens to the guy who misses a night of flossing his teeth because he was out of town for the weekend. It happens to the woman who accepts a cigarette from a friend after four weeks of not smoking. It happens to the couple who for some reason miss a night of going to the gym together as they had resolved to do. Clearly, the vast majority of behavior changers do not perform perfectly. But those who succeed never fall victim to AVE; rather, if slips occur, as they do for most people, they regret it, accept it, and immediately pick themselves up again. This makes all the difference. It is true of all successful athletes. It is true of all people successful in their work, relationships, or successful at raising families. If you slip, do not beat yourself up; do not feel sorry for yourself; do not succumb to that addictive urge, or that part of you that wants you to drink at any cost and is always looking for an excuse to do so. Stand up for yourself. Stand up to the bully of addiction like you would stand up to someone assaulting your little sister or brother.

Do not judge me by my successes,

judge me by how many times I fell down

and got back up again.

—Nelson Mandela

5   Learn to Recognize the Addictive Voice Within

This strategy was invented by Jack Trimpey. He calls it the AVRT—addictive voice recognition technique—and you can read about it in his book *Rational Recovery* (1996). It is as if we have two minds—one that wants to drink and one that wants to stay sober. Most often, it is our conscious mind that is capable of holding the standard of not drinking. The subconscious mind wants whatever feels good in the moment and it has identified drinking as the fast track. The subconscious, as discussed in Chapter 11, operates on the pleasure principle. It does not track time, does not give a fig about right or wrong, and cannot delay gratification. It wants you to avoid pain and have pleasure in every moment. It hoodwinks the conscious mind into allowing drinking. It does this by the deployment of defense mechanisms such as rationalization, justification, minimization, denial, projection, anger, humor, or whatever it takes. It can also exaggerate any emotions you may experience in order to justify drinking. Thus, you can find yourself drinking with the excuse that you are such a victim, so depressed, so mistreated, so humiliated, so angry, that therefore you can only drink. A client says to me that he has relapsed. "You remember I was telling you how disrespectful my boss was?" he asks. "Well, yesterday was the last straw. I had had it. I became so angry that I just walked off the job at noon and went straight across the street to the bar and got drunk. There was nothing else I could do." This is an example of many slip dynamics but illustrates how one can subconsciously escalate emotions to get justification for a drink.

Trimpey encourages you to regard your conscious mind that does not want to drink as the real you, and your subconscious mind that wants to drink as "it." The strategy is to consistently recognize the addictive voice within and tell it to back off or make deals with it to cope in more healthy ways.

6   Set Up a Support Team, No Matter How Small

People who are successful in their recovery tend to have one or several people in their lives who understand and support their recovery effort. Some have this automatically by virtue of already being in partnership with someone who supports them. If you have people in your life who love and respect you, you may have a natural support team. With such close people, do not be too ashamed or reserved. Share what you are doing and enlist their support. Never make others feel responsible for your recovery, but do allow their support. Let them know what your plan is and how you are doing on a regular basis. Real loved ones and friends want to help each other through good times and hard times. It is the way of human existence, and you are entitled to this support. Tell your supporters that they do not really need to do anything, but rather just be available to talk and offer encouragement. If you do not have any such recovery-supportive persons in your life, you might confide in your doctor or spiritual leader, find a private counselor, or try attending AA.

7   Set Up Fire Drills and Fire Escapes

It is a great idea to follow the lead of schools, hospitals, and emergency services of all sorts in being prepared by practicing what to do in case of emergency. In early recovery this is a good plan also. *Fire drills* in the service of relapse prevention can be solo or can involve other people in your support team. Get the phone numbers of each person on your support team and each person's agreement that you can call any time you are feeling unsafe in your recovery. Then call them each at least once per week, even on good days, just to test the system. Practice participating in the alternatives to drinking activities that you have listed on a 3×5 card (detailed below), at times *other* than when you are experiencing urges to drink.

A *fire escape* is for times when you are experiencing thoughts of drinking.

Excuse yourself from people and places where drinking begins. When struggling with a bad mood, be it depression, anxiety, frustration, or anger, change your venue, call a support person, and/or do something good for yourself.

8   Make a List of Triggers and High-Risk Situations

Discovering what people, places, situations, and moods are involved in your drinking is the sine qua non of relapse prevention. In general, it is important to stay away from people who drink and places where drinking occurs. High-risk situations that can trigger relapses include:

- Social situations, casual or formal, where drinking occurs
- Being with certain people
- Being in certain parts of town
- Certain times of the day or night
- Feeling tired
- Feeling depressed
- Feeling nervous, worried, or anxious
- Feeling angry
- Being hungry
- Certain aisles in the grocery store
- Rainy days
- Sunny days
- Feeling like celebrating
- Holidays
- Vacationing

The point is that you must develop a protective knowledge base of slippery situations, places, people, and moods that are meaningful to you as possible relapse triggers. Once you have done this, make a written list of alternative ways to handle the issue for each item. For example, if Rocky R's Restaurant is a place that triggers drinking for you, your written strategy might include staying out of that part of town and identifying other, alcohol-free, eating places, or making plans to fix nice meals at home. As time passes, add new risk situations you discover to your list. With a little practice, you will see that what at first may seem a sacrifice becomes a liberation. I cannot think of any high-risk situation that does not have a healthier and actually more satisfying alternative.

9   The 3×5 Card Technique

Research by Arnold Ludwig (1989) revealed a striking difference between recovering people who have relapses and those who do not. He found that people who did not act on their urges to drink were doing one thing that those who relapsed were not doing. They were stopping and recalling the negative consequences before succumbing to the urge to drink. For these people, it was as if the thought of drinking set off a tape recorder that reminded them of the costs to come if they were to imbibe. These vary from person to person but include things like letting down one's spouse, getting sick, disappointing other people, losing money, becoming depressed, self-disappointment, and compromised health, work, energy, leisure pursuits, and enjoyment of life. These thoughts are not only rational, they are punishing—who wants all these negative things in their lives? What these abstainers are doing is bringing the long-term aversive consequences up front where they can do what punishers normally do: extinguish associated behavior—in this instance, drinking behavior.

The 3×5 card strategy is designed to be that tape recorder, allowing you to insert rational thought and healthy behavior between urge and use. On the front side of a 3×5 card, write down the three *emboldened italicized* items listed below.

Side A (Reframing the urge)

1.   ***Urges are common and normal.*** You are not failing because you have them. Urges are a common experience in recovery. They range from flat-out crawling-the-walls craving to the simple passing thought that a drink would feel good right now. They become fewer, shorter, less intense, and farther between the longer you are in recovery. Knowing what to do with them makes all the difference.

---

2.   *Urges pass,* even if you do not drink—and *I will be glad*, not sad, that I let them pass. It is a common misperception among dependent drinkers that urges will go on forever if not acted upon. Although the duration of urges varies quite a bit, they average only about seven minutes. When considering drinking, people also have the feeling that they will only feel worse later if they do not drink now—that they will miss something and be sorry. This is a myth. No one has ever told me that they woke up in the morning and said, "Damn, I wish I would have had that drink last night when I felt like it." This is not going to happen.

3.   Make a list of *LACs* (long-term aversive consequences) that apply to you—e.g., I'll be sick and sorry, let down myself and everybody I care about, and advance costs to my health/fitness, relationships, career, leisure interests, finances, and emotional management.

<u>Side B</u> (Alternatives for coping with urges)

Write down *"Ah, there you are again, my old friend addictive urge, reminding me that I need to unwind (alter my state of consciousness). I shall do this in healthy ways, thank you."*

Now list all the alternatives that might conceivably work for you. For example,

> Change your venue (e.g., if you are inside, go outside, or if you are outside, go inside)
>
> Start a conversation
>
> Go for a drive
>
> Fix a nice meal
>
> Get some rest
>
> Watch TV
>
> Read something enjoyable
>
> Rent a movie

> Get a workout
>
> Get a massage
>
> Ride a bike
>
> Take a walk
>
> Work on a project
>
> Listen to music
>
> Call someone

Keep this 3×5 card with you at all times. Whenever you become aware of an urge to drink, anywhere, anytime, before you imbibe alcohol, read the card and follow your own instructions. Adjust it to work for you as you learn from experience. In time you will not need to have the card with you because the whole procedure becomes rewarding, and thus self-sustaining.

10 Kick Out the Tyrant

This is about self-liberation. You must *resent* that a mere chemical substance has gained so much authority in your life. The only way to have fun? The only way to not feel down or to quell anxiety? The only way to socialize? It is like having a little Hitler in your head. In many ways dependence on alcohol is like living under a tyranny, or with a destructively controlling bad boyfriend or girlfriend. It is time to stand up for yourself. Stand up to the dictator.

Remember, the reason people turn to alcohol is not so mysterious: It is to alter their state of consciousness from a less pleasant place to a more pleasant place. In the vernacular, we call this "unwinding." The phrase "altered state of consciousness" implies something somewhat more intense and is associated with addiction—that's all. Like everybody else, I too need to unwind after work and on weekends. After many years of practicing unwinding, I have myself pretty well trained. When I go home, a dozen things pop to mind: get on my mountain bike, go for a run, hit a bucket of golf balls, lift weights in my home gym, rollerblade, or get involved with any number of projects I have going. Perhaps at the bottom of my list I might think of a beer. But for the dependent drinker, this hierarchy gets inverted and the first thing that comes to mind to unwind is to have a drink. The other possibilities become distant seconds or drop off the list altogether.

Your challenge and ultimate joy in recovery is to rebuild healthy alternatives for unwinding. At first, you may have to force yourself to make a list of healthy ways to unwind. Some things do not immediately pay off. You may have to practice your alternatives for some time before they feel right—before they feel good. It is like learning to play a musical instrument. Only after hours and weeks of tedious practice do the melodies start to come and the experience becomes rewarding. Some activities, on the other hand, pay off quickly. I do not have to be on my mountain bike or hitting golf balls for very long before my consciousness is effectively altered, and in a healthy way. Really, it does not take any longer to roll the bike out of the garage, or to sit down at the piano, than it takes to fix a drink, imbibe, and feel the effects. Also, see this as an opportunity. When it comes to ways to unwind, you do not want to be a one-trick pony. You are entitled to a whole repertoire of enjoyable pastimes. When you come home in the evening, welcome this challenge. The sooner you do, the sooner you will realize the real liberation that comes with sobriety.

11 Never Drop Your Vigilance

In early recovery, one actually needs to be *hypervigilant* to relapse risk. As years pass with abstinence, you can drop the "hyper" but will still need to remain vigilant. This means working at keeping your life reasonably well balanced, which includes taking good care of yourself physically and emotionally. A good outlook is to view sobriety as the number one imperative of every day. As years pass, however, you can spend most of your daily energy on other priorities—as long as sobriety is the first priority. In my observation of countless people with many years of recovery, this seems to be the point of view they affect, whether in AA or on their own.

A good example of the importance of maintaining vigilance is the ability to consistently remain abstinent when around people who are drinking or when in places where drinking occurs. As discussed in Chapter 13, in the urgency of early recovery, anybody can remain abstinent in social situations. However, it can be all too easy to become lulled into an insubstantial sense of confidence or familiarity in such situations, and vigilance can slip precipitously, leading to relapse.

I have had clients complain that having to stay vigilant is too much work or somehow unfair. Think of it this way: For any given project or activity, accidents seldom occur at the beginning but rather later on, when the activity has become all too familiar. Last summer I had a ladder going up to the deck to install a new railing. At one point, I shifted the ladder's position from above to set a railing bolt, thinking I would reset the ladder at the ground level later. However, forgetting to do this, I turned around on the deck and jumped on the ladder. It instantly slipped out from under me and I spent the next 15 feet in a freefall contemplating my lapse in vigilance. Ladders are a great tool, but across the course of a summer of working with them, I had become too comfortable and allowed my vigilance for safety to slip. The same applies to using power tools, driving cars, and all sorts of fun recreational activities. Enjoyment and respectful vigilance are not mutually exclusive. We are able to enjoy all of these things completely while accepting a concomitant vigilance for safety. Socializing where others are drinking can be enjoyable if you are able to maintain a personal vigilance to protect your recovery.

The decay of vigilance may be related to the "willpower depletion" problem discussed in chapter 17. To avoid this, actively practice specific acts of self-control, determinedly and repeatedly. This has been shown to actually increase willpower. Certainly you will want to do this with abstinence, but it may help if you can demonstrate self-control over any other behavior. It doesn't even have to be anything that means anything. For example, practice opening your car door only with your left hand for a couple of weeks. Or try something more useful like clearing all your dishes away after each meal or taking the stairs to your office rather than the elevator for some set period of time. If you can succeed at any such effort it will likely expand your willpower in other, more important, areas of your life like quitting drinking. A good resource for you may be the new book *Willpower: Rediscovering the Greatest Human Strength*, by Roy F. Baumeister (2011).

12 Autopsy Any Slips

While you work vigilantly at not drinking, hopefully you will soon enjoy the benefits of recovery I have been talking about throughout this book. Remember, however, that slips are a common reality of early recovery. Here is what I recommend if it happens to you:

- Stop drinking right away. Preferably after the first drink, but if not then, the very next day. Do not allow yourself to fall victim to the abstinence violation effect. The goal is to prevent a lapse from turning into a relapse.
- Tell your counselor, if you have one, and/or any support persons immediately, or at least within 24 hours.
- Do an autopsy on the slip. That is, with a counselor or other support person, try to figure out what factors were related to or may have triggered the slip. Maybe you will need to avoid a certain person, place, or type of place. Perhaps you need to practice being more assertive. Since most slips are related to some negative emotional state, can you identify what feelings you may have been dealing with just prior to the slip? Could the feelings you were experiencing have been indicative of needs in your life that are not being met? Are there changes you need to make?
- Remember the *life areas model of recovery* that is the basis of this book. I have seen many individuals who continued to drink following a slip because they thought they were total failures. This is one of the important benefits of dividing recovery into several distinct functional areas of life. If your slip is related to a setback or loss in one or two areas, realizing that some other area of your life is okay can help you keep a lapse from becoming a relapse. Realizing that not all is lost has a preventive effect.

Afterword

In closing this book I hope you have found it to be useful and effective. I know firsthand that the concepts and strategies presented here have indeed helped many men and women establish very fulfilling alcohol-free life-styles. But as I stated in the Introduction, this book and its approach is a work in process. Knowledge is ever-expanding. So if you are continuing to struggle, or are not as well as you would like to be, don't give up. At the very least, I hope this book serves as a springboard to discover what eventually works for you. You have to believe you are worth it. Rest assured that I believe you are.

References

Adair, R. F., & Holmgren, L. R. (2005). Do drug samples influence resident prescribing behavior? A randomized trial. *The American Journal of Medicine, 118,* 881–884.

Alberti, R. E., & Emmons, M. L. (2008). *Your perfect right: Assertiveness and equality in your life and relationships* (9th edition). Atascadero, California: Impact Publishers.

Alcoholics Anonymous World Services (2001). *Alcoholics Anonymous: The story of how many thousands of men and women have recovered from alcoholism.* New York: Author.

American Psychiatric Association (2000). *Diagnostic and statistical manual of mental health disorders* (4th edition, revised). Washington, D.C.: Author.

American Psychiatric Association (2013). *Diagnostic and statistical manual of mental disorders,* 5th edition (DSM-5). Washington, D. C.: American Psychiatric Publishing.

Angell, M. (2011a, June 23). The epidemic of mental illness: Why? *The New York Review of Books,* 28(11).

Angell, M. (2011b, July 14). The illusion of psychiatry. *The New York Review of Books,* 28(12).

Atkins, R., & Hawdon, J. (2007). Religiosity and participation in mutual-aid support groups for addiction. *Journal of Substance Abuse Treatment, 33* (3), 321-331.

Baer, J. (1976). *How to be an assertive (not aggressive) woman in life, in love, and on the job: The total guide to self-assertiveness.* Signet.

Bandura, A. (1977). Self-efficacy: Toward a unifying theory of behavior change. *Psychological Review, 84,* 191–215.

References

Bandura, A. (1997). *Self-efficacy: The exercise of control.* Worth Publishers.

Barbui, C., Esposito, E., & Cipriani, A. (2009). Selective serotonin reuptake inhibitors and risk of suicide: a systematic review of observational studies. *CMAJ, 180,* 291–297.

Baumeister, R. F. (2011). *Willpower: Rediscovering the greatest human strength.* Penguin Press.

Beattie, M. (1992). *Codependent no more: How to stop controlling others and start caring for yourself.* Center City, Minnesota: Hazeldon.

Beck, A. T., Rush, A. J., Shaw, B. F., & Emery, G. (1979). *Cognitive therapy of depression.* New York: Guilford Press.

Berne, E. (1967). *Games people play.* Grove Press.

Bischof, G., Rumpf, H. J., Hapke, U., Meyer, C., & John, U. (2000). Gender differences in natural recovery from alcohol dependence. *Journal of Studies on Alcohol and Drugs, 6,* 783–786.

Blum, K., Noble, E. P., Sheridan, P. J., Montgomery, A., Ritchie, T., Jagadeeswaran, P., Nogami, H., Briggs, A. H., & Cohn, J. B. (1990). Allelic Association of Human Dopamine D, Receptor Gene in Alcoholism. *JAMA, 263,* 2055-2060.

Bolles, R. N. (2009). *What color is your parachute? 2010: A practical manual for job-hunters and career-changers.* Berkley, California: Ten Speed Press.

Bouza, C., Magro, A., Muñoz, A., & Amate, J. M. (2004). Efficacy and safety of naltrexone and acamprosate in the treatment of alcohol dependence: A systematic review. *Addiction, 99 (7),* 811-828.

Brown, S. A., & Schuckit, M. A. (1988). Changes in depression among abstinent alcoholics. *Journal of Studies on Alcohol and Drugs, 49,* 412–417.

Bureau of Labor Statistics, U.S. Department of Labor, *Occupational Outlook Handbook*, 2010-11 Edition, Bulletin 2800. Superintendent of Documents, U.S. Government Printing Office, Washington, DC, 2006.

Burns, D. B. (1980). *Feeling good: The new mood therapy.* William Morrow Co.

Burns, D. B. (1990). *The feeling good handbook.* Plume.

Caetano, R., Clark, C. L., & Greenfield, T. K. (1998). Prevalence, trends, and incidence of alcohol withdrawal symptoms. *Alcohol Health Research World, 22,* 73–80.

Campbell, J., & Moyers, B. (1991). *The power of myth.* Anchor Books.

Carlat, D. (2011). *Unhinged: The trouble with psychiatry—a doctor's revelations about a profession in crisis.* Free Press.

Cloud, H. & Townsend, J. (1999). *Boundaries in marriage.* Sondervan.

Cloud W., Granfield, R. (2008) Conceptualizing recovery capital: Expansion of a theoretical construct. *Substance Use Misuse;* 43: 1971-86.

Crowley, C., & and Lodge, H. (2007). *Younger next year: Live strong, fit and sexy until you're 80 and beyond.* Workman Publishing Company.

Davidson, S. (2007). *Leap!: What will we do with the rest of our lives?* New York: Random House, Inc.

Dawson, D. A., Grant, B. F., Stinson, F. S., Chou, P. S., Huang, B., & Ruan, W. J. (2005). Recovery from DSM-IV alcohol dependence: United States, 2001–2002. *Alcohol Research and Health, 29,* 131–142.

DiClemente, C. C. (2003). *Addiction and change: How addictions develop and addicted people recover.* New York: Guilford Press.

Dishion, T. J., McCord, J., & Poulin, F. O. (1999). When interventions harm: Peer groups and problem behavior. *American Psychologist, 54* (9), 755-764).

Doucet, M., & Sismondo, S. (2008). Evaluating solutions to sponsorship bias. *Journal of Medical Ethics, 34,* 627–630.

Dyer, W. (2002). *10 secrets for success and inner peace.* Carlsbad, California: Hay House.

Ellis, A. (1962). *Reason and emotion in psychotherapy:* Lyle Stuart

References

Ellis, A. (1994). *Reason and emotion in psychotherapy: A comprehensive method of treating human disturbances: Revised and updated.* Citadel.

Ellis, A., & Harper, R. A. (1975). *A guide to rational living.* Englewood Cliffs, N.J.: Prentice-Hall.

Ellis, A., & Velten, E. (1992). *When AA doesn't work for you: Rational steps to quitting alcohol.* New York: Barricade Books.

Fillmore, K., Stockwell, T., Chikritzhs, T., Bostrom, A., & Kerr, W. (2004). Moderate alcohol use and reduced mortality risk: Systematic error in prospective studies and new hypotheses. *Annals of Epidemiology, 17,* S16–S23.

Fingarette, H. (1988). *Heavy drinking: The myth of alcoholism as a disease.* Berkeley, California: University of California Press.

Fletcher, Anne M. (2013). *Inside rehab.* New York: Penguin Group.

Fletcher, A. M. (2001). *Sober for good: New solutions for drinking problems—advise from those who have succeeded.* New York: Houghton Mifflin Company.

Fournier, J. C., DeRubeis, R. J., Hollon, S. D., Dimidjian, S., Amsterdam, J. D., Shelton, R. C., & Fewcett, J. (2010). Antidepressant drug effects and depression severity. *Journal of the American Medical Association, 303* (1), 47–53.

Giles, L. C., Glonek, F. V., Luszcz, M. A., & Andrews, G. (2005). Effect of social networks on 10 year survival in very old Australians: The Australian longitudinal study of aging. *Journal of Epidemiology and Community Health, 59,* 574–579.

Gitlin, M. J. (1990). *The psychotherapist's guide to psychopharmacology.* New York: The Free Press.

Gitlin, M. J. (2008). *Therapist's guide to psychopharmacology, second edition.* Free Press.

Gladwell, M. (2008). *Outliers: The story of success.* New York: Little, Brown and Company.

Goodwin, D. W., Schulsinger, F., Hermansen, L., Guze, S. B., & Winokur, G. (1973). Alcohol problems in adoptees raised apart from alcoholic biological parents. *Archives of General Psychiatry, 28,* 238–243.

Gorski, T. T., & Miller, M. (1986). *Staying sober: A guide for relapse prevention.* Independence Press.

Gorski, T. T. (1989). *Passages through recovery: An action plan for preventing relapse.* Hazelden.

Gotham, H. J., Sher, K. J., & Wood, P. K. (1991). Predicting stability and change in frequency of intoxication from the college years to beyond: Individual-difference and role transition variables. *Journal of Abnormal Psychology, 106,* 619–629.

Gottman, J. M. (1999). *The seven principles for making marriage work.* Crown.

Gottman, J. M. (2002). *The relationship cure: A 5 step guide to strengthening your marriage, family, and friendships.* New York: Three Rivers Press.

Gottman, J. (2012). *What makes love last? How to build trust and avoid betrayal.* Simon and Schuster.

Greenfield, S. F., Hufford, M. R., Vagge, L. M., Muenz, L. R., Costello, M. E., & Weiss, R.D. (2000). The relationship of self-efficacy expectancies to relapse among alcohol dependent men and women: A prospective study. *Journal of Studies on Alcohol, 61,* 345–351.

Harris, G. (2011, March 6). Talk doesn't pay, so psychiatry turns instead to drug therapy. *The New York Times,* pp. A1, A21.

Harris, T. A. (1969). *I'm ok—you're ok.* New York: Harper & Row.

Hayes, S. C., Strosahl, K. D., & Wilson, K. G. (1999). *Acceptance and commitment therapy: An experiential approach to behavior change.* New York: The Guilford Press.

Helzer, J. E., & Pryzbeck, T. R. (1988). The co-occurrence of alcoholism with other psychiatric disorders in the general population and its impact on treatment. *Journal of Studies on Alcohol, 49,* 219–224.

Hesselbrok, M. N., Meyer, R. E., & Keener, J. J. (1985). Psychopathology of hospitalized alcoholics. *Archives of General Psychiatry, 42,* 1050–1055.

References

Imel, Z. E., Wampold, B. E., Miller, S. D., & Fleming, R. R. (2008). Distinctions without a difference: Direct comparisons of psychotherapies for alcohol use disorders. *Psychology of Addictive Behaviors, 22,* 533–543.

Jeffers, S. (1987). *Feel the fear and do it anyway.* Harcourt Press.

Johnson, B. A., Ait-Daoud, N., Bowden, C. L., DiClemente, C. C., Roache, J. D., Lawson, K., Javors, M. A., & Ma, J. Z. (2003). Oral topiramate for treatment of alcohol dependence: A randomised controlled trial. *The Lancet, 361* (9370), 1677–1685.

Johnson, V. E. (1980). *I'll quit tomorrow: A practical guild to alcoholism treatment.* New York: HarperCollins.

Johnston, L. D., O'Malley, P. M., Bachman, J. G., & Schulenberg, J. E. (2009). *Monitoring the future national results on adolescent drug use: Overview of key findings, 2008* (NIH Publication No. 09-7401). Bethesda, Maryland: National Institute on Drug Abuse.

Kabat-Zinn, J. (2009). *Full catastrophe living: Using the wisdom of your body and mind to face stress, pain, and illness.* Delta.

Kaprio, J., Koskenvuo, M., Langinvainio, H., Romanov, K., Sarna, S., & Rose, R. J. (1987). Genetic influences on use and abuse of alcohol: A study of 5638 adult Finnish twin brothers. *Alcoholism: Clinical and Experimental Research, 11,* 349–356.

Kazantzakis, N. (1952). *Zorba the greek.* Simon & Schuster.

Khan, A., Warmer, H. A., & Brown, W. A. (2000). Symptom reduction and suicide risk in patients treated with placebo in antidepressant clinical trials: An analysis of the Food and Drug Administration database. *Archives of General Psychiatry, 57,* 11–317.

Kirsch, I. (2011). *The emperor's new drugs: Exploding the antidepressant myth.* Basic Books.

Kirsch, I., Deacon, B. J., Huedo-Medina, T. B., Scoboria, A., Moore, T. J., et al. (2008). Initial severity and antidepressant benefits: A meta-analysis of data submitted to the Food and Drug Administration. *PLoS Medicine, 5*(2), e45, doi:10.1371/journal.pmed.0050045.

Kivlahan, D. R., Donovan, D. M., & Walker, R. D. (1983). Predictors of relapse: Interaction of drinking-related locus of control and reasons for drinking. *Addictive Behaviors, 8,* 273–276.

Klingemann, H., Sobell, M. B., & Sobell, L. C. (2009). Continuities and changes in self-change research. *Addiction, 105,* 1510-1518.

Koski-Jannes, A. (1994). Drinking-related locus of control as a predictor of drinking after treatment. *Addictive Behaviors, 19,* 491–495.

Kownacki, R. J., & Shadish, W. R. (1999). Does Alcoholics Anonymous work? The results from a meta-analysis of controlled experiments. *Substance Use & Misuse, 34,* 1897–1916.

Kranzler, G. D. (1974). *You can change how you feel: A rational-emotive approach.* Author.

Latt, N. C., Jurd, S., Houseman, J., & Wutzke, S. E. (2002). Naltrexone in alcohol dependence: A randomised controlled trial of effectiveness in a standard clinical setting. *Medical Journal of Australia, 176* (11), 530–534.

Leakey, R. E., & Lewin, R. (1979). *People of the lake: Mankind & its beginnings.* Avon Books.

Lester, D. (1988). Genetic theory: An assessment of the heritability of alcoholism. *Theories on alcoholism.* Toronto: Addictions Research Foundation.

Lexchin, J., Bero, L. A., Djulbegovic, B., & Clark, O. (2003). Pharmaceutical industry sponsorship and research outcome and quality: Systematic review. *British Medical Journal, 326,* 1167–1170.

Lieberman, M. A., & Borman, L. D. (1979). *Self-help groups for coping with crisis: Origins, members, processes, and impact.* Lexington, Massachusetts: Jossey-Bass.

Lorig, K., Holman, H., Sobel, D., & Laurent, D. (2006). *Living a healthy life with chronic conditions: Self-management of heart disease, fatigue, arthritis, worry, diabetes, frustration, asthma, pain, emphysema, and others* (3rd edition). Bull Publishing Company.

References

Ludwig, A. M. (1989). *Understanding the alcoholic's mind: The nature of craving and how to control it.* New York: Oxford University Press.

Mann, K., Lehert, P., & Morgan, M. Y. (2006). The efficacy of acamprosate in the maintenance of abstinence in alcohol-dependent individuals: Results of a meta-analysis. *Alcoholism: Clinical and Experimental Research, 28* (1), 51–63.

Marlatt, G. A., & Gordon, J. R. (1985). *Relapse prevention: Maintenance strategies in the treatment of addictive behaviors.* New York: Guilford Press.

Maslow, A. H. (1971). *Self-actualization.* Big Sur Recordings.

May, G. G. (1988). *Addiction and grace.* New York: HarperCollins Publishers.

McKellar, J., Stewart, E., & Humphreys, K. (2003). Alcoholics Anonymous involvement and positive alcohol-related outcomes: Cause, consequence, or just a correlate? A Prospective 2-year study of 2,319 alcohol-dependent men. *Journal of Consulting and Clinical Psychology, 71,* 302-308.

Mee-Lee, D., Shulman, G. R., Fishman, M., & Gastfriend, D. R. (2001). *Patient placement criteria for the treatment of substance-related disorders* (2nd edition, revised). Chevy Chase, Maryland: Lippincott Williams & Wilkins.

Meichenbaum, D. (1977). *Cognitive-behavior modification: An integrative approach* (Plenum Behavior Therapy Series). Springer.

Meichenbaum, D., & Turk, D. C. (1987). *Facilitating treatment adherence.* Springer.

Milam, J. R., & Ketcham, K. (1983). *Under the influence.* New York: Bantam.

Miller-Tutzauer, C., Leonard, K. E., & Windle, M. (1991). Marriage and alcohol use: A longitudinal study of "maturing out." *Journal of Studies on Alcohol, 52,* 434–440.

Miller, W. R., Wilbourne, P. L., & Hettema, J. (2003). What works?: A summary of alcoholism treatment outcome research. In R. K. Hester & W. R. Miller (Eds), *Handbook of Alcoholism Treatment*

Approaches: Effective Alternatives (3rd ed., pp. 13-63). Boston: Allyn & Bacon.

Mokdad, A. H., Marks, J. S., Stroup, D. F., & Gerberding, J. L. (2004). Actual causes of death in the United States, 2000. *The Journal of the American Medical Association, 270,* 1238–1245.

Moncrief, J. (2007). *The myth of the chemical cure: A critique of psychiatric drug treatment.* Palgrave Macmillan.

Naissides, M., Mamo, J., James, A., & Pal, S. (2006). The effect of chronic consumption of red wine on cardiovascular disease risk factors in postmenopausal women. *Atherosclerosis, 185,* 438–445.

National Institute on Drug Abuse and the National Institute on Alcohol Abuse and Alcoholism. 1998. *The economic cost of alcohol and drug abuse in the United States 1992.* Bethesda, MD: National Institute on Alcohol Abuse and Alcoholism.

Nicholas, M. (2011). *Recovery by Choice: Living and Enjoying Life Free of Alcohol and Drugs- A Workbook.* LifeRing Press.

Peele, S. (1985). *The meaning of addiction: Compulsive experience and its interpretation.* Lexington, Massachusetts: Jossey-Bass Incorporated.

Portman, T. C. (1987). Resistance in the treatment of DUI offenders. *Dissertation Abstracts.*

Project MATCH Research Group, 1998. Therapist effects in three treatments for alcohol problems. *Psychotherapy Research, 8,* 455-474.

Rand, A., & Peikoff, L. (1943). *The fountainhead.* Bobbs-Merrill Company.

Reich, T., Edenberg, H. J., Goate, A., Williams, J. T., Rice, J. P., Van Eerdewegh, P., et al. (1998). Genome-wide search for genes affecting the risk for alcohol dependence. *American Journal of Medical Genetics, 81,* 207–215.

Renshaw, D. (2004). *Seven weeks to better sex.* Westcom Press.

Roger, C. R. (1995). *On becoming a person: A therapist's view of psychotherapy.* New York: Houghton Mifflin Company.

Rotter, J. B. (1966). Generalized expectancies for internal versus external control of reinforcement. *Psychological Monographs, 80,* 1–28.

Rotter, J. B. (1992). Cognates of personal control: Locus of control, self-efficacy, and explanatory style. *Applied & Preventive Psychology, 2,* 127–129

Ruiz, D. M. (2001). *The four agreements: A practical guide to personal freedom, a Toltec wisdom book.* San Rafael, California: Amber-Allen Publishing.

Rumpf, H. J., Bishchof, G., Hapke, U., Meyer, C., & John, U. (2006). Stability of remission from alcohol dependence without formal help. *Alcohol and Alcoholism, 41,* 311–314.

Saitz, R. (1998). Introduction to alcohol withdrawal. *Alcohol Health and Research World, 22,* 5–12.

Sapolsky, R. M. (2004). *Why zebras don't get ulcers* (3rd edition). New York: Holt Publishing.

Scharch, D. M. (1997). *Passionate marriage: Sex, love, and intimacy in emotionally committed relationships.* W. W. Norton & Co.

Schuckit, M. A. (1984). Subjective responses to alcohol in sons of alcoholics and control subjects. *Archives of General Psychiatry, 41,* 879–884.

Schuckit, M. A. (1985). Ethanol-induced changes in body sway in men at high alcoholism risk. *Archives of General Psychiatry, 42,* 375–379.

Scott, P. (2008, October 1). Was the Prozac revolution all in our heads? *Men's Health.*

Seligman, M. E. P. (1991). *Learned optimism.* New York: Knopf.

Seltzer, M. A., Vinokur, A., &Van Rooijen, L. J. (1975). A self-administered short Michigan alcohol screening test (SMAST). *Journal of Studies on Alcohol, 36,* 117–126.

Skinner, R. B. (1987, July/August) A Humanist alternative to A.A.'s 12-steps: A human centered approach to conquering alcoholism. *The Humanist.*

Sobell, L. C., Cunningham, J. A., & Sobell, M. B. (1996). Recovery from alcohol problems with and without treatment: Prevalence in two population surveys. *American Journal of Public Health, 86,* 966–972.

Spring, J. A. (1996). *After the affair: Healing the pain and rebuilding trust when a partner has been unfaithful.* HarperCollins.

Steiner, C. (1974). *Scripts people live: transactional analysis of life scripts.* New York: Grove Press.

Sullivan, J. T., Sykora, K., Schneiderman, J., Naranjo, C. A., & Sellers, E. M. (1989). Assessment of alcohol withdrawal: The revised Clinical Institute Withdrawal Assessment for Alcohol scale (CIWA-AR). *British Journal of Addiction, 84,* 1353–1357.

Thombs, D. L. (1999). *Introduction to addictive behaviors* (2nd edition). New York: Guilford Press.

Trimpey, J. (2010). *The Art of AVART: Addiction Voice Recognition Technique.* Lotus Press.

Trimpey, J. (1995). *The small book (rational recovery systems).* New York: Dell Publishing.

Trimpey, J. (1996). *Rational recovery: The new cure for substance addiction.* New York: Pocket Books.

Watkins, C., Moore, L., Harvey, I., Carthy, P., Robinson, E., & Brawn, R. (2003). Characteristics of general practitioners who frequently see drug industry representatives: National cross sectional survey. *British Medical Journal, 326,* 1178–1179.

Wegscheider-Cruse, S. (1989). *Another chance: Hope and help for the alcoholic family.* Science and Behavior Books.

Weil, A. (2005). *Healthy aging.* Knopf.

Whitaker, R. (2011). *Anatomy of an epidemic: Magic bullets, psychiatric drugs, and the astonishing rise of mental illness in America.* Broadway.

Yalom, I. (1980). *Existential psychotherapy.* Basic Books.

Yapko, M. (1998). *Breaking the patterns of depression.* New York: Main Street Books.

References

Young, J. E., & Klosko J. S. (1994). *Reinventing your life: The breakthrough program to end negative behavior ... and feel great again.* New York: Plume.

Young, J. E., Klosko, J. S., & Weishaar, M. E. (2003). *Schema therapy: A practitioner's guide.* New York: Guilford Press.

Zailckas, K. (2005). *Smashed: Story of a drunken childhood.* Viking Adult